Waging The War
of the Worlds

Waging *The War of the Worlds*

A History of the 1938 Radio Broadcast and Resulting Panic, Including the Original Script

JOHN GOSLING

Radio script by HOWARD KOCH

McFarland & Company, Inc., Publishers

Jefferson, North Carolina, and London

LIBRARY OF CONGRESS CATALOGUING-IN-PUBLICATION DATA

Gosling, John, 1967–
Waging *The War of the Worlds* : a history of the 1938 radio
broadcast and resulting panic, including the original script /
John Gosling ; radio script by Howard Koch.
p.   cm.
Includes bibliographical references and index.

ISBN 978-0-7864-4105-1
softcover : 50# alkaline paper ∞

1. War of the worlds (Radio program)   2. Welles, Orson,
1915–1985 — Criticism and interpretation.   3. Science fiction radio
programs — Psychological aspects.   4. Radio audiences.
I. Koch, Howard. Invasion from Mars.   II. Title.
PN1991.77.W3G67   2009   791.44'72 — dc22   2009025945

British Library cataloguing data are available

On the cover: *foreground* Orson Welles post-broadcast press conference
on October 31, 1938 (Mary Evans Picture Library); *background* illustration
of the Martian war machines by Frank R. Paul (Wood River Gallery)

Manufactured in the United States of America

*McFarland & Company, Inc., Publishers
Box 611, Jefferson, North Carolina 28640
www.mcfarlandpub.com*

With love to my wife Juliet
and daughter Holly.
I could not have done it
without your unflagging
support and patience.

TABLE OF CONTENTS

ACKNOWLEDGMENTS

I would like to begin by thanking the librarians and archivists of the world. They are the unsung heroes of the long-distance researcher, and time and time again I have been bowled over by their cheerful willingness to dig into dusty records on behalf of a complete stranger. In no particular order then (for all are equally worthy of praise) may I express my considerable appreciation to: The Buffalo Library Service, Princeton University Library, the New Jersey State Library, Barbara Laub at Maplewood Memorial Library in New Jersey, Carol Uhrmacher at the Marin County Free Library, Liliana Gavilanes of the Universidad San Francisco de Quito Library, Karen at the Seattle Public Library, Henrique Barreto Nunes, director of the Biblioteca Pública de Braga at the Universidade do Minho, Nathaniel DeBruin at the Marshall University Library, Anne Louise Attar of the Providence Public Library, Maureen Neville at Trenton Public Library and Janet Lorenz at the Margaret Herrick Library.

A major challenge in writing this book has been the requirement to research material in languages I have not the slightest fluency in. My profuse appreciation therefore goes out to my translators, whose tireless work has helped to shine a light on so many forgotten and fascinating stories. Thank you Catherine Barber and Janice Moreira in Chile, Shikha Raikundalia in Portugal and Steven William Mahoney in Brazil.

For assistance with photographs, I would like thank Ana Leal of the Costa do Estoril tourist office for her help in searching out local sources of photographs and to express my great appreciation to Celestino Domingos for kindly allowing access to his fantastic collection of vintage postcards of Portugal. I would also like to thank Laura Anderson, administrative director of the Grand Island Chamber of Commerce, for her help in locating a photograph of Grand Island, and Antoinette Beiser of Lowell Observatory, who greatly assisted in obtaining images pertaining to Percival Lowell and his work. Adam Fielding of George Mason University Library provided invaluable assistance in obtaining images of John Houseman and Orson Welles from the archives of the Federal Theatre Project. Thank you also to James Ragucci for the picture of the Grover's Mill monument and to Mauricio Jaramillo for assistance in locating photographs of Gonzalo Benítez and Luis Alberto Valencia.

For providing firsthand recollections of their experience of the 1938 broadcast, I would like to pay tribute to the memory of the late Professor Sheldon Judson and to thank his daughter Anne Judson for kind permission to use material obtained in personal correspondence with the professor. I would also like to thank Norman Corwin for sharing his recollections of October 30, 1938. My gratitude to Jenny Rector at the *Daily Progress* newspaper in Charlottesville, Virginia, for locating material in its archive and to David Fill of the comprehensive website WKBWradio.com for help in researching the WKBW broadcasts of 1968 and 1971. In regard to the WPRO broadcast of 1974 I would like to express my appreciation to the following persons who gave up their time to answer my questions: Jim Pemantell (Jamestown Police Chief, retired), Chief Thomas Tighe (Jamestown Police), Jay Clark, Holland Cooke, Gary Berkowitz and Paul Giammarco. In regard to the 1949 broadcast in Quito, my heartfelt appreciation goes to Ximena Páez, whose fascinating recollections of her father's role will, I hope, serve to shed new and important light on the events of that tragic night.

This book would not be what it is without the contributions of writers far more talented than myself, and so I would like to express my thanks to the estates of H. G. Wells and Howard Koch for kindly allowing me to reproduce the work of these wonderful writers in the pages of this book. Specifically, I would like to express my gratitude to Norman Rudman, the legal representative of the family of Howard Koch, for his great patience in negotiating with me the rights to the 1938 play, and to Peter Koch for supplying (to my very great delight) a copy of an original script of *The War of the Worlds*. Thanks also to A. P. Watt Ltd, literary executors for the estate of H. G. Wells, for permission to quote from *The War of the Worlds*. My thanks also to Greg Martin at Border Media for granting permission to publish the transcript of the meeting between H. G. Wells and Orson Welles recorded in 1940 by KTSA San Antonio.

The following persons have all offered their time, knowledge and enthusiasm in the course of my research: Fran Ruch of the West Windsor Senior Center, Joan S. Parry of the Historical Society of West Windsor, and Larry French of the fantastic Welles resource Wellesnet. Thanks to Lulu Miller of WNYC, New York Public Radio, who assisted in the vexing quest for a picture of the perpetrators of the Quito scare, Douglas S. Wilson of O'Gara & Wilson, Ltd., for kindly verifying the existence of an early draft of the 1938 script, Mark W. Falzini of the New Jersey State Police Museum for providing pages from the Trenton police logbook and José Rivera for assistance in searching the UCLA Library Department of Special Collections repository for material pertaining to John Houseman.

I fear that this is not a complete acknowledgment of all those who have in some fashion over the years helped to shape this book, and if by chance I have missed you, I can only apologize and assure you of my deep appreciation.

PREFACE

There is arguably no more important book in the history of science fiction than *The War of the Worlds*. It has influenced and informed generations of writers, artists and filmmakers, but when H. G. Wells set out to chide the hypocrisy and complacency of the British Empire with his pointedly observed tale of alien invasion, surely not even in his wildest dreams could he have predicted how the story would worm its way into the public psyche, nor could he possibly have foreseen how a marvelous new invention — radio — was to become intimately entwined with his creation. In 1898, when *The War of the Worlds* was first published, Guglielmo Marconi had only just opened his first radio factory in Britain, yet just 40 years later via a radio drama *The War of the Worlds* would intrude directly into the lives of a huge number of frightened Americans.

In the intervening years the story of the 1938 Orson Welles "panic broadcast" has attained a near-mythic quality among social commentators, but in our haste to heap well-deserved plaudits on Welles, a complacency has crept into the telling of the tale, such that perfectly preventable inaccuracies have entered the record by a simple process of casual repetition. This is not to say that this book intends to downplay or diminish one of the great stories in the history of American broadcasting, but it will provide a measured analysis of the public reaction, and a clearer understanding of the genesis, production and aftermath of that extraordinary Halloween eve.

Similarly, while researchers have focused on the 1938 broadcast, a much larger story has been ignored, sidelined and all but forgotten. This book, then, is an attempt to redress the balance and tell for the first time the full extraordinary story of how a work of fiction was able to assume a tangible life of its own and spread terror and confusion, not just in America, but all across the world, for the "Martian attack" of 1938 was just the opening salvo in a largely unknown war that has been raging for the past seven decades. From the streets of New Jersey to remote corners of Brazil and to the shores of Europe, this is a murky story that has involved in equal part politics, religion, spies, dictators, UFOs, alleged government conspiracies, giant egos, uncanny coincidences, wooden puppets and a not inconsiderable measure of paranoia and deception.

In short, this is a story of many parts, and while it will certainly not skimp on the dramatic details, this book will also endeavor to provide the reader with a deeper understanding of the numerous factors that have contributed to the seemingly inexplicable success of a military campaign launched from a dead and far distant world. We will see how it is that an ancient association between Mars and the art and act of war has provided fertile ground for the imagination of both scientists and fantasists (though sometimes the distinction has become strangely blurred) and how that great and profound outpouring of thought found its ultimate zenith of expression in the seminal work of H. G. Wells.

1

The story of how *The War of the Worlds* migrated from the printed page to the radio airwaves is every bit as fascinating, dominated by the looming presence of Orson Welles, though, if we look beyond his legendary instinct for self-aggrandizement, the 1938 production was in truth a highly collaborative effort by the hardworking cast and crew of the Mercury Theatre on the Air. This book is therefore concerned with putting the record straight and ensuring that men like Howard Koch (whose rightful authorship of the 1938 broadcast is often eclipsed by the sheer wattage of Welles' luminescent personality) are given due credit for their work. We will also meet some other equally important people virtually unknown outside of their native countries, radio pioneers like Portugal's Matos Maia and Brazil's Sérgio Brito, as well as one or two characters history has recorded less favorably, notably Leonardo Páez, author of the calamitous 1949 *War of the Worlds* broadcast in Quito, Ecuador, who, so legend has it, was last seen atop the burning roof of his radio station.

How it is that a story written in the twilight years of the Victorian era could cause such violent upheavals forms an ongoing thread of discussion throughout this book, and as the reader will discover, there are answers unique to the countries that endured these scares. Undoubtedly *The War of the Worlds* has at heart a truly unusual plasticity that has allowed it to be restructured and molded to suit the prevailing themes and moods of the times. The stroke of genius in reworking the narrative into a series of breaking news stories for the 1938 broadcast also contributed greatly to its portability. This basic template when transplanted to other countries and times always retains the essential elements of the original story, but taps seamlessly and effortlessly into local vogues, sensibilities and concerns, such that as the years have rolled by the dance band rhythms of the 1930s have been replaced with more up-tempo beats and the illusion of breaking news has been utterly perfected, until in 1968 the terror was improbably bookended by the Beatles and the Vietnam War!

This book therefore offers the reader a selective insight into the social, political and religious dynamics that have driven the citizens of several different countries to believe they were facing an invasion from Mars. We will see how in Brazil a rash of UFO sightings convinced both civilian listeners and the military that the end of the world was nigh, and how in Portugal deeply held religious beliefs were instrumental in amplifying fear. We also learn how different countries reacted to the maverick activities of their radio personalities, with some not nearly so forgiving as the American authorities.

The book concludes with a warning that voices dismissive of the possibility of another Martian scare are very possibly deluding themselves, and that governments should take very seriously the possibility that a new broadcast might yet trigger fresh pandemonium. They may not strike in America, but the Martians have a whole world to choose from, and there are plenty of countries yet to experience what it is like to be told by those you trust the most that civilization as you know it is coming to an end. This is the legacy bequeathed to us by Orson Welles and the Mercury Theatre on the Air. Let us hope that a future edition of this book is not in need of a new chapter.

1

GOD OF WAR

A Brief History of Mars in the Mind of Man

This is the true story of one of the most unusual chapters ever experienced in the annals of warfare. Ever since 1938, when the first skirmish was fought on American soil, the conflict has repeatedly reignited, plunging cities on three continents into a state of chaos and fear. The very fate of worlds has hung in the balance, yet the invading armies that fought these battles have been no more corporeal than a bank of fog, and though an immense ethereal gulf has separated them from their goals, in reality they have traveled no measurable distance at all. It has been a war without the physicality of bombs or bullets, yet blood has been shed and property damaged and, while not a single inch of territory has been seized, the invaders can justifiably claim to have won many stunning victories. For the art of war has always been as much about the application of terror as it is brute military strength, and these invaders have been uniquely successful in applying the principles of psychological warfare to their campaigns. This is the story of a war of the worlds fought between Earth and Mars, a war all the more incredible for the fact that it has been waged not on a battlefield, but over the radio airwaves and in the hearts and minds of millions of frightened listeners.

The origins of this extraordinary conflict had actually been millennia in the making, for the inhabitants of the third world from the Sun have long held a special place in their imaginations for the Red Planet. From the home of warlike gods and scientific supermen to a symbolic embodiment of the communist red menace, humans have long projected their hopes, dreams and nightmares onto the face of Mars, though given our violent nature it was perhaps inevitable that the planet would come to be regarded most often as a herald of doom and destruction. But as primitive superstition gave way to scientific pragmatism and the first telescopes were trained upon the distant planet, optimism began to grow that we might not be alone in the universe.

As these scientific instruments improved, the Moon was swiftly dismissed as a dead and lifeless world, but Mars, a distant and indistinct object in even the best of telescopes, seemed to offer some hope of companionship. There were things that looked like seas, an apparent shifting of the seasons and even a tantalizing hint of vegetation, so in these inspiring circumstances it was hardly surprising that minds both scientific and visionary would seize upon the possibilities to create a living, breathing Mars. Yet no sooner had the prospect of a Martian civilization captured the public imagination than a terrible tragedy was visited upon our nearest neighbors. This ancient world seemed to be suffering a slow and lingering death, and as desperate Martian engineers drove colossal canals from the dwindling polar caps to irrigate their parched cities, we could only watch helplessly from afar and sympathize with their plight.

This romantic vision of Mars would soon come under threat by the advance of science, and the voyage of *Mariner 4* in July 1965 seemed to be the death knell for any prospect of a meeting of minds. *Mariner*'s grainy images showed no canals and no struggling Martian civilization, though even now some diehards cling to the belief that the planet once harbored intelligent life. Yet this crushing disappointment has been tempered by recent discoveries. Ever more powerful probes and robotic rovers have revealed Mars as a place of wonders, a fantastic landscape of giant volcanoes larger than any on earth, canyons miles deep and, most remarkable of all, clear evidence that water once flowed in the open. The very real possibility that microbes may yet cling precariously to life beneath the surface has reenergized our fascination with the Red Planet, and we still hope to one day travel there in person. When we do, it will be the culmination of a voyage of discovery that began thousands of years ago, when it first became apparent that the stars in the sky were not in fact all the same.

Mars as imaged by NASA's *Mars Global Surveyor* in late June 2001. Visible is the Tharsis volcanic region (left), Valles Marineris chasms (right) and the late winter south polar cap (bottom) (NASA/JPL/Malin Space Science Systems).

Lacking a means of close observation or the mathematics to make sense of what they saw, our ancient ancestors could make no appreciable distinction between the light of the stars and that of the planets, but they knew that Mars was among a handful of celestial objects that behaved in a most peculiar fashion. Generation after generation they saw that most of the things they could observe kept the same relative positions in the night sky. So slowly do they move that the night sky we know today would have been equally familiar to an ancient Babylonian or Roman. This is simply because as incredibly distant objects the individual, or "proper," motions of the stars are impossible to distinguish with the naked eye. In comparison, the nearby planets of our solar system shift position at a far more rapid pace. It was such a stark discontinuity that the Greeks would come to call these mysterious objects *planetes asteres*, meaning wandering stars. The behavior of Mars was especially perplexing. After a period of time moving in one direction it would appear to shift into reverse! Naturally the complex celestial mechanics involved were beyond the abilities of early observers to explain, but the effect was startling enough that the ancient Egyptians dubbed Mars the "backward traveler."*

The scientific term for this aberrant behavior is called retrograding[†] and has to do with the way the orbits of Earth and Mars interact. At the point of closest approach, when the orbits of the two planets bring them to what is known as opposition, the Earth is for a time effectively catching Mars up and overtakes it. At this point Mars appears to reverse direction in our night sky. This retrograde motion is one reason the planet has been ascribed with such a violent personality. To the Greeks, the very movement of the planet was indicative of disorder and distrust. That the color of the planet (due to high concentrations of iron oxides on the surface) is also deeply suggestive of blood is another reason that so many cultures have imbued Mars with warlike connotations. It is an association that is clear from the very earliest recorded observations.

Those first tentative observations can be accredited to the Babylonians who noted the existence of Mars in approximately 400 B.C. They named it Nergal, the underworld personification of the sun god Utu and the god of the netherworld, the harbinger of war, pestilence, fever and devastation. The Greeks named the planet after their god of war Ares, but we derive the modern name, Mars, from the Romans and their god of war.

The scientific age of observation of Mars began in the early 1500s, when the Danish astronomer Tycho Brahe made some surprisingly fine orbital calculations over a 20-year period of time. Brahe was an odd character to say the least. He owned a pet moose, fathered eight children out of wedlock and, after getting into a duel, reportedly over a fine point of mathematics, lost a portion of his nose. This he allegedly replaced with a self-made prosthesis of gold, silver and wax! His startling eccentricities aside, his observations, which he made entirely by eye (the astronomical telescope not yet having been invented) were the most comprehensive yet attempted and as a result his student Johannes Kepler was able in 1609 to demonstrate that the orbit of Mars must be elliptical rather than perfectly circular according to the classical assumption.

---

*The ancient Egyptians also named it *Har decher* (The Red One) and the city of Cairo in modern Egypt is named after the Arabic word for Mars, *Al-Qahira*, meaning "The Victorious One."

[†]All the outer planets exhibit this retrograde motion, but their much greater distance from Earth makes it far harder to observe.

This was an important discovery, and it placed Mars firmly at the heart of a raging controversy over the nature of the solar system. In the 1520s, the Polish-born astronomer Nicolaus Copernicus had begun formulating an extremely dangerous theory that challenged the belief that the Earth was at the center of creation and hence all other celestial objects must revolve around it in perfect circles. The Greek astronomer Ptolemy had codified this idea centuries earlier. To dare challenge this was to challenge the Church itself, for surely the Ptolemaic system was representative of the perfection of creation? Copernicus was dismissive of the Ptolemaic system because, in order to explain the motion of the planets, Ptolemy had had to resort to some rather complex mathematical sleights of hand. It was simply far less troublesome and a great deal more elegant to place the Sun at the center of things, but Copernicus sensibly published this heretical notion on his deathbed and with a certain amount of irony proceeded to put himself comfortably beyond the reach of the Church, whose reaction in these cases was generally fatal in nature.* He is said to have received the first printed copy of his book, *De revolutionibus orbium coelestium* (On the Revolutions of the Heavenly Orbs), on the day he died, May 24, 1543. Legend has it that he awoke from a coma as the book was placed in his hands, looked at it, and then died contentedly.

Copernicus' ideas, though severely suppressed, were singularly persuasive and inevitably gained support, even if they did not quite explain all the observed ambiguities in the motion of the planets. In further refining our knowledge of the motion of Mars, Kepler had added weight to the Copernican view and paved the way for others to hammer in the final nails. Most famously, the Italian scientist Galileo Galilei fought the Church through his writings in support of the Copernican view, though he was forced several times to recant his beliefs under threat of the Inquisition and late in life spent much of his time under a form of house arrest. The Church would continue to punish and intimidate scientific heretics such as Galileo, but the writing was on the wall (or more accurately in the stars), and the publication in 1687 of Sir Issac Newton's *Principia*[†] chiseled into place an epitaph that would finally bury centuries of religious dogma.

Galileo had also begun studying Mars in 1609, which is thought to be the first time the planet had been seen through a telescope. The telescope he used was incredibly primitive by modern standards, but on December 30, 1610, he was able to write to his friend Benedetto Castelli, "I ought not to claim that I can see the phases of Mars; however, unless I am deceiving myself, I believe I have already seen that it is not perfectly round."[1] The invention of the telescope and the gradual erosion of Church authority ushered in a new age of observation, though the first drawings of Mars were rudimentary in the extreme. Another Italian, Francisco Fontana, was perhaps the first to draw Mars as seen through a telescope, but his sketches of 1636 and 1638 show no detail and are marred by defects introduced by his flawed optics. It is Christiaan Huygens, a Dutch astronomer and scientist, who is credited with identifying the first verifiable feature on Mars, when in 1659 he sketched what is thought to be the area now known as Syrtis Major. He also

---

*The Italian philosopher Giordano Bruno was a vocal proponent of the Copernican model of the universe. In 1600 he had an iron spike hammered through his jaw and tongue and was burned at the stake after refusing to recant.

†*The Principia* is generally considered the greatest scientific book ever written, providing a detailed explanation of the motion of bodies under centrifugal force and the law of universal gravitation.

calculated the duration of the Martian day at 24 hours, a respectably accurate figure further refined a few years later (in 1666) by the Italian Giovanni Cassini to 24 hours and 40 minutes.*

In 1698, Huygens became the first to speculate about the existence of life on Mars in a posthumously published treatise entitled *Cosmotheros*. He imagined that Mars would be colder than the Earth due to its greater distance from the Sun, but that life would have adapted to these difficult conditions. This was an idea far ahead of its time, especially given recent discoveries of life in the most inhospitable areas of the Earth, such as sub–sea thermal vents. Huygen's ideas were subsequently given some credence by the observations of the British astronomer Sir William Herschel.

Herschel set out his thoughts in a 1784 presentation to the Astronomical Society of London, laboring under the prodigiously weighty title *On the remarkable appearances at the polar regions of the planet Mars, the inclination of its axis, the position of its poles, and its spheroidal figure; with a few hints relating to its real diameter and atmosphere*. Herschel imagined a planet similar in many ways to our own, but beset by frozen conditions and periodic melting of the caps. Dark areas he interpreted as sea and light areas as land, but he went even further, stating, "Mars has a considerable but modest atmosphere, so that its inhabitants probably enjoy a situation in many ways similar to our own." This was something of a leap of faith, but then he believed that the entire solar system was inhabited, including the Sun. That particular idea is patently ludicrous in the light of modern knowledge, but Herschel was by the standards of his time an accomplished scientist and had for instance conducted a quite brilliantly conceived experiment that if anything should have dissuaded him of the possibility of life on Mars. He had observed the passage of two stars behind Mars and saw that as they slipped behind the disc of the planet they were undimmed by the obscuring haze of an atmosphere. His perfectly cogent conclusion was that the atmosphere must then be very thin by earthly standards.

Undaunted by any evidence to the contrary, many other astronomers would continue to postulate the existence of life on the planet. France boasted several ardent Mars watchers. Emmanuel Liais proposed in 1860 that the dark regions were vegetation and Camille Flammarion suggested much the same in 1873, though he attributed the red color of Mars itself to vegetation.[†] It was also during this period that the idea that Mars might be crisscrossed with artificial canals came to prominence. The concept was to make a lasting impression on many writers and on *The War of the Worlds* in particular, yet if not for a simple mistake of translation, it is likely that the idea would never have taken hold.

Observing Mars in 1858, the Italian Angelo Secchi saw features he called *canali*. This actually translates from the Italian as "channels" but poor translation into English meant that the more provocative idea of canals stuck. When Giovanni Virginio Schiaparelli also used the term *canali* in reporting his 1877 observations he was certainly thinking of them as natural channels through which meltwater flowed, but even he was not opposed in principle to the idea that they might be artificial. In a carefully worded statement, he said, "Their singular aspect, and their being drawn with absolute geometrical

---

*The precise rotational period of Mars is 24 hours, 37 minutes, 23 seconds.
[†]An idea that found its way into *The War of the Worlds*, when the Martians transplant their red weed vegetation to Earth.

precision, as if they were the work of rule or compass, has led some to see in them the work of intelligent beings, inhabitants of the planet. I am very careful not to combat this supposition, which includes nothing impossible."[2] Schiaparelli went even further in later statements to support the idea that the canals were artificial, but equally espoused his views with a degree of careful circumspection, such that he never fully committed to one side or another of the argument. However, his observations on the debate made a considerable stir, helped in part because the Suez Canal had been completed in 1869 and the public was thus predisposed to appreciate the engineering splendor that a Martian canal system implied. However, nothing did more to popularize the cause of the canals and intelligent life on Mars than the books of the American astronomer Percival Lowell.

As a Christmas present in 1893, Lowell had received Flammarion's epic compendium of Mars observations. Wildly enthused by the subject, he moved in 1894 to Flagstaff, Arizona, where he constructed an observatory and began his own detailed observations. What

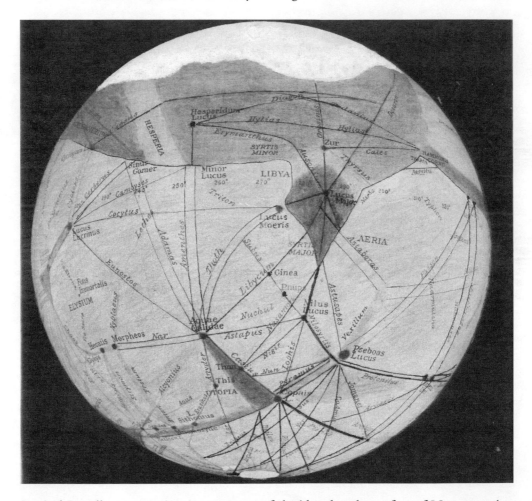

Percival Lowell was a passionate proponent of the idea that the surface of Mars was crisscrossed with a network of artificially created canals. These can be seen in this illustration of Mars sketched by Lowell in 1905 (Lowell Observatory Archives).

he saw stunned Lowell, and the following year he published the first of three sensational books on Mars in which he argued that the canals represented the work of a Martian civilization and was in fact a vast irrigation system. In his first book he wrote, "The lines form a system; that, instead of running anywhither, they join certain points to certain others, making thus, not a simple network, but one whose meshes connect centres directly with one another, is striking at first sight, and loses none of its peculiarity on second thought. For the intrinsic improbability of such a state of things arising from purely natural causes becomes evident on a moment's consideration."[3]

Lowell was passionate in his belief in a Martian civilization that was fully focused on the urgent task of redistributing a dwindling water supply to every corner of their world. The fact that other observers saw no canals at all, or saw entirely different features, cast significant doubt on his credibility, but for Lowell the logic of the situation was unassailable. He believed unequivocally that Mars was inhabited. From that basic precept he reasoned that since conditions were clearly extremely inhospitable, the inhabitants would need to correct matters by their own hand. Hence the existence of a canal network became, not only perfectly plausible, but also essential. It was a wonderfully persuasive argument to the public, though he was clearly seeing exactly what he wanted to see and did not escape fierce disagreement from his fellow astronomers.

In a way Lowell can actually be considered something of a science fiction writer, though at the time such stories were known as scientific romances. Of course he really believed in the Mars he saw through his telescope, but as any good novelist would, he took the available evidence of his observations and extrapolated them into a plausible vision of life on an alien world. Astronomers are no longer expected to be quite so cavalier with their pronouncements, but Lowell was not alone in letting his imagination get the better of him. Flammarion had gone so far as to describe the clothing and eating habits of the Martians in his 1862 book *La Pluralité des mondes habités* (The Plurality of Inhabited Worlds). Lowell and Flammarion were in a sense the scientific superstars of their time, and their lurid speculations made for great copy.

Influenced by Schiaparelli, Flammarion and Lowell, a number of

Portrait of Percival Lowell, June 3, 1904 (Lowell Observatory Archives).

Percival Lowell observing at his telescope at Flagstaff, Arizona, circa 1897 (Lowell Observatory Archives).

scientific romances were published. In 1880 Percy Greg's *Across the Zodiac* visited a Mars of canal builders, and Robert Cromie discovered a utopian civilization in his 1890 novel *A Plunge into Space*. Earlier still, in his comic fantasy *Gulliver's Travels*, Jonathan Swift made a remarkably accurate guess as to the existence of two small moons around Mars, and even came close to predicting their size and orbital characteristics. That he did this in 1726, some 150 years before the discovery of Phobos and Deimos, is quite an achievement. It has even been suggested (in jest, of course) that he must have been a Martian.

But then in 1898 came the book that would forever cement the reputation of the planet as a portent of doom. Until this point, no one had considered the possibility that a Martian civilization might seek less benign solutions to their problems than canals, that a world overflowing with a plentiful bounty of resources was close at hand and that the means might exist for the Martians to reach out and take what was needed. Separated by an immense gulf of space, we had not reckoned that the old gods retained their baleful influence, and that our marvelous scientific flights of fancy might one day assume a nefarious life of their own. The Martians conjured up by Lowell were after all nothing more than a distant intellectual curiosity, and could never trouble the inhabitants of the Earth. It would surely take nothing less than an extraordinary leap of the imagination to bridge that gap.

2

MARS ATTACKS
H. G. Wells Declares War

The architect of the first full-scale alien invasion of Earth was born into entirely unremarkable circumstances on September 21, 1866, in Bromley, England. Herbert George Wells, or Bertie, as friends and family knew him, was the youngest of three brothers, a bright and inquiring child who by the age of seven had become a voracious reader. It was a trait he developed while laid up in bed with a broken leg. With nothing else to do but read, he had his first intensive exposure to astronomy and biology, both of which would figure prominently in his future writings. From an early age his potential stood out to those around him. His brother Frank remembered him as a "masterful child" and "unorthodox and critical,"[1] but a promising future was in danger of being snuffed out for lack of money to finance a suitable education.

His parents, Joseph and Sarah, would have harbored ambitions that their sons might rise in life somewhat above their station, for while not exactly poor — rather lower-middle-class — the specter of poverty was a constant worry. By 1879 Joseph's crockery shop was failing and Sarah was forced to take work as a housekeeper. With no money to pay for the young Herbert's schooling, he was apprenticed like his brothers before him to a draper. It was a desperately unhappy experience for the bookish child, and after several years of intolerable servitude he threatened suicide if his mother did not have him released from his apprenticeship. Thankfully the ploy worked and, free at last to pursue his dreams, he began the determined fight to better himself.

Luckily his obvious talents had come to the attention of a local school headmaster, who encouraged him to qualify to become a science teacher. This led to a government scholarship place at the Normal School of Science in London, where one of his teachers was the great T. H. Huxley, the foremost proponent at the time of Darwin's theories of evolution. It was a fortuitous encounter that was to deeply affect his writing, and it was at the Normal School that Wells began writing his scientific romances. The earliest version of his first novel, *The Time Machine*, was published in the school magazine, which he also edited.

As he moved now in rarefied academic circles, it is no surprise that Wells would involve himself in the question of life on Mars. On October 19, 1888, he spoke to the debating society at the Royal College of Science in London. His topic was "Are the Planets Habitable?" and on the subject of Mars he opined, "There was every reason to suppose that the surface of Mars was occupied by living beings."[2] He returned to the subject in an unsigned article for the April 4, 1896, issue of the *Saturday Review*, proposing that any Martians (were they to exist) would have little in common intellectually with humans. The pieces were falling into place for the creation of his greatest novel.

The story Wells was preparing to spin in *The War of the Worlds* was undoubtedly a radically new departure in literature, though he was not quite the first to postulate a visit to Earth from the Martians. This honor belongs to the German author Lasswitz Kurd, but while the Martian visitors in his 1897 novel *Auf Zwei Planeten* (Two Planets) were essentially benign,* Wells chose to create a race of warlike beings with no interest at all in dialogue or coexistence. His son Anthony West suggests, "The seed idea for *The War of the Worlds* is to be found in *The Time Machine*, in the passage that describes the fears that crowded in on the Time Traveler as he hurtled into the future...."[3] It is then that the traveler ponders if the human race might in the far future evolve into something so utterly powerful and inhuman that they would look upon him with undisguised contempt, seeing him not as an equal

H. G. Wells, author of *The War of the Worlds* (Library of Congress, Prints & Photographs Division).

but as a primitive beast, "a foul creature to be incontinently slain."[4] It is not unreasonable to suppose that Wells expounded upon this idea in *The War of the Worlds*. His Martians do look contemptuously upon the human race as cattle, but there is much more to Wells' thesis than this, for though they are utterly inhuman in appearance, in some important respects the invaders are all too human in character.

Wells was quite deliberate in this regard. Science fiction is now routinely regarded as a legitimate vehicle for social commentary, specifically as a way of sneaking criticism beneath the radar of societies not well disposed to unwelcome home truths, and Wells was a pioneer of this underhand form of denunciation. While the motive for the Wells' Martian invasion was also clearly inspired by the work of Percival Lowell and other canal proponents, the main thrust of the story had been influenced by events closer to home and a chance conversation between Wells and his brother Frank.

Walking in the countryside one day, they had discussed the calamity visited upon the aboriginal Tasmanians when English settlers arrived. What followed was nothing less than a bloody campaign of genocidal proportions, with the settlers committing appalling acts of violence on the aboriginals. It has even been reported that native Tasmanians were hunted and trapped like animals. By the time of the brothers' conversation they had been all but wiped out. It was another shameful episode in the history of colonialism. "Are we

---

*Almost benign. The Martians impose a Utopian peace on Earth, but wipe out the British navy in the process.

such apostles of mercy as to complain if the Martians warred in the same spirit?" Wells would ask in the opening chapter of *The War of the Worlds*.

During the same walk, Wells credits Frank with a crucial observation. "Suppose some beings from another planet were to drop out of the sky suddenly," mused Frank, "and begin laying about them here!"[5] Thus inspired, Wells was now able to begin fashioning a dire warning for his readers, that the comfortable existence they took so much for granted could be revoked on a cosmic whim, or indeed by something much closer to home. The British Empire was then facing resurgent threats from abroad, notably from France and Germany, but Wells was of the opinion that people had their heads buried in the sand as to the nature of the threat. Reflecting on this in 1920, Wells had this to say on the subject of his fellow citizens' casual indifference. "Tragedy, people thought, had gone out of human life for ever. A few of us were trying to point out the obvious possibilities of flying, of great guns, of poison gas, and so forth in presently making life uncomfortable if some sort of world peace was not assured, but the books we wrote were regarded as the silliest of imaginative gymnastics."[6]

The opening chapter of *The War of the Worlds* sets the scene, introducing a dying Martian civilization and an England that is firmly convinced of its place as a great power upon the Earth. Upon a serene and indolent corner of that unsuspecting country comes the fall of what at first is taken to be a meteorite, but as the unnamed narrator of the book soon discovers, it is in fact a manufactured cylinder of metal. From within emerge the horrifying Martians. At first it seems these creatures can be contained within the pit gouged out by the arrival of their cylinder, but this conceit is quickly banished and a furious battle for supremacy erupts. Rifle and cannon are pitched against a foe armed with giant mechanical walking machines, devastating heat-rays and a choking black gas. The fighting is vicious and uncompromising, and shows to merciless effect how thin the veneer of civilization is. The scenes of refugee columns, frantic stampedes and selfish acts of brutality are among the most harrowing passages of the book. They are also horrifyingly timeless.

Another equally important influence on Wells' writing was his innate dislike of the society he lived in and the appalling social inequities he saw about him. His early experiences as an apprentice had taught him that that there much to deplore in capitalism and his country of birth was not nearly as great as it liked to pretend. The relish with which he would knock down the great edifices and symbols of authority in *The War of the Worlds* is abundantly apparent in a letter he wrote to his lifelong friend Elizabeth Healey. "I'm doing the dearest little serial for Pearson's new magazine, in which I completely wreck and destroy Woking*—killing my neighbours in painful and eccentric ways—then proceed via Kingston and Richmond to London, which I sack, selecting South Kensington for feats of peculiar atrocity."[7]

The tone is both macabre and cheerful, but while Wells happily pedaled about the countryside on his bicycle selecting targets for obliteration, he was finding a way to work in yet another of his pet hates. As he wrote in his autobiography, "To most Londoners of my generation these rows of jerry-built unalterable homes seemed to be as much in the

---

*Wells lived in Woking when he was writing the book, and his house was near to Horsell Common, where the Martians first land.

nature of things as rain in September.... It is only with the wisdom of retrospect that I realise the complete irrational scrambling planlessness of which all us who had to live in London were the victims."[8] In *The War of the Worlds*, those houses were anything but unalterable. This was urban regeneration the Martian way.

Not unsurprisingly, given the influence upon him of his teacher Huxley, Wells was also a vocal proponent of Darwinism and viewed the Martian subjugation of the human race as a perfectly natural outcome in the battle for survival of the fittest. His Martians therefore had no interest in negotiation or truce. They fought total war and literally viewed the human race as cattle to be herded, bred and consumed.

Not many books can boast such a tangle of underlying currents as *The War of the Worlds*, and few are as dark and deep flowing. Wells spent much of his formative years in a basement kitchen with a domineering mother whose fierce faith in God was in stark contrast to his own low opinion of religion. This stygian existence was continued when she took up her housekeeping job. The servants' quarters of the great house where she had found work were also underground, and then once again during his apprenticeships, Wells usually found himself working or lodged in grim cellars. That these experiences were imprinted upon his mind and emerged in his writing is incontestable. The subterranean Morlocks and surface-dwelling Eloi in *The Time Machine* are the most obvious example, but there is a more disturbing parallel to be found in *The War of the Worlds*. The narrator and a curate find themselves trapped beneath a house upon which a Martian cylinder has crashed. They are imprisoned in a kitchen, which has effectively been turned into an underground tomb, and there they bicker, argue and ultimately learn to hate each other. Is it reading too much into the novel to ask what Wells was thinking when he has his hero attack the curate with a meat cleaver?

All of these bleak ideas may be central planks of the book, but Wells was not obsessed with lecturing his readers. He was first and foremost a social commentator of great skill, but he could also write a story of unsurpassed pace and excitement. Even read today, over 100 years after its publication, *The War of the Worlds* has hardly dated at all. The action scenes read as if from the latest science fiction blockbuster. Take, for instance, an attack by a Martian war machine on the sleepy English town of Shepperton:

> In another moment it was on the bank, and in a stride wading halfway across. The knees of its foremost legs bent at the farther bank, and in another moment it had raised itself to its full height again, close to the village of Shepperton. Forthwith the six guns which, unknown to anyone on the right bank, had been hidden behind the outskirts of that village, fired simultaneously. The sudden near concussion, the last close upon the first, made my heart jump. The monster was already raising the case generating the Heat-Ray as the first shell burst six yards above the hood.
>
> I gave a cry of astonishment. I saw and thought nothing of the other four Martian monsters; my attention was riveted upon the nearer incident. Simultaneously two other shells burst in the air near the body as the hood twisted round in time to receive, but not in time to dodge, the fourth shell.
>
> The shell burst clean in the face of the Thing. The hood bulged, flashed, was whirled off in a dozen tattered fragments of red flesh and glittering metal.
>
> "Hit!" shouted I, with something between a scream and a cheer.
>
> I heard answering shouts from the people in the water about me. I could have leaped out of the water with that momentary exultation.

The decapitated colossus reeled like a drunken giant; but it did not fall over. It recovered its balance by a miracle, and, no longer heeding its steps and with the camera that fired the Heat-Ray now rigidly upheld, it reeled swiftly upon Shepperton. The living intelligence, the Martian within the hood, was slain and splashed to the four winds of heaven, and the Thing was now but a mere intricate device of metal whirling to destruction. It drove along in a straight line, incapable of guidance. It struck the tower of Shepperton Church, smashing it down as the impact of a battering ram might have done, swerved aside, blundered on and collapsed with tremendous force into the river out of my sight.

A violent explosion shook the air, and a spout of water, steam, mud, and shattered metal shot far up into the sky. As the camera of the Heat-Ray hit the water, the latter had immediately flashed into steam. In another moment a huge wave, like a muddy tidal bore but almost scaldingly hot, came sweeping round the bend upstream. I saw people struggling shorewards, and heard their screaming and shouting faintly above the seething and roar of the Martian's collapse.

By the middle of the book, the Martians are well on their way to completing what Wells called "the rout of civilisation." His narrator finds himself traveling through an England undergoing a hideous transformation as a virulent Martian Red Weed begins to choke and overwhelm our native vegetation.* After his encounter with the curate, (who is driven mad by the affront to his religion represented by the Martians) and a young soldier with implausible plans to retreat underground (Wells once again fixating on the subterranean) and plot revenge, he reaches a devastated London. It seems that the human race

Illustration by the Brazilian artist Henrique Alvim Correa from a 1906 Belgian edition of *The War of the Worlds*. H. G. Wells is said to have felt it matched very closely his conception of the Martian tripod war machines (Mary Evans Picture Library).

*Perhaps influenced by Flammarion's suggestion in 1873 that the red color of Mars was caused by the spread of vegetation.

is finished but, just at the moment of his greatest despair, the Martians are revealed to have perished, laid low not by human ingenuity or force of arms but microbes. For all their scientific superiority, they could not contend with the germs and pathogens that we take for granted.

Perhaps the most intriguing aspect of the book is that Wells does not take sides. The Martians are portrayed without any real rancor. The narrative does not implore us to hate them or even root for humanity but rather to observe events dispassionately, just in fact as Wells had his Martians scrutinize us like "the transient creatures that swarm and multiply in a drop of water." Yet despite the innate pessimism of the novel, humanity gets a second chance, for Wells remained at heart an optimist. He was a committed socialist, a campaigner for world peace and women's rights who dreamed of a utopian paradise on Earth if only we could settle our petty squabbles. The novel thus ends on a cautious note of optimism, with a world rebuilt, society restored and a newly gained respect for our tenuous place in the universe.

Critical reaction in England was generally extremely positive. "One reads and reads with an interest so unflagging that it is positively exhausting"[9] wrote the reviewer in the January 1898 issue of the *Spectator* magazine, and from *Academy* came the laudatory "Mr. Wells has done good work before, but nothing quite so fine as this."[10] *The Guardian* newspaper (January 25, 1898) was somewhat less fulsome, acknowledging that "Mr Well's [sic] strength lies in his grave wielding of the scientific manner...." while observing, "We miss in this book, however, much of the delicate fancy of his earlier books." However, this does appear to have been a relatively isolated opinion, and in the United States the novel was well received. *The New York Times* (April 2, 1898) said, "Mr. Wells's dramatic power is of the strongest, and though 'War of the Worlds' deals with death, desolation and ruin, he has known how to manage a terrible topic in a clever and ingenuous way."

The War of the Worlds began official serialization in America within the pages of *Cosmopolitan Magazine** in April of 1897, but it was prescient of things to come that *The War of the Worlds* would be unofficially reproduced within the pages of a newspaper in the months after its American debut, and that the story itself was substantially altered to suit the viewpoint of local readers. This was a technique that would contribute greatly to the scare that would occur in 1938, and as will become clear in subsequent chapters, it is fascinating to observe just how easily the novel lends itself to such reinvention, both in terms of locale and more importantly in regard to the social and political happenings of the time. This would happen again and again over the years. Witness the moment in Steven Spielberg's 2005 film version of the story, where the son asks of his father "Is it the terrorists?" as all about them is reduced to rubble and ruin.

It was the *Boston Post* that was the first to tap this rich vein of reinvention, though the preposterously named *Fighters from Mars: The War of the Worlds in and near Boston* is hardly a tour de force of the imagination. The creation of a now-unknown editor at the *Post*, the first installment ran on January 9, 1898, and hacks up the original text

---

Cosmopolitan Magazine in 1897 was utterly unrecognizable compared to its modern incarnation. With a circulation of 1,700,000 in the 1930s, the magazine had a marked emphasis toward quality fiction, with writers of the caliber of Rudyard Kipling and Jack London contributing. A second Wells story, "The First Men in the Moon," appeared in 1900.

with ruthless abandon, renaming English place-names to those in and around Boston and cleaving out whole sections of text. Despite the prominent copyright notice proclaiming H. G. Wells as the author, it seems doubtful in the extreme that Wells ever saw a cent in compensation, or for that matter would have condoned such brutal butchery of his work.

It seems equally certain that Wells would have been horrified to discover that this ransacking of his imagination was to continue in the weeks that followed, though this time we can put a name to the perpetrator. Garret P. Serviss was already a popular astronomy writer at the time, but the January 12, 1898, edition of the *New York Evening Journal** carried nothing less than his unofficial sequel to *The War of the Worlds*. Entitled *Edison's Conquest of Mars*, it starred (and was apparently endorsed by) the great inventor himself, Thomas A. Edison, and in the weeks to come had him lead a counter-invasion of Mars in an avenging fleet of spacecraft. It is a pretty terrible sequel (if indeed it deserves the term) in that it ignores much of the original novel. The Martians are not even as described by Wells, but rather giant humanoids, and the main intent of the story seems to be to inflict as much punitive damage on the Martians as possible while portraying American forces as the sole saviors of mankind.

So *The War of the Worlds* had arrived in America and, apparently unbeknownst to its author, had fallen victim to some rather sharp business practices by the newspapers of the time. But if H. G. Wells was blissfully unaware of the skullduggery taking place in his name in the late 1890s, he could hardly fail to notice what happened some 40 years later when his story was once again reimagined. Indeed, the whole world was destined to sit up and take notice when the story was dramatized to calamitous effect by an upstart young radio star named Orson Welles.

---

*The *Boston Post* began daily serialization of the story on February 6, 1898.

3

ORSON WELLES
Larger Than Life

The first *War of the Worlds* radio broadcast can be judged a remarkable event for any number of reasons, not least that the guiding force behind its inception, production and execution was just 23 years of age at the time and yet already a renowned figure on both stage and radio. How Orson Welles was able to arrive at this celebrated position in such a remarkably short time is a story that combines all the best elements of a well-written radio show: tragedy, drama, dogged determination in the face of adversity, exotic travel and a traumatized tortured hero. It was to be a script that he would rewrite many times during his life, each draft more exciting and farfetched than the last. An appreciation of Welles as both showman and fantasist is therefore vital to our understanding of how he came to be associated with the most infamous radio broadcast of all time.

It is difficult to say precisely why Welles chose to make the story of his life so opaque to analysis. Was it vanity or hubris? Did he take devilish amusement in keeping people guessing, or was he just trying to compensate for issues that went to the heart of a troubled upbringing? Certainly the phrase "like father like son" seems to apply particularly well. Just as the son would go on to embroider the story of his life into a rich tapestry of half-truths and entertaining tall tales, so his father, Richard Head Welles, left behind a tangled weft and weave of uncertain facts and hearsay.

Depending on your source, Richard was either the owner of Badger Brass, a Kenosha bicycle lamp manufacturer, or a flamboyant inventor in the style of Ian Fleming's Caractacus Potts. The truth seems to be that he was the treasurer and general secretary of Badger Brass but did not, as has been suggested by Welles, invent its main claim to fame, a million-selling bicycle lamp, nor for that matter the automobile!

To exactly what degree his son helped to create the myth of a highly successful businessman and inventor is left open to question, but speaking in a moment of unguarded frankness he had this to say. "My mother and father were both much more remarkable than any story of mine can make them. They seem to me just mythically wonderful."[1] Welles biographer Frank Brady describes Richard Welles as "a minor legend in his own time"[2] and talks of a restaurant named after him and a private brand of cigars. Then there are the inventions. There is, for instance, the story of a servant sent aloft in a steam-powered aircraft which promptly crashed, and the mechanical dishwasher that succeeded only in smashing dishes. But it is still not unreasonable to credit Richard Welles with some sporadic success with his innovations, including a patented automobile jack.

However, the sad truth was that Richard Welles was a heavy drinker and serial womanizer with a moth-like attraction to the dark light of nearby Chicago. All the stranger, then, is the fact that the woman he married was far more deserving of the pedestal upon which their son placed them both, though she too had her dark side. Beatrice Ives was by all authoritative accounts a pioneering woman. Her family had acquired some wealth and prestige through commercial means, but hard times had afflicted her father's coal merchant business. Though they maintained the trappings of former wealth in the shape of a large house just outside Kenosha, by the time Richard Welles began to court her, Beatrice (and her mother) were giving music lessons to keep the wolf from the door. Beatrice was in fact an accomplished concert pianist and in later life performed to considerable acclaim under the name Trixie Ives, but her rather shallow suitor was likely more attracted to her beauty than her musical talents and aspirations. Exactly what she saw in Richard Welles is harder to fathom, but it is likely that she anticipated the opportunity to pursue her interests without fear of financial restraint. Richard was not at the time lacking in funds, and so she was thus able to achieve this goal though at the considerable personal cost of a generally unhappy marriage.

A passionate and articulate public speaker on anything from Buddhism to the Spanish-American War, Beatrice was apparently arrested and briefly jailed in 1914 for speaking out at a pro-pacifist demonstration. The same year, her political convictions propelled her to seek public office and make history as the first woman to be elected as head of the Kenosha board of education. The local paper reported her victory on its front page and described her as "one of the most prominent members of Kenosha clubs and societies,"[3] a position she clearly relished, holding court regularly at her home as one of the leading doyennes of the artistic scene. It was a lifestyle that Richard Welles found incomprehensible. To him, she was engaged in social climbing and snobbery while to her, his continuing dalliances and boorishness were an ever-present embarrassment. This curious partnership of opposites between Richard and Beatrice may do much to explain Orson's erratic behavior throughout his life.

George Orson Welles was born on May 6, 1915, the second child of this peculiar union. Of their first son, born ten years earlier, little has been written or is known. Unfortunately for Richard Welles junior, he was eclipsed in life by the brilliance of his younger brother and seems to have been abandoned by his mother as a lost cause at an early age, a strong indication that for all her talent, maternal instinct was not nearly so important to Beatrice as the need to have produced a child who lived up to her own impossibly high standards.

Orson Welles was apparently everything his older brother was not, though the stories of his precociousness are so many and varied that they should be taken with a liberal pinch of salt. Perhaps most extraordinary was the first reported instance of his genius, when at the age of eighteen months he is said to have flabbergasted Maurice Bernstein, the family doctor, with the utterance "The desire to take medicine is one of the greatest features which distinguishes men from animals."[4] This was an astonishing thing for a child so young to say, but it also served as an excuse to draw Bernstein into the orbit of Richard and Beatrice Welles. One might speculate that as the only witness to the pronouncement, he had engineered the entire thing for that very purpose, for in order to assume the role of mentor to this miraculous child he became a regular visitor to the house and Beatrice.

Doctor Bernstein was not without some alleged skeletons in his closet, not least for a scandal in Chicago that involved a violent attack on a clinic supervisor and a failed four-month marriage of dubious intent. The latter left him significantly enriched thanks to a generous dowry, but if, as seems likely, he was something of a scoundrel, he was also a complex and intelligent man who saw something genuinely remarkable in the young Welles. Thus in the years that followed he very likely did much to develop Welles' potential out of a genuine wish to help, though equally encouraging Beatrice's belief that she had sired the genius she so strongly desired. (The latter was clearly to his advantage in maintaining a close relationship with her.) That he was also stoking a massive ego in the child was a fact not lost on Welles himself in later life. "The word *genius* was whispered into my ear the first thing I ever heard while I was still mewling in my crib, so it never occurred to me that I wasn't until middle age!"[5]

In 1917 a Detroit competitor bought up Badger Brass, and in settlement for the dissolution of his partnership, Richard Welles was suddenly far wealthier to the tune of $100,000. After a number of years of increasing financial woes for the family, they were now snugly secure in their needs, of which his were now largely alcoholic in nature. As such he would doubtless have been happy to waste away in parochial Kenosha but for the insistence of Beatrice that they move somewhere where the beating heart of her beloved arts was stronger. Chicago was then undergoing painful spasms of economic growth and development and was enjoying an equally powerful cultural awakening, and so it was that the whole family, including the now firmly entrenched Dr. Bernstein, was relocated to the Windy City.

For the child Orson, who by the age of three was already apparently speaking like an adult, the stimulation provided by the move to a vibrant city like Chicago was pure grist for the mill. His mother harbored fervent aspirations that he would follow in her footsteps and become a great musician and so took him to numerous stage performances, exposing him to a cultural smorgasbord of music and opera. Meanwhile at home, the ever-present Dr. Bernstein lavished his young ward with gifts intended to encourage both intellectual and cultural development.

The list of achievements that flowed forth is as impressive as they are varied. A puppet theater became an obsession for Welles, with many a happy hour spent writing, planning and staging his own little dramas. A magic kit fueled a lifelong passion for illusion and sleight of hand, and a theatrical makeup kit would open his eyes to the possibilities of disguise and deception, a particularly sensitive topic for a child who felt more at home in the company of adults and spent much of his formative years trying to look and behave as if far older than he actually was.

His parents finally and acrimoniously separated when he was five. Beatrice took the children and continued to lavish attention on her favorite son, though Welles claimed her relentlessness once drove him to the ledge of a high window and there threaten suicide rather than face another music lesson.* But Beatrice's plans were to be curtailed, for on his ninth birthday Welles found himself called to her deathbed. She died aged only 43 on May 10, 1924, in Chicago Memorial Hospital, though somehow Doctor Bernstein was so interwoven into the Welles family fabric that he continued in his role of parallel father figure.

---

*An uncanny parallel with that of his namesake, H. G. Wells.

It should be noted that Richard Welles was not entirely an absentee father in regard to his sons' development and had tried over the years to wrest Orson from the detested influence of his mother and surrogate father. The school of life he favored was, of course, in stark opposition to that of his wife. After Beatrice's death, Welles apparently joined his father in sampling some of what that life had to offer, such that he was smoking cigars at the age of ten and would sit up late into the night listening to his father's tall tales. Richard also introduced him to his friends and acquaintances, numbered and noted among them several eminent cartoonists, including Bud Fisher, the creator of the comic strip *Mutt and Jeff*, and George McManus of *Bringing Up Father* fame. He even encouraged his son to try his hand at becoming a cartoonist, a career he thought much more appropriate and potentially lucrative than the musical one Beatrice had mapped out for him. As a result Welles would develop a not inconsiderable talent as an illustrator, which he would later put to good effect in stage design. But though he clearly resisted any attempt to mold him in the image of either parent, he would always be torn between the two contrasting lifestyles.

In the aftermath of his mother's death, Welles once again joined his father in traveling the world, primarily, one suspects, to escape the morbid attentions of Dr. Bernstein, for whom he was now the only remaining link to his beloved Beatrice. The pair fetched up in a variety of exotic places including Jamaica and the Far East, returning eventually to face the nagging question of what to do about the boy's formal schooling. For a genius, there were some quite astounding gaps in his knowledge, including a virtually nonexistent grasp of mathematics, a pointless distraction, he thought, for one who had already decided that the theater was to be his lifework.

Neither Dr. Bernstein nor Richard was in favor of this, so putting aside their mutual loathing for each other; they agreed to send him at the age of 11 to the Todd School for Boys, located in Woodstock, Illinois. Both hoped Todd would knock some sense into him, Bernstein because the school had a strong reputation for music teaching (Beatrice's influence reaching from beyond the grave) and Welles senior because the headmaster ran an authoritarian institution that almost succeeded (at least in the father's view) in straightening out his wayward younger son — that is, until he was expelled.

The plan might have worked, but for the fact that in 1926 the school was undergoing a change of leadership that completely turned the old regime on its head and presented Welles with an environment entirely suited to his own aspirations. The catalyst for this fortuitous change was to be the next in the series of influential figures that were to prove pivotal in his life. Following on from the confused ménage à trois that had characterized his early years, Todd headmaster Roger "Skipper" Hill was a wholly new and conventional kind of father figure, a man settled in a stable, loving relationship with a devoted wife. Both were intensely focused toward the goal of encouraging their young charges to maximize every talent they possessed.

Welles biographer Simon Callow suggests that from an early age, Welles was aware on some level, conscious or otherwise, of the power he possessed to charm those around him and thus made full use of his natural abilities to achieve his aims. He would brandish his intellect, flaunt his charisma and even use his burgeoning sexual magnetism if it would draw the object of his attention. Skipper Hill was no less immune to the charismatic Svengali in his midst and, like those before him, crossed the dangerous line from praise into adulation. Orson was continuing to charm and bludgeon his way through life, taking control of the Todd theatrical department as if it were his own private fiefdom and beginning to build his thoroughly deserved reputation as a prodigy and master of stage-craft. A fellow student recalled that "the theatre was totally Orson's, it was a one-man band."[6]

It was quite clearly a magical time for him. Under Skipper Hill, the school was more akin to a miniature community than an educational facility. It offered all manner of facilities and opportunities with a relaxed attitude to teaching that allowed Welles to drift through those lessons that disinterested him and dominate those that inflamed his passions. Roger Hill effectively gave his wayward charge free rein and admitted to a reporter, "He pretty much educated himself. I don't take any credit for Welles at all."[7]

But then during the Christmas holidays of 1930 came another defining moment. Welles' father was discovered dead in a room of the Bismarck Hotel in Chicago. It can hardly have come as a surprise to him that heart and kidney disease were cited as the cause. At the suggestion of the Hills, he had recently cut contact with his father in an attempt to dissuade him from his increasingly heavy drinking, having spent what must have been a dispiriting foreign adventure with him a few months previously.

The deceptively breezy dispatches of their travels in the Far East in 1930 (they departed for Shanghai in July) were published in a small newspaper called the *Highland Park News*, an early example of Welles' acute talent for self-publicity, but what they did not tell was the embarrassment meted out to him by his father's drunkenness, when for instance on a ferry out of Hong Kong he was so intoxicated as to require his son to pull his trousers back up in front of a crowd of local potentates. Yet on the same trip Richard had berated his son for rolling back to their cabin in a state of inebriation, a case perhaps of a despairing old drunk seeing the seeds of his disease sown in the son. However, if his father imparted one positive legacy in his son, it was a love of travel. So when the specter of continuing education loomed and resistance stiffened to his determination to act, it was agreed with Dr. Bernstein (who had assumed the position of legal guardian) that a painting tour of Ireland would be a suitable compromise cause of action.

The painting tour was another triumph of Welles' indomitable will to succeed in his chosen profession. (The painting was soon abandoned.) Finding himself in Dublin after a series of frivolous adventures, he was drawn to the Gate Theatre. The Gate was and still is a theater of considerable standing. Lacking both a reputation and qualifications that might induce the theater to hire him, Welles simply breezed in as if the Gate should be honored to make his acquaintance. Again, he created his own reality. As he himself later admitted to Peter Bogdanovich, "I lied like a maniac."[8] He fooled no one, but pure bravado got him an audition for a plum role in the forthcoming production of *Jew Süss*, a darkly comic satire of anti–Semitism in 18th-century Germany.

Cofounder of the Gate Theatre Micheal MacLiammoir has this to say of Welles' audition: "It was an astonishing performance, wrong from beginning to end but with all the qualities of fine acting tearing their way through a chaos of inexperience. His diction was practically perfect, his personality, in spite of his fantastic circus antics, was real and varied; his sense of passion, of evil, of drunkenness, of tyranny, of a sort of demoniac authority was arresting; a preposterous energy pulsated through everything he did."[9] It is an extraordinary description, though Welles has himself poured good-humored cold water on the story, stating in an interview for the BBC arts program *Arena* that Micheal MacLiammoir was not actually present at the Gate Theatre that day, and it was MacLiammoir's partner Hilton Edwards who gave him his break. Regardless of who was present to see his audition, Welles duly got his chance and created an overnight sensation, but one can't help but think Welles is giving a tip of the hat from one fantasist to another when he acknowledges of MacLiammoir, "He couldn't have told the story as well if he hadn't put himself in it as an eyewitness."[10]

The critics were unanimous in their praise of Welles' debut, and with the adulation still ringing in his ears, he prepared in February of 1932 to return home to what were surely even greater glories. But it was not to be. News of his triumphs in Ireland had not traveled back to New York, and struggling to be taken seriously as an actor at just 17 years of age left him adrift with neither income nor hope of finding one. It must have been a terrible letdown for someone so convinced of his own innate worth, so when Skipper Hill came to his rescue with the suggestion that they coauthor a play, he gratefully took up the challenge. A play was written (and cautiously commended in theatrical circles) but the necessary backing failed to materialize. It was another disappointment, but the irrepressible teenager was not about to give up his dreams and so instead embarked on another audacious trip abroad.

The details of his travels, of how he took a freighter to Morocco and from there engaged in a wild series of adventures among Arab princes, enjoyed the pleasures of harems and fought bulls in Spain, all while simultaneously illustrating a book on the plays of Shakespeare, would be extraordinary if even half true. One of the few certainties of this period is the book, a well-received work intended as a plain-speaking guide to Shakespeare that was coauthored with Skipper Hill.

Returning in 1933 to Chicago, Welles was to enjoy another of the lucky breaks that so characterized his early career and would desert him so spectacularly in later life. A chance encounter at a party got him an introduction to Guthrie McClintic, husband of Katharine Cornell. Cornell was considered the first lady of American theater and with her director husband had founded a repertory company that was about to go on a nationwide tour with Shakespeare's *Romeo and Juliet*. Welles again wove his magic, convincing McClintic to hire him without even a formal audition and then making a typically lasting impression on those who worked with him. Writing in her autobiography, Cornell enthused, "We were all struck by his beautiful voice and speech and always provocative acting methods."[11] They were also struck by his more unfortunate qualities: sleeping till noon, drinking late into the night and even becoming involved in barroom brawls. Nevertheless, Welles soaked up the minutiae that went into the production of a stage play. No detail was too small; he even noted the number of cough drops made available to the audience before a performance and filed it away for future reference.

After a summer hiatus, the company made a triumphant Broadway debut, though Welles was not so pleased. Another actor was assigned the role of Mercutio instead of Welles, and he was "demoted" to what he felt was the lesser role of Tybalt. The role of Mercutio had gone to a movie star named Brian Aherne whom Welles thought a terrible actor. As Aherne recalled, Welles was pleasant enough to him, but their fight scenes often seemed a little too intense. Welles broke his prop sword on two occasions. But what he also did was take a minor character and, charged with his anger and resentment, imbue him with a power and presence that stole the show. The very strength of that performance was to have an unexpected impact on his career.

Present in the audience one evening was a relative newcomer to the world of theater and indeed to America; a recent immigrant from England named John Houseman. He had come to America in 1925 as a grain merchant, but was now hoping to become a theater producer and writer. Writing in his autobiography, he describes his first sight of Welles in ebullient terms.

> That glossy and successful evening was marked for me by one astonishing vision: not Miss Cornell's fervent Juliet, nor Edith Evan's admirable nurse, nor Basil Rathbone's polite, middle-aged Romeo, nor Brian Aherne's Mercutio, exuberantly slapping his yellow tights as he strutted through Jo's* bright Italiante scenery — those were all blotted out by the excitement of the two brief moments when the furious Tybalt appeared suddenly in that sunlit Verona square: death in scarlet and black, in the form of a monstrous boy — flat-footed and graceless, yet swift and agile; soft as jelly one moment and uncoiled the next, in a spring of such furious energy that, once released, it could be stopped by no human intervention. What made this figure so obscene and terrible was the pale, shiny child's face under the unnatural growth of dark beard, from which there issued a voice of such clarity and power that it tore like a high wind through the genteel, modulated voices of the well-trained professionals around him.[12]

Houseman was captivated and rushed backstage to meet this Tybalt, but the amazing actor was nowhere to be seen. He could not, however, soon forget him, and when some three weeks later a new project presented itself, his first thought was to secure Welles in the starring role. Another backstage visit and a bribed doorman finally got him into Welles' presence. It was a crucial encounter for both men. Houseman was, like Welles, something of an everyman in the theater (he would later reinvent himself as an actor and win an Oscar† at the age of 70) but he also had two important qualities that Welles lacked: a good head for business and the tact and management abilities that went with it.

He was just the kind of complementary collaborator that Welles needed. Those around him recognized this. Actress Geraldine Fitzgerald recalls the relationship in colorful terms. "They said [it] was like a busted water main, his talent, and it went all over the streets and down alleys and filled up holes and made shapes and patterns, that was Orson. And John comes along and then with buckets and jugs and pots and pans he collects all this wonderful wonderful material and allows it to have more shape than Orson would have bothered to give it."[13] The two became friends, and together they would enjoy some unparalleled successes. However, the relationship was fraught with disagreements and arguments. It would last only a few highly charged years and end on an appalling note of acrimony and bitterness,§ but for now, a bright future beckoned.

---

*Stage designer Jo Mielziner.
†*The Paper Chase*, 1973.
§Simmering resentments came to a head in 1939, when at a tense meeting at a Hollywood restaurant, Welles refused to acknowledge the Mercury Theatre's financial difficulties, and in a fit of rage hurled a flaming plate warmer at Houseman, as well as a tirade of abuse.

By 1935, Roosevelt's New Deal program was well under way and one surprising development was the creation of the Federal Theatre Project. Under this ambitious plan, the government would fund theatrical projects across the country, offering work for thousands of struggling actors, actresses and technicians, while providing affordable quality entertainment for the masses. It was to one of these endeavors, the Negro Theatre Project in Harlem, that John Houseman was appointed head that year. It was a daunting job. Crime, deprivation and bigotry were endemic in the neighborhood and Houseman had to contend with both the suspicions of the local population at the appointment of a white face and the prejudices of wider society.

It was while searching for a suitable play that would fit the sensibilities of his actors and audience (generally accustomed until then to either being patronized or insulted onstage), that he called upon Welles for suggestions and to fill the crucial role of director. The breathless answer came at 2 A.M. one morning with the ringing of the phone. Welles had recently married, and his wife Virginia had provided the inspiration. They would produce an all-black version of *Macbeth* set on the island of Haiti during the reign of Henri I (Henri Christophe). The witches would become voodoo priestesses! It was a stunning and original vision, but Houseman was uncomfortable. He had originally proposed the laudable aim of producing a classical play acted out with no reference or concession to the actors' skin color, yet this highly charged reinvention of Macbeth seemed

to imply the very opposite. It was a possibility not lost on some in the community, and the controversy that dogged the production resulted in much impassioned debate and on one occasion a late-night attack on Welles by four irate citizens.

No one need have worried. Welles was committed to the idea of giving the black actors their equality on the stage, and the play was a smash with its Harlem patrons, though as Houseman noted, one white critic asked that he and his wife should not be seated next to any Negroes. It was an offensive request rendered laughably impracticable on opening night, April 14, 1936, as Harlem came out in force and mobbed the Lafayette Theatre in a supportive crowd 10,000 strong. The *New York Times* of April

John Houseman, photographed in New York during the production of the Federal Theatre Project play *Horse Eats Hat* (Theatre of the Thirties Collection, Special Collections & Archives, George Mason University Libraries).

15, 1936, reported on the scene. "As the hour grew near for the performance, Police Lieutenant Samuel Battle and twelve policemen, including two on horses, found it almost impossible to open a way to the lobby. All northbound automobile traffic was stopped for more than an hour." The article goes on to describe how Welles was practically dragged from the wings to take a bow upon his professional directorial debut.

The acclaim was intoxicating, but functioning within the bureaucracy of the Federal Theatre Project had become more and more difficult for Welles and his now committed partner John Houseman. The last straw had come when a long-rehearsed production of a socially controversial play called *The Cradle Will Rock* was cancelled from on high. The reason was given as financial cutbacks to the program, but the suspicion must be that the government had become nervous about a publicly financed organization

Orson Welles at age 21, photographed in New York during the production of the Federal Theatre Project play *Horse Eats Hat* (Theatre of the Thirties Collection, Special Collections & Archives, George Mason University Libraries).

performing a play that drew attention to corruption at all levels of society. Leading their actors past security guards who had effectively locked them out of their own production, the pair staged what amounted to a guerrilla performance in a hastily procured and dilapidated theater. The play was performed before a large and freely admitted audience, but the cast were under instructions from their union not to perform onstage without contracts. Welles and Houseman could not afford to comply, so in a daring and unique event in the history of theater, the cast delivered their lines from their seats scattered among the audience. It was an extraordinary swan song for both men in that it signaled the end of their association with the Federal Theatre Project. The obvious next step was for the pair to form a repertory company of their own.

The Mercury Theatre arose metaphorically from the ashes of the Federal Theatre but specifically from the fireplace of a small house Welles and his wife were renting at Sneden's Landing in Rockland County, New York. In a corner of that fireplace, he and John Houseman had found an old copy of *American Mercury* magazine and, borrowing the name, set out to reinvent American theater. With Welles at the controls, it was to be another typically exhilarating flight of dizzying highs and terrifying lows. They began

Orson Welles (left) and John Houseman, photographed in New York during the production of the Federal Theatre Project play *Horse Eats Hat.* For several years Houseman and Welles were inseparable, but their relationship became increasingly strained (Theatre of the Thirties Collection, Special Collections & Archives, George Mason University Libraries).

with $100 in the bank, yet at the height of its powers, the company was considered the brightest light on Broadway. With plays such as their production of *Julius Caesar* they did indeed do much to energize and revitalize theatrical conventions. Their Caesar wore a business suit, not as a cost-cutting exercise, but to emphasize the parallels that Welles discerned between the original work and modern times. Other hits followed, but the threat of bankruptcy and ruin was never far from their thoughts.

To keep the wolf from the door, Welles had been cultivating another creative avenue for his talents, one that was to prove spectacularly lucrative. New York City was then the center of the radio broadcasting industry and with his distinctive voice and command of the spoken word Welles was soon in great demand. It also helped that he could land on his feet no matter what he was presented with and could switch effortlessly from character to character with little or no preparation. In conversation with Peter Bogdanovich, Welles paints a picture of an industry dominated by few such able actors. "Soon I was doing so many I didn't even rehearse. I'd come to a bad end in some tearjerker on the seventh floor of CBS and rush up to the ninth (they'd hold an elevator for me), where, just as the [on-air] light was going on, somebody'd hand me a script and whisper 'Chinese mandarin, seventy-five years old' and off I'd go again."[14] It was an ability that would earn him upwards of $1,500 a week, an unheard-of sum of money at the time, much of which Welles would plow back into his productions.

Bizarrely, as Welles himself has noted, his roles were frequently uncredited, but that did not stop the money rolling in. The radio role that most suited his extraordinary voice was that of the Shadow, a mysterious crime fighter with a supernatural power to cloud the minds of his enemies, a somewhat ironic ability for the character given that Welles was capable of that very trick away from the microphone. He was not the first actor to take the role; Frank Readick, with whom he would later work on The *War of the Worlds*, had preceded him. In fact, Readick provided the spine-chilling trademark laugh of the Shadow even after Welles took over in September 1937. Surprisingly, Welles could never quite nail it (though he subsequently laid claim to the laugh in conversation with Peter Bogdanovich) but more than any other actor, his rich tones became synonymous with the role and were

Orson Welles, March 1937 (Library of Congress, Prints & Photographs Division, Carl Van Vechten Collection).

instantly recognizable to his millions of fans. A visit Welles made to his lawyer nicely illustrates his fame as upon entering the premises he was preceded by the excited office boy, who shouted out, "The Shadow is here, the Shadow is here!"[15]

The sheer number of roles that Welles was taking on necessitated that he find a novel way of getting from one performance to the next, and he did. He delighted in explaining, though it seems too fantastic to be true. Welles claims that he had discovered there was no law in New York to prevent people using an ambulance to get from place to place, even if they were not sick. So he hired an ambulance and shuttled back and forth from studio to studio, cutting through the traffic with ease. How exactly one went about hiring an ambulance in New York City Welles never explained, but annoying little details like that would have only ruined the telling of a great tale. It seems likely that the truth of the matter was a little more prosaic, with John Houseman providing the somewhat sarcastic observation that Welles "would be delivered in a taxi by one of his slaves barely in time for the dress rehearsal."[16] Houseman's antipathy toward Welles should not however discourage an appreciation of the tale, and it is perfectly understandable why the ambulance story has retained so much currency with biographers.

For a brief time and despite the constant adversity and worries about money, things could not have been better. The joy of pure creativity and critical acclaim sustained the Mercury in the darker hours, and the next season should have been even bigger and better, but then came a fresh blow. Hiram Sherman, who next to Welles was the most valuable member of the repertory cast, had defected to another producer. To Welles, who counted Hiram as his oldest and most trusted friend, it was a betrayal of unimaginable magnitude.

Houseman described Welles' reaction on learning of the news. "When I got to Sneden's Landing I found Orson lying limp and huge in a darkened room with his face to the wall. Locked in his room, Orson refused to discuss the future. I spent two days in the theatre canceling our commitments before I started back to Sneden's." It was a trip he was not to complete. "I saw an oversized black limousine coming up the hill at high speed. As it approached, it began to sound its horn and I became aware of Orson's huge face sticking out of the window with its mouth wide open and of his gigantic voice echoing through the surrounding woods."[17] Welles was bringing news of his latest coup, an offer of unparalleled opportunity that would subsequently plunge the pair into more hot water than either could ever have imagined. The CBS radio network had come to him with an offer he could hardly ignore. He was to have a radio show of his own, it would be creatively and artistically his to command, and John Houseman and the rest of the Mercury Theatre regulars were coming along with Welles for what proved to be the ride of their lives.

4

PREPARING TO END THE WORLD
The Making of the Broadcast

Producing a broadcast of the Mercury Theatre was a study in the art of organized chaos and barely restrained hostility. At the very center of this weekly maelstrom stood the elemental force that was Orson Welles, not exactly the calm in the eye of the storm but rather a conductor of lightning. John Houseman describes a typical day of preparation for a broadcast in terms that might just as usefully illustrate a riot. "Often violence broke out. Scripts flew through the air, doors were slammed, batons smashed."[1] Yet somehow week after week, these turbulent energies were marshaled, shaped and channeled by Welles into an astonishing and smoothly performed masterpiece.

The proposed format was simple. Each hour-long show would present an adaptation of a classic literary property. Welles would naturally take the lead, plus read any expositional passages, a technique he had developed the previous year when he had brilliantly adapted Victor Hugo's *Les Misérables*. At first glance, CBS could be considered quite daring in promoting such an artistic endeavor, but in truth radio was then undergoing a serious crisis of conscience and the network had sound reasons for securing the services of Welles. In her insightful book *Radio Voices*, Michele Hilmes paints a picture of despairing network executives lamenting the decline in standards. Wrote NBC head of continuity Burke Boyce in a 1936 memo, "Certainly our programs are of a lower standard of taste and humor than they were a year ago."[2] This sorry state of affairs was blamed on the powerful advertising agencies that supplied much of the programming to the networks and fought hard to evade and subvert what standards there were. Even Congress was becoming concerned at the concessions to quality made at the behest of sponsors, and ominous threats of legislation had prompted the networks to try repositioning themselves as patrons of the arts. It wasn't an enormously disruptive adjustment. The networks still had plenty of essentially vacant airtime filled with musical interludes and could easily afford to pad out their schedules with what became known as "sustaining shows," to the point in 1938 where up to two-thirds of the CBS output met this criteria.

These low-cost shows were usually aired opposite unassailable sponsored competitors and were produced on very tight budgets. Welles was therefore to be paid a flat rate of $50,000 for the first nine shows, from which he had to meet all expenses except for the use of the CBS orchestra, though if the monetary rewards were thin, then conversely the opportunity to push the creative envelope was incredibly enticing, since without the interfering presence of a sponsor they were blissfully free to experiment and innovate.

It was the beginning of the golden age of radio, and for the fiercely independent Welles the situation was heaven sent. He was to be at the helm of a new and exciting venture with which he intended to challenge the moribund conventions of radio, and at the same time he would further cement his reputation as an artistic prodigy. His agent had declared emphatically, "You got to do it all, Orson,"[3] and Welles willingly obliged by billing himself as writer, director, producer and star, hence the original working title for the series, *First Person Singular*.* Meanwhile CBS was equally pleased to make capital of the unique fact that they had a highly regarded theatrical company in their employ, though Welles was wary of revisiting past glories. His approach was spelled out in a manifesto presented to the *New York Times* on June 12, 1938.

> The Mercury has no intention of reproducing its stage repertoire in these broadcasts. Instead, we plan to bring to radio the experimental techniques that have proven so successful in another medium and to treat radio itself with the intelligence and respect such a beautiful and powerful medium deserves.

Bold, challenging words, but it was John Houseman who effectively found himself saddled with the job of breathing life into this singular vision, for Welles was if anything an accomplished delegator of tasks and besides rather busy at the time in pursuit of a ballerina with whom he had become enamored. After discarding the first choice of *Alice in Wonderland* (felt to have too many childish connotations) CBS and Welles settled on *Treasure Island* as an appropriate inaugural broadcast. Though Houseman complained that he knew nothing at all of the conventions and styles of radio, Welles set him to work with the rather careless rejoinder that he had better start learning.[4] After Houseman had spent days cooped up in his one-room apartment laboring to fashion a script, Welles then threw a typical curveball and announced that they would instead premiere with Bram Stoker's *Dracula*, to which he had just secured the rights. Three weeks had been wasted. It was now less than one week to the first broadcast.

Buying up half a dozen copies of the book and arming themselves with paper, paste and scissors, the pair retired to an all night diner on 59th Street called Reubens and over steak and cognac fell upon the story, disemboweling it into key component moments and creating the storyboard to a serviceable script in a single marathon 12-hour session. It was now just two days to airtime, and though it would prove to be the first of many successful broadcasts, this precarious brush with a deadline set something of a pattern. The progress of *The War of the Worlds* would be no less stressful, and indeed this was one storm that was almost extinguished in the rarefied creative atmosphere that characterized the Mercury Theatre on the Air.

After the initial nine broadcasts for which Welles was contracted, the show was swiftly renewed and to considerable acclaim continued to deliver its broad spectrum of classic adaptations, though listening figures remained disappointing. Planned for the seventeenth show was *Lorna Doone*, by R. D. Blackmore, a turbulent novel of love and larceny set in late 17th-century England. A draft script had been prepared by Houseman but as the broadcast date of October 30 approached, second thoughts began to plague Welles. Was this really such a suitable story? The role of the driven hero John Ridd had seemed perfectly suited to his dramatic flair, but in the cold light of day the script was

*From the very beginning, the show was more commonly known as The Mercury Theatre on the Air and by the second season the network had effectively dropped any reference to "First Person Singular."

lacking the vigor that Welles had originally imagined. It now seemed dull and slow. Fearing that it would be impossible to polish enough to meet his high standards in time for the broadcast (yet again just over one week away), Welles decided to shelve *Lorna Doone* and replace it with *The War of the Worlds*, the only other property to which he had secured the rights at the time.

With the notable exception of *Buck Rogers*, for a juvenile audience, science fiction was at the time a relatively untried genre on radio, but Welles and Houseman had already sized up a number of potential stories. Sir Arthur Conan Doyle's *Lost World* would have provided Welles with a suitably larger-than-life role in the person of Professor Challenger, as would M. P. Shiel's *The Purple Cloud*, in which the human race is all but suffocated by cyanide gas released by volcanoes. This story would have suited Welles immensely, concerning as it does the travels and travails of a lone and thoroughly amoral survivor who goes on an orgy of godlike destruction in the depopulated world. Ultimately both stories were passed over in favor of the Martians. The decision does not seem to have been made for any particularly compelling reason, other than it was generally held that a pseudo-scientific tale would provide a good contrast with the more serious offerings of the season. Houseman subsequently acknowledged the possibility that neither he nor Welles had even read *The War of the Worlds* prior to the decision to dramatize it, though in his biography of Welles, Frank Brady suggests that Welles had come across the story several years previously in the pages of a pulp magazine called *The Witch's Tale*.*

As the season progressed, Houseman was finding the pressure of managing the Mercury both on and off the air plus writing a weekly sixty-minute script an increasingly wearisome burden. "There was a time when I never got out of bed, because I never had time to get out of bed. So I would lie in bed and write the radio shows, lie in bed and administer the Mercury Theatre, simply because I had no time to get up."[5] So it was that that the exhausted Houseman came to add to the Mercury roster a largely untried but talented young playwright named Howard Koch. Koch was an almost total unknown when a desperate Houseman hired him. Having had a play recently performed by the Federal Theatre Project in Chicago, he had arrived in New York with his family with the ambition of becoming a writer. His starting salary with the Mercury was $75 a week, and for this he was expected to turn out some 60 pages of script every seven days.

For his third project he was assigned *The War of the Worlds* and instructed to reset the novel in contemporary America and to use the device of breaking news flashes to dramatize the story. There is no consensus as to who came up with this idea, Welles or Houseman, but such interruptions were becoming commonplace as the storm clouds of war gathered in Europe. Not even Welles had escaped unscathed, having had his September 25 broadcast of *Sherlock Holmes* interrupted with word of the Munich crisis.

Armed with his instructions, Koch set about the task, but after several days' work phoned Houseman in considerable torment. In his autobiography Koch explains how difficult he was finding it to adapt the story. "Reading the story, which was set in England

---

*Investigation reveals no magazine of this name, but there was a long-running radio drama called *The Witch's Tale*, which was the brainchild of Alonzo Deen Cole, a radio pioneer who was writing, directing and starring in his own show several years before Welles made such effective capital of the concept. However, *The Witch's Tale* radio series did not adapt *The War of the Worlds*.

and written in a different narrative style, I realized I could use very little but the author's idea of a Martian invasion and his description of their appearance and their machines. In short, I was being asked to write an almost entirely original play in six days. I called Houseman, pleading to have the assignment changed to another subject." Houseman's secretary Annie Froelisch, who was on loan to Koch to transcribe his handwritten pages, chimed in on the phone to add her own succinct opinion to the debate. "Those old Martians are just a lot of nonsense! It's all too silly! We're going to make fools of ourselves! Absolute fools!"[6]

As recalled by Koch, Houseman called back after discussing the situation with Orson. Unfortunately for the writer, Houseman said, "The answer was a firm 'no,' it was Orson's favorite project."[7] In retrospect it looks like this may have been a white lie on the part of Houseman. Writing in *Harper's Magazine* in 1948, he indicates that he was never actually able to contact Welles that evening as he was then entering into his 36th hour of dress rehearsals for *Danton's Death*. Acquiescing to Koch's request for a change of assignment did not seem possible, as the only available replacement at this short notice was the leaden *Lorna Doone*. Houseman shared Welles' deep reservations about the quality of the *Lorna Doone* script, and so to swap at this late stage would surely be a case of dodging the heat-ray and falling into the fire. Cajoling the despondent writer to persevere, Houseman promised to come to his aid later that evening.

Koch certainly had his work cut out for him. As he had correctly anticipated, moving the action to America and reimagining the story as a series of news flashes required

a complete rethink of the story's structure and the invention of a whole new set of characters, a problem Koch endeavored to address in the earliest known draft of the script. One key addition to the cast is the reporter Carl Phillips, who would be played superbly by Frank Readick, but Welles not unnaturally bags the plum role of Professor Pierson, who can best be described as an amalgamation of two characters from the novel, those of the unnamed narrator and the astronomer Ogilvy. It would only be in the second act of later drafts that more familiar material would come to the fore, with Welles (continuing in the role of Professor Pierson) meeting a deranged artillery-

Howard Koch, author of the 1938 *War of the Worlds* **radio script (courtesy Peter Koch).**

man who has grandiose dreams of fighting back against the Martians by creating an underground resistance (literally and figuratively) in the sewers and cellars beneath the occupied cities.

An intriguing question quite naturally arises during this period of incredibly stressful effort. How many drafts of the script did Koch produce, and by how much did they differ from the final version that was aired? Regretfully, no record exists in any account of the making of the broadcast to help answer this important question, but one early draft of the script was purported to have emerged briefly in 2003, before sinking out of sight again. The description of the 17-page script[8] (which was auctioned on eBay by a highly reputable antiquarian bookseller in Chicago called O'Gara & Wilson) is radically different than the final version that was broadcast, and offers an astounding insight into the way the story evolved in those hectic few days allowed to Koch.

The first disparity to note is that this version goes by the rather unwieldy title *An Attack by the Men from Mars.** At just 17 pages the script is considerably shorter than the broadcast version, and while it apparently shares some similar passages, these were much more developed in the final version. However, the most striking difference pertains to the cast of characters. The broadcast version features an all-male cast, but this earlier draft has four female characters. Unfortunately only two of these characters were described in the sale brochure, but we do learn that one was to be named Wilma Reynolds and that her role was that of a reporter working alongside the character of Carl Phillips. Hence the dialogue eventually delivered in its entirety by Frank Readick as Phillips was in this earlier version divided equally between the characters of Reynolds and Phillips. The other female character described was based loosely on the deranged artilleryman that the narrator of the novel meets in his travels, but rather than planning on retreating underground to form a new society, this new character proposes the rather preposterous idea of training an army of sewer rats to chew through the armored hulls of the Martian war machines. In hindsight, the loss of this character might be considered a blessing rather than a curse.

The provenance of this version of the script seems to be extremely convincing. The script was part of a large collection of radio ephemera amassed by James Jewell, a well-known director, actor and writer credited as one of the co-creators of *The Lone Ranger*. It was Jewell who selected the *William Tell* Overture as the famous theme for the series and he often directed and occasionally wrote episodes. He also directed many episodes of *The Green Hornet*. In 1938 he was working for the CBS radio affiliate WBBM in Chicago and it was here he was said to have found the copy of *The War of the Worlds* script, though it is entirely unclear what such an early draft version of the script would have been doing so far from New York. As to the fate of the script itself, it failed to reach its reserve in the auction, but was then sold to a private collector who was allegedly planning to publish it. Alas, nothing further has been heard of it.

The precise place this earlier script occupies in the development of the story can only be guessed at (though it must surely have been very early in the process) but we can

---

*It may be entirely coincidental, but Houseman wrote an article about the *War of the Worlds* broadcast for *Harper's* in December of 1948 that he called *The Men from Mars*. Could it be that this harks back to the earlier draft name of the script?

with some confidence reconstruct the sequence of events that occurred after John Houseman finally arrived at Koch's apartment in the early hours of Tuesday morning. Much to his relief, he found the mood had altered for the better and the moribund campaign was now making rapid military progress. As Koch described in his account of the writing of the script, he was just like H. G. Wells before him, reveling in his role. "I deployed the opposing forces over an ever-widening area, made moves and countermoves between the invaders and the defenders; eventually I found myself enjoying the destruction I was wreaking like a drunken general."[9]

Koch was gleefully laying fictitious waste to real places, but how he came to choose his beachhead for the Martian invasion was down to one of those random quirks of fate that no one could have predicted, least of all the inhabitants of an unsuspecting little New Jersey hamlet. With no script to hand, Welles had risked announcing at the conclusion of his Sunday, October 23, broadcast, that *The War of the Worlds* would be the next Mercury presentation, and Koch had duly been handed the rush assignment that very night. He generally took Monday off and despite the urgency of the assignment still managed to snatch a few hours away to visit his family, but on the return journey Koch began to mull over the requirements of the story. He realized that in order to make good on his instructions, he would need to provide his invaders with adequate intelligence on the lay of the land.

In search of a map he stopped off at a New Jersey gas station on Route 9W. That evening he spread out his new map and, with eyes closed, brought a pencil point down at random. This entirely arbitrary method alighted on Grover's Mill, a name that Koch felt very satisfied with. It had an authentic ring and was also sufficiently close to Princeton that he could plausibly bring in the real astronomical observatory to be found there as an additional location.

With additional help from Houseman and Froelisch a draft script was completed by Wednesday evening, a process described by Koch as "a nightmare of scenes written and rewritten, pages speeding back and forth to the studio, with that Sunday deadline staring me in the face."[10] There now began a well-practiced if highly stressful process of revision and refinement. On Thursday the Mercury's Paul Stewart (a Broadway actor turned director) led and recorded a rehearsal, without music and with only the most basic of sound effects, which would be replayed for Welles that evening in his hotel room. These rehearsals were in themselves opportunities to rework the script and discover what worked and did not. The cast was encouraged to contribute in this regard with suggestions to make the dialogue more natural and free flowing. So for instance, in the part of the story where the key character of Professor Pierson meets the soldier, it was pointed out that the original line as inspired by the novel, "I've been thinking about the drains" would be inappropriate to American audiences. The word *drain* was more likely to conjure up visions of the drainer in a sink, so the line was changed to "I've been thinking about the sewers."

At the gathering late Thursday night in Welles' room at the Regis Hotel, the considered consensus was that for all this effort the result remained dull and if it were to be made to work in any reasonably dramatic way, the use of news flashes would need to be further accentuated. Welles was particularly insistent on this, likely because that same night he had listened to and was greatly impressed by a dramatic play called *Air Raid*. Written by the poet Archibald MacLeish and presented by the well-regarded *Columbia Workshop* (another CBS "sustaining show"), the play was in the style of a live news broadcast from a European town under attack by enemy forces. Welles had even lent to the *Columbia Workshop* the Mercury player Ray Collins to serve in the role of announcer, and Welles was himself intimately familiar with the work of MacLeish, having previously starring in his play *Panic** onstage, and *The Fall of the City* on radio.

It was the work of MacLeish that evidently most influenced Welles in pursuing the idea of presenting *The War of the Worlds* in the style of a news broadcast. Since he had lent Collins to the *Columbia Workshop* and knew MacLeish personally it is entirely plausible to suppose that he knew in advance the subject and style of *Air Raid*, but MacLeish's previous work would also have heavily informed Welles. *The Fall of the City* had been broadcast just over a year earlier, on April 11, 1937, with Welles taking the role of a reporter observing the reactions of a huge crowd[†] in a city square as an invading force approaches. The parallels are impossible to escape.

Clearly, Welles knew exactly what he wanted, but he was not best positioned at the time to help in any substantive way. He was now deep in rehearsals for the Mercury stage production of *Danton's Death* and also directing and editing filmed interludes for another stage play called *Too Much Johnson*. So intent was he on this project that Houseman recalls that on entering Welles' hotel room, people had to "wade knee-deep through a crackling sea of inflammable film."[11] With Welles so heavily occupied it was essentially left to Houseman, Koch, Stewart and Froelisch to battle on with both script and Martians. It was close, but after another late night, victory was declared and on Friday afternoon they were able at last to deliver a script to the network for approval by Davidson Taylor, a CBS producer attached to the Mercury broadcasts, and then finally the CBS legal department. Much to everyone's surprise, this was the beginning of a whole new set of troubles.

The script was returned. The legal department was emphatically against the use of real names for institutions and organizations, fearing that someone might take exception and sue for defamation. Frank Brady suggests that there were also concerns voiced as to the excessive realism of the play. In total, to be excised at the network's behest were 28 specific items pertaining to names of persons and institutions. Also removed were several instances apparently deemed just too frightening or disturbing for the listening public, including the Martian cry of "ULLA ULLA ULLA" and a line about fleeing citizens trampling each other. The requests seem to have been rather arbitrary in nature. Civilians trampling each other was considered too visceral an example of the way in which the veneer of civilization could be stripped away in a crisis, yet a description of carnage on the battlefield that was broadcast includes talk of soldiers "trampled to death under the metal feet of the monster."

A copy of the script kindly provided to the author by the estate of Howard Koch provides ample illustration of this editing process, with handwritten changes and

---

*The title is coincidental. The "panic" in question relates to a Wall Street crash.
[†]The first verse play written for radio, *The Fall of the City* was a gigantic undertaking, with over 200 volunteer cast members filling Seventh Regiment Armory at East 67th Street and Park Avenue in midtown Manhattan, which had been secured especially for its acoustic properties.

timings penciled in. A note on the front of the manuscript states, "This script of my radio play WAR OF THE WORLDS was the one used in the broadcast. Corrections made by Orson Welles." Alas, this may not be accurate; comparing another script known to have been hand annotated by Welles, it is clear that the handwriting does not match.* It therefore seems more likely that the annotations are the work of either Houseman or Paul Stewart. Regardless of the hand involved, the insight provided is priceless.

Surviving in this version of the script, roughly penciled out, is the scene apparently excised for its unpleasant suggestion of man's inhumanity to man and, fascinatingly, it is an almost verbatim quote from the original novel. In the script, it occurs when Professor Pierson meets the soldier in the deserted streets of New York. The soldier has some very clear ideas about the art of survival upon a devastated Earth under the dominion of the Martians.

> I've been doing some thinking. I saw what was up. Most of the people were squealing, but I'm not so fond of squealing. At the best and worst, death, it's just death. And it's the man that keeps on thinking comes through. I saw everyone tracking away south. Says I: "Food won't last this way" ... And I turned right back. I went for the Martians like a sparrow goes for man. Up in Westchester and Northern New Jersey, they're starving in heaps ... bolting ... trampling on each other.

It is a shame this powerful dialogue was lost, but it is interesting to observe how much attention was paid to the scenes featuring the soldier. By and large the editor has exercised a light touch on the script, but the alterations to the soldier's dialogue are by far the most extensive. The intention seems quite clear: to make the dialogue more colloquial in keeping with the character's working-class background, and as such this insightful revision is extremely effective. An equally perceptive edit comes during the conversation between the reporter Carl Phillips (originally called Dick Philips in the script) and the owner of the Wilmuth farm, where the first Martian cylinder has crashed to earth at Grover's Mill. Here, squeezed into a margin, is added the short but very effective sequence of dialogue in which Philips has to encourage a nervous Mr. Wilmuth to speak up into a microphone. This inspired addition to the script adds greatly to the sense that one is listening not to scripted dialogue but to a live and unrehearsed event.

Most excitingly, the previously mentioned scene featuring the call of the Martians also survives in the original copy of the script, struck out with a heavy black marker but still legible. It occupied a position near to the beginning of Welles' closing soliloquy, as Professor Pierson walks through the Holland Tunnel to Manhattan Island and records his observations of the abandoned city. This passage too is lifted almost word for word from the original novel.

> In some places plunderers had been at work, but rarely at other than the provision and wine shops. A jeweler's window had been broken open in one place, but apparently the thief had been disturbed, and a number of gold chains and a watch lay scattered on the pavement. I did not trouble to touch them. Farther on was a tattered woman in a heap on a doorstep; the hand that had hung over her knee was gashed and bled down her rusty

---

*In 1994, what was described as the official directorial copy of *The War of the Worlds* script went under the hammer at Christie's auction house. The script, which came with a letter from Welles affirming its provenance, is notable for numerous charming illustrations by Welles, but there appear to have been few handwritten changes to the text, indicating it was a final draft used in the broadcast.

brown dress, and a smashed magnum of champagne formed a pool across the pavement. She seemed asleep, but she was dead. The farther I walked up town the profounder grew the stillness until near Washington Square I first heard the howling. It crept almost imperceptibly upon my senses.

At this point the script calls for the unearthly "ULLA ULLA ULLA" howl of the Martians to reverberate across the city; however, an examination of the heavily annotated script calls into question the idea that this scene was removed because of some misplaced squeamishness on the part of a network censor. It seems just as likely that it was cut because the show was running (as often happened with Welles' productions) well over its allotted time of 60 minutes. The script contains minute-by-minute handwritten timings that must have been established in rehearsals, and the final page stands at just over 67 minutes. Something had to go, and the various passages shortened or removed brought the running time to a new and more favorable figure of 58 minutes.*

As for the alterations to institutions, the suggestion that the censor demanded this appears to be entirely vindicated, as the changes were made carefully and consistently throughout the script. For instance, "The United States Weather Bureau" becomes "The Government Weather Bureau," and "Princeton University Observatory" is altered to "Princeton Observatory." Specific place-names survived unscathed, including the soon-to-be-infamous Grover's Mill, but the other alterations provide a very strong clue as to the place this version of the script occupies in the evolution of the story. Since we know that the demands from the censor came on Friday afternoon, this then must logically be the last iteration before the final version was produced, and certainly if one strips out all the indicated edits, one is left with a script that is almost identical to the transmitted version. As John Houseman recalls, "Under protest and with a deep sense of grievance we changed the Hotel Biltmore to the non-existent Park Plaza, Trans-America to Intercontinent, the Columbia Broadcasting Building to Broadcasting Building. Then the script went over to mimeograph and we went to bed. We had done our best and, after all, a show is just a show."[12]

With the script having now passed muster with Taylor and the lawyers, Paul Stewart oversaw another studio rehearsal on Saturday, including sound. Houseman remembers, "He worked for a long time on the crowd scenes, the roar of the canon echoing in the Watchung Hills and the sound of the New York Harbor as the ships with the last remaining survivors put out to sea."[13] Stewart also crossed swords with Bernard (Benny) Herrmann, the CBS head of music who had been somewhat reluctantly assigned to write and conduct music for the Mercury Theatre. Several years previously, Herrmann and Welles had endured a bruising first encounter. During Welles' radio production of *Macbeth* he had intensely irritated the composer by bringing in a set of bagpipes to the studio and all but drowning out Herrmann's music. Now Herrmann and Stewart found themselves at odds. Recalls Stewart,

> We had such a limited budget for the program that we could not get the dance band from CBS, who were suffering our unsponsored show on Sunday night; so we had to use the symphony men, many of whom worked with Toscanini and the New York Philharmonic. To get Benny to conduct the dance songs I had suggested (including "Stardust" and "La

---

*The page numbering of the second act suggests that five pages of Professor Pierson's travels in the war-ravaged countryside had been completely removed by this stage.

Cumparasita") was almost an impossibility. He didn't understand the rhythms at all. I said, "Benny, it's gotta be like this" and snapped my fingers — and he got very upset. He handed me the baton and said, "*You* conduct it!" I got up on the podium. All the musicians understood Benny's personality, so when I gave the downbeat they played it just the way I wanted it. I said, "Now that's how to do it!" I handed the baton back to Benny, who was crestfallen. The moment in the broadcast when Herrmann conducts "Stardust" with the symphony orchestra is one of the most hysterical musical moments in radio.[14]

Yet despite their fiery personalities, Welles and Herrmann produced a remarkable collaboration. Sound was to Welles an incredibly important component of his shows and he went to great lengths to achieve the exact effects he wanted. By blending sound, music and actors seamlessly together, Welles and Herrmann developed an aural vocabulary that was truly groundbreaking, an achievement for which Mercury actor William Alland lavishes praise on Welles, though Herrmann was just as important to the process. "What he brought was, first of all, a complete ensemble style of performance, a completely integrated musical score. The musical bridges and transitions which are the equivalent of fades and dissolves in film are miraculously good."[15]

Aptly illustrating Welles' perfectionism, Houseman tells of hours spent trying to find the exact right way to sever a human head for *A Tale of Two Cities*. "Various solid objects were tried under a cleaver wielded by one of the best sound men in the business: a melon, a pillow, a coconut and a leg of lamb. Finally it was discovered that a cabbage gave just the right kind of scrunching resistance."[16] On another occasion, Welles had hundreds of feet of audio cable strung up to the roof of the building and had four extras firing handguns for a battle scene in *Beau Geste*. It was a great idea, except for the arrival of squad cars full of irate police who threatened to arrest everyone for illegal possession of firearms. One can only wonder what people of this caliber and inventiveness might have achieved had they been allowed to work on the blood-chilling call of the Martians.

But who were these unsung soundmen who labored to satisfy their perfectionist master? A number of names are generally associated with Mercury Theatre on the Air productions, among them John Dietz, James Rogan, Ray Kremer, Bill Brown and Henry Gauthierre, but most famously one of them was a woman! Ora Daigle Nichols and her husband Arthur (whose name does not seem to be associated with the Mercury in this instance) had learned their trade providing live sound effects in silent film theaters, but with the advent of the talkies they found their unique talents transferred well to the burgeoning radio industry. So well regarded was Nichols (who was the only woman at the time earning a living in the male-dominated world of sound effects) that she was voted one of the most influential women in radio, an honor she shared with the likes of Amelia Earhart and Eleanor Roosevelt.

Nichols' precise role on *The War of the Worlds* broadcast is not entirely clear, but in the film *The Night That Panicked America*, about the making of the broadcast, it is suggested that Nichols was the senior sound person on the show and that she and another soundman (possibly her husband) achieved the sinister reverberating sound of the Martian hatch opening up by slowly unscrewing the lid of an empty pickle jar in a nearby toilet cubicle. In the light of the previous stories it certainly seems plausible that Welles would have had his sound team try anything to get the right effect, and an additional account does exist to verify the unique acoustic properties of the CBS men's room.

For *The Count of Monte Cristo*, Houseman recalls that Welles and costar Ray Collins crouched by a toilet bowl to acquire a suitably subterranean timbre to their voices, while at the other end of the building, a microphone picked up the flushing of another toilet to simulate waves "breaking against the walls of the Chateau d'If."[17] Alas for the veracity of this wonderful tale, the surviving recording of *The Count of Monte Cristo* does not seem to feature waves crashing against rock, though several other sounds, such as the splash of oars in a boat ride to the chateau, have about them an unfortunate porcelain quality.

Adding further credence to the unorthodox use of toilet plumbing by Welles is a similar tale told by Mercury member Richard Wilson. Liederkranz Hall is located on the north side of East 58th Street, between Park and Lexington Avenues, and as described by Wilson was an "ancient turn-of-the-century building with lots of toilets and urinals." During the making of *Les Misérables*, Welles "put a microphone in there to represent the sewers of Paris, because all the johns and urinals leaked, dripped and so forth. Somebody made his way through and on the program; on a coast-to-coast broadcast we heard this toilet flushing.... That went out over the national broadcast. Orson as usual had his headphones on to monitor all the sound and he heard this and the look on his face was extraordinary, it was incredible."[18] And yes, if you listen carefully to the recording of that show, you really can hear that flush.*

The Saturday rehearsal wrapped at around 6 P.M. and with the cast gone, a soundman packing up equipment was left to answer the phone. It was Welles calling, and he can hardly have felt encouraged when the soundman said that in his opinion it was not one of their better shows. This was a not uncommon opinion. In his memoir *I Looked and Listened*, *New York Times* columnist Ben Gross recollects a Mercury actor declaring a few days prior to the broadcast that the show was "lousy"[19] and Welles himself was advised not to go ahead from Skipper Hill.

Welles had himself already derided the script as corny in the Regis Hotel meeting. When he arrived for the crucial Sunday afternoon rehearsal his mood had not improved for the better. Writing in his unpublished memoirs, Mercury cast member Richard Baer describes the tense scene in the studio. "Orson railed at the text, cursing the writers and at the whole idea of his presenting so silly a show."[20] This might seem very unfair given his largely hands-off approach to the process of preparation for the broadcast, but though he had been unusually distracted in this case, it was essentially Welles' established method of working. With his time spread so thinly, he gave others within his repertory company a great deal of freedom to create and improvise from his basic guidelines and then, when all the ideas and tension reached a boiling point, he stepped in at the last minute to impose dictatorial order in his own inimitable style. "Sweating, howling, disheveled and single-handed he wrestled with chaos and time — always conveying an effect of being alone, traduced by his collaborators, surrounded by treachery, ignorance, sloth, indiffer-

*One can hear what may be the very first recorded toilet flush in history some six minutes and 50 seconds into the first episode of *Les Misérables*.

ence, incompetence and — more often than not — downright sabotage"[21]: thus John Houseman described a typical final rehearsal.

Now, with just hours to go before he was due live on the air, Welles had to come
up with something fast to salvage *The War of the Worlds*. His solution was to accentuate
the very things that were the antithesis of good radio drama. Rather than speed up the
pace he slowed it even more, stretching out the pregnant pauses, reinstating dialogue that
had been cut in earlier rehearsals precisely because it had been felt to be dragging down
the story, and piling on the banal piano music. It was a move that Houseman protested
strongly, arguing that there would not be a listener left if he continued with this apparently suicidal course of action. It was only in retrospect that Houseman came to realize
what Welles intended with his editing and how devastatingly effective it would prove.
That piano, recalls Houseman, "became a symbol of terror, shattering the dead air with
its ominous tinkle ... that piano was the neatest trick of the show."[22]

At the time, however, Welles ignored Houseman's protests and kept his own coun-
sel. For better or worse, the die was now irrevocably cast, and as the seconds ticked away
he swigged down a carton of pineapple juice, climbed onto his podium in Studio One
at 485 Madison Avenue, and, donning earphones, prepared to cue the opening music. It
was 8 P.M. EST on Sunday, October 30, 1938, and America was about to experience a
night of terror like no other that had gone before. The men from Mars were coming.

5

WAR

8 P.M., October 30, 1938

On the 20th floor of the New York studios of the Columbia Broadcasting System it was zero hour for Orson Welles. Perhaps the most difficult and certainly the most contentious script ever attempted by the Mercury Theatre was about to be performed. It had been argued and fought over by those who had crafted it, suffered setbacks and rewrites at the hands of censors, and was considered by some a failure before it had even been broadcast, but now there was no time left for doubt or hesitation. Welles stood ready, his cast and crew arrayed around him as the announcer Dan Seymour introduced them to their waiting audience: "The Columbia Broadcasting System and its affiliated stations present Orson Welles and the Mercury Theatre on the Air in *The War of the Worlds* by H. G. Wells." This was the moment for Welles to cue the familiar Mercury Theatre theme music. As the strains of Tchaikovsky's Piano Concerto No. 1 faded away, his distinctive voice took over the airwaves.

> We know now that in the early years of the twentieth century this world was being watched closely by intelligences greater than man's and yet as mortal as his own. We know now that as human beings busied themselves about their various concerns they were scrutinized and studied, perhaps almost as narrowly as a man with a microscope might scrutinize the transient creatures that swarm and multiply in a drop of water. With infinite complacence people went to and fro over the earth about their little affairs, serene in the assurance of their dominion over this small spinning fragment of solar driftwood which by chance or design man has inherited out of the dark mystery of Time and Space. Yet across an immense ethereal gulf, minds that are to our minds as ours are to the beasts in the jungle, intellects vast, cool and unsympathetic regarded this earth with envious eyes and slowly and surely drew their plans against us. In the thirty-ninth year of the twentieth century came the great disillusionment.

This introduction was adapted closely from the original novel, but the show then took its own unique direction and segued into the first of the banalities that had so worried John Houseman, the tail end of a weather report followed by a link to the Hotel Park Plaza and the first of many musical interludes provided by Bernard Herrmann. As the fictitious orchestra of Ramón Raquello played, listeners across America were lulled into a false sense of security, and even a short time later when the first interruption of normal service occurs, it is in itself fairly innocuous and not likely to pique much more than mild curiosity in the listener. Apparently, the "news flash" said, there have been reports of explosions on the surface of the planet Mars. More music follows and then an announcement that an interview has been arranged with a Professor Pierson at "Princeton Observatory." This is followed by yet more music and then, finally, fully six minutes into the broadcast, the hookup to Princeton.

Frank Readick, in the guise of reporter Carl Phillips, begins by describing the scene in the observatory to the listeners, warning that the forthcoming interview may be interrupted by the arrival of messages for Professor Pierson. From the outset Welles as Pierson delivers a typically nuanced performance, his words uttered in measured tones that to listeners must have sounded like the very voice of reason. As he begins to explain what he sees through the telescope, the shrewdness of the adaptation also begins to make itself evident. Welles' lines are written to impart gravitas. He talks compellingly of Mars being in opposition to the Earth, the point of closest approach between the two planets,* and makes a caustic comment on the implausibility of the surface features turning out to be canals. Koch had clearly done his homework or at least had read something of the canal theories, for H. G. Wells does not directly mention the concept in his novel. In accentuating what was still firmly in the public imagination, this nicely judged addition cleverly plants the very idea it purports to decry in the mind of the listener.

After further denouncing the odds of life on Mars at a thousand to one against, Pierson is handed a note, which with his permission is read on the air. Something has triggered a seismograph recording of earthquake intensity within 20 miles of Princeton. Pierson is equally dismissive of the idea that the events on Mars are linked to this new occurrence. It might be a meteorite of unusual size, but he insists it's just a coincidence, though the adroit listener will have anticipated by now that the professor is due to have his convictions sorely tested.

Welles is ratcheting up the tension brilliantly. The reports are becoming more ominous and the pace of events quickening. Now there comes apparent confirmation that a meteorite has indeed struck farmland near Grover's Mill. After another brief musical interlude we rejoin the professor and Phillips, who have arrived at the scene of the impact. Here on the Wilmuth farm they are confronted by an amazing sight, a huge cylinder embedded in the ground and surrounded by a large crowd of curious onlookers and police.

What could so easily have descended into farce now instead climbs towards a truly dramatic crescendo, thanks in large part to the foresight of Frank Readick. As research for the role he had dug out a seminal recording from the archives, the disastrous explosion of the German airship *Hindenburg*, which had occurred on May 6, 1937. A local reporter by the name of Herbert Morrison had been at Lakehurst, New Jersey, to record the arrival of the giant craft and found himself witness to the fiery destruction of the pride of Nazi Germany. His heart-rending description of the scene, a mixture of incredulity, choked-back sobs and courageous reportage in the face of unimaginable horror became the blueprint for the scenes Readick was now called upon to describe at the Wilmuth farm.

Just as Morrison began his report on the arrival of the *Hindenburg* with a monologue on the dimensions and appearance the airship, so Readick sets the scene with a "word picture" of events at Grover's Mill. What really nails the scene is that Readick behaves exactly as one might expect a reporter would if dropped unprepared into an incred-

---

*Mars was not in opposition in 1938, but whether by design or coincidence, the script actually set the story in October of 1939, and Mars was due to for opposition that year, with closest approach set for July.

ible live situation, apparently making up his lines on a wing and a prayer as events unfold. Spectators jostle the reporter for a better view, a question is asked but is drowned out in the melee, and the local landowner is drolly asked to comment on "this rather unusual visitor that dropped in your backyard."

It's all very exciting but not necessarily yet alarming, as in the novel when the

Orson Welles at the CBS microphone, circa 1938.

onlookers initially treat the whole thing as a jolly Sunday afternoon outing. Then, with a crash, the lid of the cylinder comes loose and the carnival atmosphere turns to horror. "Ladies and gentlemen," cries Readick, "this is the most terrifying thing I have ever witnessed.... Wait a minute! Someone's crawling out of the hollow top. Some one or ... something. I can see peering out of that black hole two luminous disks ... are they eyes? It might be a face. It might be—" From this point on, the situation turns grim and wholly chaotic. The Martian emerges, a tentacled monstrosity of glistening leathery skin and drooling jaws before which the panicked crowd retreats. Readick briefly cuts his transmission to reposition himself behind a wall and from here is witness to the doomed approach of a peace delegation to the Martians. Like a modern war reporter pinned under enemy fire, Readick describes the Martian heat-ray lashing out toward the men, who are horribly incinerated, and then the beam moves toward him. Vehicle gas tanks explode at its touch, buildings burn, people scream. The beam is now a scant 20 yards from the reporter; it comes closer and closer still, and then there is a sudden deathly silence.

Pregnant with implication, the seconds tick ominously by and then finally we hear a voice. "Ladies and gentlemen, due to circumstances beyond our control, we are unable to continue the broadcast from Grover's Mill. Evidently there's some difficulty with our field transmission." This brilliant piece of understatement underlines the awful uncertainty of the situation. The network doesn't know what happened to their reporter and neither do the listeners. One can imagine families huddled about their radios filling in the blanks. They know in their hearts something horrible has happened, but hope it isn't true and the uncertainty is driving them crazy. Report after frantic report follows. Welles' slow-moving freight train of a story is now a runaway express. The reporter's charred body is identified in a hospital. Martial law is declared, the broadcast system appropriated by the military and, after the first detailed description of a Martian war machine, comes the anxious news that a major battle has been fought and lost. Thousands of soldiers lie dead and the Martians control a great swath of the New Jersey countryside.

In the studio there was a feeling among the cast that the uncertainties and reservations that had plagued the rehearsals had been overstated and that the broadcast was going better than anyone could have imagined. How much better it was going was about to become abundantly clear, but for now it was the turn of Kenny Delmar to take the microphone in his role as secretary of the interior, originally scripted to be the president of the United States until vetoed by the legal department. That Delmar did a pretty good impersonation of President Roosevelt in mocking defiance of the lawyers can be ascribed to what Houseman called the "strange fever that seemed to invade the studio — part childish mischief, part professional zeal."[1] It had begun at about 2 P.M., when Welles started to work his magic, and by now the atmosphere in the studio was electric. But then, as Delmar was busy springing his little joke on the listeners, urging calm and resourceful action in support of "the preservation of human supremacy on this earth," the phone rang in the control room.

Davidson Taylor took the call, blanched and suddenly left the room. He returned pale as death and insisted that they had to stop the show. In the outside world something appalling was happening. People were taking the broadcast entirely too seriously, as if an invading force of Martians was actually advancing upon them and the president really had put the nation on high alert. The CBS switchboard was overwhelmed by the volume of frantic calls, as were police stations. One swamped local precinct that did get through to the CBS control room asked if the invasion was real and was scornfully dismissed by a harassed technician. CBS night news manager Hal Davies was one of those manning the phones that night. "About 10 or 15 minutes into the broadcast and the phones started ringing. And I began to get hysterical calls, saying, 'Where are the invaders?' and 'What's happening?' And I said, come on, this is just Orson Welles' Mercury Theatre, because I had the program on the monitor. Just a regular show, take it easy ... don't panic, there are no invaders."[2]

Meanwhile, Taylor was trying to get into the studio to order Welles to cut short the broadcast, but was physically blocked by Houseman. He was not about to let him ruin a fantastic show and besides, how bad could it possibly be outside? As Houseman describes him, Taylor was not the most statuesque or demonstrative of men and so was reduced to watching helplessly as Welles and his players continued on, apparently oblivious to the dramatic standoff taking place a few feet away or the mounting chaos outside in the real world. Taylor did, however, eventually get a message to Welles that he and his cast should deliver their lines with less verisimilitude. Welles complied, though he must have been acutely conscious that something very strange was happening. Legend has it that as time ticked by, the control booth filled up with uniformed beat cops intent on finding someone to arrest.

Normally a 60-minute broadcast like *The War of the Worlds* would be interrupted at the halfway point by a station break, and if it had been a sponsored show it would have been interrupted even more frequently. But as usual with Welles, things were running long and thus it was not until some 42 minutes of the broadcast had elapsed before the following statement was read out: "You are listening to a CBS presentation of Orson

Welles and the Mercury Theatre on the Air in an original dramatization of '*The War of the Worlds*' by H. G. Wells. The performance will continue after a brief intermission."

As the uproar outside the studio continued (at least for those who had missed the intermission statement) Welles soldiered on with his role of Professor Pierson. A refugee now after the attack at Grover's Mill, he sets out across a devastated countryside in search of other survivors. This portion of the broadcast has an entirely different narrative structure than the first half. It is devoid of tense news flashes, which for those still listening in a rational state of mind should have let the cat out of the bag. Following, in essence, the novel, Welles' character survives his travails and at the conclusion of the story discovers that earthly bacteria have defeated the Martians, for they have no natural defense against them.

As the closing music faded, Welles stepped back before the microphone to deliver a statement that must have provided scant comfort to the many shocked and infuriated listeners:

> This is Orson Welles, ladies and gentlemen, out of character to assure you that "The War of the Worlds" has no further significance than as the holiday offering it was intended to be. The Mercury Theatre's own radio version of dressing up in a sheet and jumping out of a bush and saying Boo! Starting now, we couldn't soap all your windows and steal all your garden gates, by tomorrow night ... so we did the next best thing. We annihilated the world before your very ears, and utterly destroyed the C. B. S. You will be relieved, I hope, to learn that we didn't mean it, and that both institutions are still open for business. So good-bye everybody, and remember, please, for the next day or so, the terrible lesson you learned tonight. That grinning, glowing, globular invader of your living room is an inhabitant of the pumpkin patch, and if your doorbell rings and nobody's there, that was no Martian ... it's Halloween.

But Welles' words disguised the growing sense of urgency and alarm permeating the CBS building, as the full enormity of the situation began to strike home and the phone continued to ring off the hook. As the final theme was playing, Welles took one such call in the control room. Houseman describes the one-sided conversation that ensued: "...a shrill voice announcing itself as the mayor of some Midwestern city, one of the big ones. He is screaming for Welles. Choking with fury, he reports mobs in the streets of his city, women and children huddled in churches, violence and looting. If, as he now learns, the whole thing is nothing but a crummy joke — then he, personally, is coming up to New York to punch the author of it on his nose!"[3]

Welles judiciously hung up as the bedlam continued in the studio. By now the police had arrived (though they had no idea whom to arrest or indeed if there is anyone to arrest) and CBS managers frantically confiscating scripts and recordings. Welles and Houseman were put under a sort of house arrest by CBS and hustled into a small back office where they were and held incommunicado for thirty minutes while the network tried to marshal a response for the press. Eventually they saw no option but to offer up Welles and Houseman to the pack of baying reporters. It was by all accounts a bruising encounter. Were they aware, asked the press, of the deaths? What of the fatal stampedes, the suicides and the family of five killed in a traffic accident? Welles and Houseman had no answers to give, and though it all proved to be the worst kind of hyperbole it left the two convinced for a time that they were in effect mass murderers.

Both men were eventually able to flee the CBS building by a back door and, since the show must go on, rushed to a late-night rehearsal of their forthcoming *Danton's Death*. Toward midnight, a late-arriving member of the cast reported that the famous ticker sign in Times Square was reporting on the broadcast. On hearing this, Welles and a few others walked to the southeast corner of 42nd Street and watched as the ticker scrolled the words "ORSON WELLES CAUSES PANIC." Joseph Cotten, the star of *Danton's Death*, was certain that Welles had bitten off more than he could chew. "He was finished, washed up, a dead pigeon; show business would have no more of him from then on."[4] But Cotten could not have been more wrong. Welles would survive and miraculously emerge even more famous and powerful than ever, but at the time the words he watched in Times Square must have seemed ominous. Yet the true scale of events would not become apparent until the following morning, with the publication of newspaper headlines that would be echoed around the world.

6

"It's Just a Radio Show"
Dispatches from the Front Lines

Howard Koch had listened to the broadcast at home and then, exhausted by the deprivations of the previous seven days, retired to his bed. He slept soundly that night and could not even be roused on the telephone by John Houseman, who had attempted to deliver an urgent warning that something had gone horribly wrong. Strolling to his barber on Monday morning Koch was therefore blissfully unaware of the pandemonium he had helped unleash. He assumed that the palpable air of excitement on the street and talk of an invasion referred to some new act of aggression by Hitler, whose territorial ambitions were only too well known to the American public. It was only when his barber showed him a shocking headline on the front page of a morning newspaper that the full enormity of the situation struck him. "I stared at the paper while the confused barber stared at me. Centre page was a picture of Orson, his arms outstretched in a gesture of helpless innocence, and underneath was the opening scene of my play."[1]

The newspapers that morning and for days afterwards were jam-packed with sensational accounts of the terrified public reaction to the broadcast. We will examine in the next chapter the reliability of that reporting, but the sheer volume of stories in the press leaves little doubt as to the immense and sustained interest it generated across the nation. With an embarrassment of riches to choose from, the newspapers were at liberty to fill hundreds of column inches with a bewildering variety of stories that painted a sweeping picture of a nation teetering on the brink of chaos.

Reactions to the broadcast appear to have varied considerably depending on age, gender and circumstances. For many, the irresistible imperative was to gather up their loved ones and seek safety elsewhere. Older people seemed to have sought comfort in religion, younger people railed against the injustice of a life cut short, and a few brave souls took up arms in preparation to defend their homes. Still others tried to locate or warn friends or family, fearing that they might already have succumbed to the attack or be in imminent danger. As has already been established, a barrage of calls assailed the CBS switchboard, and other telephone services appear to have been equally overwhelmed.

Totaled and taken at face value, the number of calls various switchboards across the country are reported to have received is nothing short of astounding. The *New York Times* of October 31 tallied a total of 875 calls, a figure easily matched and exceeded by the *Newark Evening News*, which claimed in its October 31 edition to have been deluged with more than 1,000, and that in total the New Jersey Bell telephone company handled between 75,000 and 100,000 extra calls above and beyond the normally expected demand between 8 and 9 P.M. The majority of calls apparently originated from the north of Trenton. The same article further reported that in Philadelphia the police took 3,000 calls and the local CBS affiliate WCAU another 4,000. The October 31 edition of the *Seattle Star* quoted a San Francisco operator as saying that during and immediately after the broadcast they were virtually swamped with "requests for cross-continent telephone connections with New York and New Jersey." But no matter how impressive the figures, behind the numbers are a multitude of personal stories, and who better to tell some of these than the switchboard operators who bore the brunt of this extraordinary surge in traffic.

Anne O'Brian Lamb was an operator for the long-distance toll exchange at the Bell Telephone office in Trenton. In a letter published in a special commemorative edition of the *Trentonian** newspaper on October 21, 1988, she recalled in fascinating detail the volume and nature of the calls she and her fellow telephone operators had to contend with that night, with a sudden massive flood of calls from people desperate to reach their children at Lawrenceville and Princeton schools. The calls came thick and fast and were extremely alarming. "'Do you know anything about this green gas that is coming from Grover's Mill?' 'I'll pay you any amount of money if you will get me through to my son in Princeton.'" At first the operators had no idea what to say until finally their supervisor told them to say it was just a radio show.

Edna M. Bohn was also a telephone operator and related a similar story to the *Trentonian* of her experiences at the Princeton office of New Jersey Bell: "All of a sudden I think every subscriber in Princeton lifted their receivers." She described the switchboard lighting up and how frightening it was to receive calls from people who thought that the Martians were landing. Eventually she called her husband. Clearly of sounder mind than her callers, he was finding it very funny that people were fleeing with their possessions.

Writing in his own account of the making of the broadcast and its aftermath, Howard Koch also offers an example of the extraordinary nature of the calls said to have flooded telephone exchanges, ending his story on a punch line that in the circumstances is the very model of professional conduct. Koch knew a woman who was on duty as a supervisor in an exchange that evening. The telephone company was promoting improved customer service and the supervisor, having overheard an operator sign off with a very polite and commendable "I'm sorry, sir, we haven't that information here," asked what the caller had been inquiring about. The operator replied, "He wanted to know if the world was coming to an end."[2] Conversely, the *Hartford Courant* of October 31 recorded that newspaper switchboard operators in some cities "quit saying 'hello.' They merely plugged in and said without pause or preamble: 'It's just a radio show.'"

Naturally, numerous concerned citizens turned to the emergency services for reassurance and advice, clogging police telephone lines or rushing in person to their nearest station. The *Newark Evening News* of October 31 reported that calls were coming in so fast that two extra operators had to be provided to help cope with the unprecedented volume. New York City was said to have experienced a particularly intense reaction, doubtless because it appeared to be the ultimate goal of the Martian invasion and was thought likely to bear the full brunt of the poison gas attack. The *New York Times* reported a num-

---

*On October 21, 1988, the *Trentonian* newspaper issued a special commemorative edition, which collected together a superb selection of firsthand accounts of the broadcast from Trenton-area residents.

ber of instances of people rushing in great distress into police stations in search of advice and safety, with one man shouting that enemy planes were crossing the Hudson. The West 135th Street station in Harlem had to contend with a crowd numbering 30 men and women who arrived to tell officers they had their possessions packed and were ready to be evacuated.

In the chaos caused by fleeing residents, jams were said to have formed as frantic families tried to get clear of the approaching war front. The *Newark Evening News* recorded a major incident at Hedden Terrace and Hawthorne Avenue that involved upward of twenty families and required the presence of three radio cars, an ambulance and a police emergency squad of eight men to calm the situation and clear traffic. Under the command of a Lieutenant Seery, the police discovered a scene of pandemonium. Tenants had fled onto the street in their underclothes, dragging terrified children along with them and, in fear of the Martian gas, had wrapped "wet towels and handkerchiefs around their heads." It took police 15 minutes to restore a semblance of order and over a dozen people were said to have required treatment for shock at St. Michael's Hospital.

Many newspapers were particularly keen to report on those cases where people had decided to leave home in search of safety. The October 31 *Seattle Daily Times* reported that a woman in Boston had "called her brother here to say she heard the broadcast and was leaving home immediately. She told him many others in her neighborhood also were leaving in haste." The *Hartford Courant* carried the story of Samuel Tishman, a resident of Riverside Drive in New York. Said Tishman, "I grabbed my hat and coat and a few personal belongings and ran to the elevator." He then joined "hundreds" who had begun running toward Broadway. It was only when he and others stopped taxis whose drivers had heard the whole broadcast on their radios that a semblance of calm was restored.

Margaret Cleary Leedom of Hamilton, New Jersey, was quoted in the *Trentonian* recalling frantic preparations to flee. Her neighbors told her they had packed the car, woken the children and set out for Philadelphia. Leedom's family was also caught up in the excitement. Her brother had gone out to put gas in the car, leaving her mother and sister alone in the house. When a knock came at the door, it was opened to reveal an innocent gang of trick-or-treaters or, as Leedom's sister assumed, "Martians!" When she recovered her wits, the trick-or-treaters were on the receiving end of the trick to end all tricks. "Do you dammed fools know what's going on?" demanded Leedom's mother, and after she explained that the Martians were invading, the trick-or-treaters took to their heels.

If there were any people in the country who should have kept their nerve it was the military, but Marine Corps officials were forced to issue denials that troops based at Quantico had been spooked. Quoted the *Washington Post* of November 2, Major General James C. Breckinridge said officers and enlisted men of his command understood a play was being broadcast and not an account of a foreign invasion. The story seems to have gained currency because one of the enlisted men had turned on a radio in one of the barracks as a joke on his comrades, but luckily no one bought into the deception. Breckinridge was not the only high-ranking soldier to be annoyed. The *Newark Evening News* of November 1 reported that unnamed army and navy officials had been critical of the broadcast, voicing the concern that in the event of a real attack by a foreign power on the country, people might not heed the warnings, believing it to be just another radio fake.

The evening of October 30 held particular powerful memories for Lillian R. Ruder of Bordentown, New Jersey, who described in poignant terms to the *Trentonian* how she happened to be in Mercer Hospital that night. Having previously lost a baby by miscarriage she was overjoyed to give birth that night to a healthy baby. But then she started to hear a strange murmuring in the hallway. Buzzing the nurse to find out what was happening, she was told that people were coming into the hospital with the incredible news that the world was coming to an end. With her newborn baby to care for and a whole future together to look forward to with her husband, she could only pray, "Dear God, don't let it end like this."

Faced with what appeared to be the end of the world it is hardly surprising that a great many took solace in religion. Midwesterner Joseph Hendley was convinced of the need for prayer, saying, "That Hallowe'en boo sure had our family on its knees before the program was half over. God knows we prayed to Him last Sunday."[3] The *New York Times* of October 31 reported that a service at the First Baptist Church in Caldwell, New Jersey, was interrupted by the arrival of a terrified parishioner with the fearful news that "a meteor had fallen, showering death and destruction." Led by their pastor, the Reverend Thomas, the congregants all prayed for deliverance. According to the *Trenton Evening Times*, one Kingston church "closed a bit early to give the congregation time to prepare for Judgment Day. Recollecting a similar experience to the *Washington Post* of October 31, 2001, Mabel "Lolly" MacKenzie Dey remembers she was playing the piano at the Plainsboro Presbyterian Church when "Someone, I think it was a fella, came barging in and started shouting, 'Martians have landed at Grover's Mill!' ... So I stopped playing the piano, and I just bowed my head, and I prayed to the Lord."

For younger people with an entire hopeful future in front of them, the broadcast was particularly terrifying. Princeton juniors Pete Lauck and Bob Boone were returning home when they picked up the broadcast on the car radio. It is unrecorded which of the two should be attributed with the following account. "My roommate was crying and praying. He was even more excited than I was — or more noisy about it anyway ... I remember also thinking there wasn't any God ... I thought the whole human race was going to be wiped out — that seemed more important than the fact we were going to die. It seemed awful that everything that had been worked on for years was going to be lost forever."[4]

All across the nation, people took what comfort they could from one another's company. Helen Anthony was a high school girl from Pennsylvania. "I was really hysterical. My two girlfriends and I were crying and holding each other and everything seemed so unimportant in the face of death. We felt it was terrible we should die so young."[5] At a southwestern state college, girls in the sorority houses gathered together for comfort and made emotional phone calls to their parents, "saying goodbye for what they thought might be the last time."[6] Girls, however, seemed to be a lot more pragmatic in the face of danger, as the *Seattle Post-Intelligencer* reported in its edition of October 31, 1938, that five boys at Brevard College in North Carolina had fainted as fights broke out among students desperate to phone their parents to rescue them.

It seems that many parents across America were on the receiving end of frantic calls from their children that night, and as recorded in the October 30, 1988, edition of the

Charlottesville Daily Progress, at least one enterprising father did set out on a rescue mission. John W. Wilkens was well aware as a World War I veteran what a gas attack could do, so when his daughter Therese called in hysterics to tell him that she and her friends were about to be gassed by the Martians, he wasted no time in setting out to collect her from William and Mary College in Williamsburg, Virginia, though he did take time to remove the doors from his 1935 Studebaker so he could cram more people into the car. When he got to the school, he and a helpful state trooper started loading up as many of the girls as they could. "I packed them in like sardines and wrapped a rope round the car so they wouldn't fall out and even lashed a few of them to the hood." This must have made an extraordinary sight as he made the 100-mile journey home, only to find out on arrival that he was another hapless victim of Orson Welles. "I felt real foolish," said Williams. "After I got over that, I put my car doors back on."

Not everyone that evening was willing to jump in an automobile and take matters into their own hands. Some were quite resigned to their fate, such as one mother who calmly roused her young children. When they asked why they had been awakened, she replied serenely, "Because we're going to die, children, and if we are going to die, then we are all going to die together."[7] That calm mother was not the only person to take a markedly differing attitude to the prevailing view of events. There was, for instance, the man drowning his sorrows at a Harvard football victory over Princeton, who became so dispirited that according to the *Trenton Evening Times* he called the *Daily Princetonian* from a New York bar to find out if any of the players had been stricken by the poison gas. Then there was the man whose proposal of marriage had been rejected several times previously, but (reported the October 31 *Newark Evening News*) was accepted with a yes when he managed to convince his girlfriend that it was the end of the world.

It was not recorded if in the cold light of day her acceptance still stood, but perhaps the drollest story of the evening belongs to the renowned radio personality Norwin Corwin. He was present in the CBS building on the night of *The War of the Worlds* broadcast, working on rehearsals for his own show *Words Without Music* just one floor above Studio One. As Corwin recalls, he knew someone who worked in the master control room and the following day had called him to get some firsthand details of what had occurred. Corwin asked how long the calls had continued to come into the station, and was told that the phone was still ringing at 2 A.M. Corwin then inquired what the last call had been about. His colleague said it came from someone who sounded like a New Jersey truck driver. The man demanded to know if he was speaking to the people responsible for the broadcast about the Martians. On being told it was, the caller spoke with great emotion. "Well, I want to tell you something, mister. My wife heard that broadcast and she got so excited, she opened the door and fell down a whole flight of stairs. Jeez, it was a wonderful broadcast!"[8]

Of course, not everyone found something to laugh about. The *Newark Daily News* recorded many indignant callers, including one who declared, "You ought to register a complaint with the radio station. Something should be done about it. Not only we but our children became frightened and hysterical. This story was so realistic it seemed true. It should have been censored." But not everyone was upset. According to the *Newark Evening News* of November 1, police in Collingswood, New Jersey, reported they had received not a single call from frightened listeners. "People don't listen to that kind of radio program on Sunday in Collingswood," said a police spokesman enigmatically.

If a regular listener saw through it, then the head of the Warner Brothers location department should have spotted it immediately for the fraud it was, yet as recalled by Howard Koch, both were completely hoodwinked. The location head and his wife were far from any sign of civilization, driving through the redwoods of northern California, when they tuned into the broadcast: "...soon the things were landing all over, even in California. There was no escape. All we could think of was to try and get back to L.A. to see our children once more. And be with them when it happened. We went right by gas stations but I forgot we were low on gas. In the middle of the forest our gas ran out. There was nothing to do. We just sat there holding hands expecting any minute to see those Martian monsters appear over the tops of the trees."[9]

Such dignified resignation in the face of adversity and apparently imminent death was not shared by every listener, as in this account from a young man who had been at a party which had broke up in terror and disarray. "I drove like crazy up Sixth Avenue. I don't know how fast—fifty, maybe sixty miles an hour. The traffic cops at the street crossings just stared at us, they couldn't believe their eyes, whizzing right past them going through the red lights. I didn't care if I got a ticket. It was all over anyway. Funny thing, none of the cops chased us. I guess they were too flabbergasted. My apartment was on the way so I stopped off just long enough to rush in and shout up to my father that the Martians had landed and we were all going to be killed and I was taking my girl home. When I got to her place, her parents were waiting for us. My father had called them. Told them to hold me there until he could send a doctor as I'd gone out of my mind."[10]

This momentary kind of madness was said to have afflicted many listeners. Connie Casamassina was enjoying her wedding reception when news of the invasion broke among the guests. "Everyone ran to get their coats. I took the microphone and started to cry — 'Please don't spoil my wedding day'— and then my husband started singing hymns, and I decided I was going to dance the Charleston. And I did, for 15 minutes straight. I did every step there is in the Charleston."[11] Others are reported to have reacted in an even more disturbed fashion. The *Seattle Daily Times*, like many other papers, reported a Pittsburgh man returning home just in time to prevent his wife swallowing a bottle of poison as she screamed, "I'd rather die this way than like that."

It should, however, be noted that other listeners are reported to have acted with great bravery. The *New York Times* reported that many members of the emergency services responded as if there was a genuine attack under way, with hundreds of physicians, nurses and city officials calling in to offer their services. Most impressively, some civilians were more than willing to take up arms, such as Henry B. Sears, whose description to the *Trentonian* of his adventures that night makes for a truly gripping tale.

Henry Sears was 13 years old at the time and completing his homework with the radio on by his side. At the time he lived over a tavern called the Green Gables Inn,* which his mother owned and ran. But his homework was forgotten as he became gripped

---

*The Green Gables Inn was located on Applegarth Road in Cranbury, New Jersey, but as of this writing was derelict and awaiting demolition.

by news of the Martian invasion. Grover's Mill was only eight miles away, so he rushed downstairs to the tavern and announced to his mother and the dozen or so customers that something incredible was happening. He plugged in the radio, and sure enough the Martians were invading. All the men leapt up and (perhaps armed with more than a little Dutch courage) announced their intention to go and fight the aliens. Grabbing his own gun, Henry headed after them, the frantic words of his mother ringing in his ears. "Henry, you're not going."

The heroically impulsive response of Henry Sears serves to demonstrate that the events of October 30 amounted to far more than a blind mob panic, which is the way the evening has been sometimes portrayed. Indeed, in the years following the broadcast, the suggestion has gained currency that it provoked vast numbers into panicked flight, but while this supposition has been challenged in recent years, it is clear from the stories of people like Henry Sears that no simple explanation can suffice for the behavior recorded that night, and so a thorough reappraisal is clearly required. Not for nothing have these stories become a cherished part of family histories and entered into the annals of American folklore, but if we are to afford these stories the respect they deserve, our next task must be to shine a light on the battlefield and do our best to penetrate the fog of war.

7

THE FOG OF WAR
What Really Happened?

So what actually happened on the night of October 30, 1938? Did the world really come to an end (temporarily at least) for millions of people, or has the myth grown out of proportion to the true scale of events? This is a contentious question. The accounts in the previous chapter provide an extremely convincing body of anecdotal evidence supporting the argument that the broadcast caused widespread fear and distress, but it is equally fair to acknowledge that all great stories suffer in the telling and by the passing of time; memories fail, events are distorted and — sadly, it must be acknowledged — the truth is sometimes tarnished. This brings us to the vexing question of how much faith we should place in the original press reports of 1938.

Over the years a great deal of information about the broadcast and its effect has been derived from newspaper reports of the time, but the accuracy and impartiality of these accounts has been called into question by the suspicion that the newspapers had an axe to grind with radio. It is certainly true that in the years prior to the broadcast the wire services and newspaper publishers had fought (and lost) a bitter battle with radio, one that had many parallels with the conflict now brewing between the Internet and television. Until the advent of radio, the print press had enjoyed an unchallenged monopoly on the distribution of news and information within the United States, but who, wondered the journalists, would want to read a newspaper with day-old news when you could hear it live and fresh on the radio? Fearful press journalists were losing sleep over just this vexing question, but reduced readerships and falling revenues were not their only concern; also at stake was the power to guide and shape public opinion.

This particular conflict had actually been simmering since the early 1920s, when there arose a growing conviction among print journalists that this newfangled invention called radio might be more than a passing fad and could yet prove a serious competitor. This was despite the fact that there had been no real impact yet, and indeed some newspapers had even bought into radio stations, seeing them as a useful new advertising medium. In any event, newscasts were seldom a feature of the radio schedules and, lacking reporters and journalists of their own, the stations were largely beholden to the wire services for any provision of news. However, in 1922, the Associated Press (AP), one of the biggest wire services, opened hostilities by notifying its members that AP news bulletins were to be withheld from radio broadcasters.

The AP's action would prove relatively ineffective, since there were other wire services willing to deal with the radio stations, and the newspapers themselves were still divided on their opinion of radio; some, as we have already established, had already entered into close relationships with broadcasters. The difference of opinion between newspapers that partnered with radio stations and those that did not therefore prevented any serious conflict from breaking out in the short term, but the onset of the Great Depression in 1929 would be the uniting force that brought the rival newspapers and wire services together to take concerted action against radio.

Prior to the Depression, newspapers had enjoyed healthy advertising revenues and there was more than enough money to go around, but between 1929 and 1933, the estimated annual advertising revenue of the newspaper industry plummeted. From a national total of $800 million before October 1929, it dropped to $450 million in 1933.[1] Yet in essentially the same period and despite the detrimental effects of the Depression, radio managed to double its advertising revenue from $40 million to $80 million dollars.

At the same time, radio was also starting to show its true potential as a news gatherer and disseminator in its own right. Several key stories of the period elevated the medium in the eyes of the public, most notably the kidnapping of the Lindbergh baby on March 1, 1932, and the attempted assassination of president-elect Franklin D. Roosevelt on February 15, 1933. The Lindbergh case was especially galling to the newspapers, as it marked the moment that the near instantaneous and more intimate quality of radio really caught the public imagination. The radio stations sent their own reporters to the Lindbergh estate and in the course of the crisis hundreds of reports were aired. The newspaper press reacted angrily by criticizing the quality of reporting, but this, of course, disguised their real motives.

The year 1932 was also a presidential election year, which reignited a smoldering dispute that had first flared up at the last election. The problem was election returns. Previously the wire services had agreed to supply their returns data to the radio stations for free, but in 1932 the United Press (UP) balked at this and asked instead for $1,000 to supply the information. NBC refused, but after CBS agreed, the UP suddenly upped the ante by demanding upwards of $35,000 to help defray the cost of gathering the returns. At the same time the AP announced that it would not supply news to any chain that obtained news from another organization, and International News Service (INS) president J. V. Connolly announced that the INS "would neither sell nor give its service to radio." For as Connolly decreed, the INS "had no business furnishing material to the radio that could be used in competition with the client newspapers."[2]

As it happened, no one was willing to pay the enormous UP fee. The wire services blinked at the eleventh hour and the returns did go out on the radio, infuriating many of their newspaper clients. This anger would be given voice in April 1933, when the annual meetings of the Associated Press and the American Newspaper Publishers Association convened in Washington. The headline in the May 1 issue of *Broadcasting Magazine* said it all: "AP AND ANPA DECLARE WAR ON RADIO."[3]

In fact, what they had done was to pass a number of resolutions that would place radio with its back firmly against the wall. The AP membership voted almost overwhelmingly to cease all provision of news to radio while also mandating that newspapers with a broadcasting interest must limit any news segments to no more than occasional 30-second bulletins. The ANPA also passed a nonbinding resolution that radio schedules, previously published in newspapers free of charge, would now require a fee.

It can be argued fairly persuasively that the actions of the AP (which were swiftly duplicated by the other wire services) and, to a lesser extent, the ANPA, actually caused them more harm than good. Faced with little choice but to either abandon news or make their own, the NBC and CBS radio networks sensibly chose the latter, and set up their own news-gathering organizations. This, of course, only served to inflame passions even more. Speaking about the establishment of the CBS news service, Edward Harris, chair of the ANPA Radio Committee, said "A general attack has been launched by broadcasters against newspapers."[4]

Yet at the end of 1933 the networks unexpectedly sued for peace. At a meeting in December at the Hotel Biltmore in New York, the so-called Biltmore Agreement was drafted, outlining a plan that the broadcasters would suspend their own news-gathering services and receive in return limited bulletins from the wire services. It seemed an odd agreement to make given that the broadcasters were in the position of strength, but behind the scenes, the wire services and print journalists had been ratcheting up the pressure, primarily by threatening to lobby Washington just as the 1934 Communications Act was coming before legislators. Crucially, this was the first major overhaul of American telecommunications policy in over 60 years and the potential for mischief by the newspaper and wire services was of considerable concern for the networks, who were fearful that these still very powerful lobbies might persuade legislators to pass laws unfavorable to their burgeoning businesses. It also appears that there was a serious intent to finally make good on threats to suspend radio listings in newspapers, which would have deprived millions of radio owners of a means of planning their listening time.

But the Biltmore Agreement was in every important particular a lame duck. It was an agreement in name only, with no binding signatories and it covered only the CBS and NBC networks. This left a great number of small independents free to do as they please, and into this vacuum stepped others willing and able to compete with the wire services. One of key personalities in this arena was Herbert Moore, formerly the CBS news editor — until the Biltmore Agreement suspended his operations. His Transradio Press Service soon became highly successful as an independent news gatherer and aggregator, and with that, the writing was swiftly on the wall for the Biltmore Agreement. As the years rolled by, it was watered down more and more as commercial pressures grew against it, until in the spring of 1937 *Broadcasting Magazine* was able to announce that the conflict was over, ending not with a bang, but a whimper.

So if the battle was all but over, was there by October of 1938 any real antipathy left toward radio that might explain sensationalist reporting about the *War of the Worlds* broadcast? Anecdotally speaking, it seems that the reporters who confronted Welles and Houseman in the hours after the broadcast were baiting the pair, and if the account told by Houseman is accurate, telling them that there had been deaths seems a particularly cruel and unpleasant tactic. But another consideration is not that there was any particular antipathy toward radio but that Welles had made himself something of a target. Only a few months before the *War of the Worlds* broadcast, a heavily made-up Welles had graced the cover of *Time* magazine, and his reputation as a "boy wonder" preceded him wherever he went. He was given to making bold announcements in the press and clearly was a master showman and manipulator, convinced of his own brilliance and invulnerability. It is entirely possible that, as he had effectively placed himself on such a lofty pedestal, the press took satisfaction in giving it a hearty shake.

But what of the actual tone and content of the newspapers? Is there any indication or proof that they were exaggerating events in order to embarrass radio? The *New York Times* of October 31, in line with probably every other newspaper in the country, led with reports of the broadcast and the anger of listeners, turning up irate residents such as a Mr. Warren Dean, who was quoted as saying, "I've heard a lot of radio programs, but I've never heard anything as rotten as that." Or Samuel Tishman, last seen running down Broadway, who proclaimed it "the most asinine stunt I ever heard of." However, a thorough reading of the edition of the *Times* and a further large story on November 1 reveals no overt signs of bias; indeed, in the story Welles is given considerable room to defend himself. In fact, as we have already seen, Welles had used the *Times* to make announcements about the Mercury Theatre and so could hardly be said to be on bad terms with the paper. Indeed, none of the malicious allegations reportedly put to Welles and Houseman by a baying pack of journalists on the night of the broadcast were repeated in the *Times* the following day.

A better barometer of feelings toward the broadcast are the letters from the public published in the *Times* of November 2. Had the *Times* really harbored any antagonism toward Welles or radio, one feels it unlikely they would have published the letter of Alvin J. Bogart of Cranford, New Jersey, who wrote, "May we hope that no action will be taken against the Columbia Broadcasting System for the brilliant dramatization." Nor would they have given column space to H. G. W. Sundelof (a suspicious set of initials, it must be conceded) who declared, "Orson Welles should be complimented on his dramatization of the Martian descent on Newark and New York over CBS last night. It was an outstanding piece of work." In truth, the letters betray a wide degree of feeling and the hand of an editor keen to present all possible shades of opinion. Another letter writer, George Bellamy, for instance declared it a "boring and rather inane production" while others took exception to the apparent stupidity of the listening public.

The *Washington Post* of October 31 is a little more sensationalist in its reporting, claiming, "So unnerved were Americans at the prospect of invasion that at least two persons suffered heart attacks, hundreds fainted, men and women fled their homes, would-be fighters volunteered, hysteria swept the nation for a long and fearful hour." It is highly unlikely there were any heart attacks and "hundreds fainted" seems a fanciful exaggeration. Indeed, the tone of the *Post* story seems designed to highlight the mad panic that allegedly took place, rather than present any actual facts, a suspicion reinforced by its misidentification, twice, of Grover's Mill as "Grover's Corner."

The *Post* of November 2 calmed down a bit, publishing an editorial with the interesting comment that "if the radio industry continued to permit the presentation of imaginative drama in the form of news, its value as a disseminator of factual information might be seriously impaired." The comment certainly seems to suggest some latent hostility toward radio, but the rest of the editorial is rather complimentary, praising the speed of response from CBS, which had swiftly announced that it would not allow dramatists to repeat the same mistake, and observing that this had occurred with "...greater speed and effectiveness than could be expected from any body of censors."

The *Post* did apparently make capital of the broadcast a few days later, when according to Welles biographer Frank Brady, it ran on November 15 a full-page ad aimed at advertisers, mocking the ability of radio to deliver a message with any degree of clarity. "Who listened to him?" asked the *Post*, and, rubbing salt into the wound, "Who listens to what your announcer tells them about your product?"[5]

So if the premier newspapers in the nation were not exactly baying for blood, what of the smaller local newspapers? The *Trenton Evening Times*, reporting from the very heart of the "war zone," carried the story on its front page of its October 31 edition, though it shares fairly equal billing with other events, and a donation to a state finance survey by a wealthy pair of socialites was clearly of sufficient importance that they received top billing and had their photographs printed. The paper did print well over a dozen tales of varying scales of terror and confusion, though there is a sense that in saying, "The panic reached its peak in the metropolitan New York section," the provincial paper was enjoying the fact that its large neighbor had been so soundly frightened and embarrassed.

The *Trenton Evening Times* does provide one particularly illuminating and authoritative-sounding account, a letter of protest from city manager Paul Morton, in which he complains of the unprecedented drain on his resources by people clogging up his phone lines. Morton was so infuriated that he wrote a formal letter of complaint to the Federal Communications Commission (FCC), a copy of which luckily still resides in the FCC archives, so we know for certain that his complaints were reported accurately by the *Trenton Evening Times*. In the letter, Morton states that some 2,000 calls were received in about two hours and that the emergency communications facilities of Trenton were crippled for three hours. Had there been a real emergency, says Morton in his letter to the FCC, "it could have easily caused a more serious situation."

The concern shown by a senior city administrator seems perfectly genuine and there is no obvious reason for him to exaggerate the scope of events. He thus provides us with one of the most authoritative insights into the true scope of events that night. But if Trenton was in turmoil, then what of Grover's Mill? Surely it must have been in a veritable frenzy, yet strangely the evidence is a lot less certain than one might imagine. The *Washington Post* of October 31 reported an anonymous girl from "Grover's Corners" ringing the Princeton Press Club to cry out, "You can't imagine the horror of it! It's Hell!" The *Trenton Evening Times* carried the exact same quote, but reported that the call came into the Trenton police radio room, casting some doubt on its verity. Also in the *Trenton Evening Times* was an extraordinary account of what a squad of state troopers encountered when they arrived at Grover's Mill. So many people were either trying to get to the scene or escape from it "that traffic was almost at a standstill for miles around."

Yet someone who was at Grover's Mill that night flatly contradicts this account. Sheldon Judson,* then a 20-year-old student member of the Princeton Press Club, was alerted to the possible fall of a meteor by the city desk of the *Philadelphia Inquirer*. He enlisted the help of Arthur F. Buddington who was then chair of the Princeton Geology

*Sheldon Judson became a professor of geosciences at Princeton University.

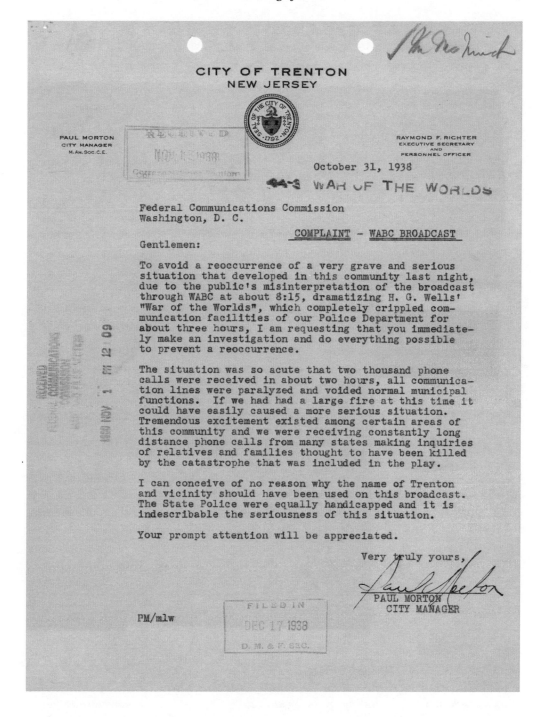

CITY OF TRENTON
NEW JERSEY

PAUL MORTON
CITY MANAGER
M. AM. SOC. C. E.

RAYMOND F. RICHTER
EXECUTIVE SECRETARY
AND
PERSONNEL OFFICER

RECEIVED
NOV 15 1938

October 31, 1938

WAR OF THE WORLDS

Federal Communications Commission
Washington, D. C.

COMPLAINT - WABC BROADCAST

Gentlemen:

To avoid a reoccurrence of a very grave and serious
situation that developed in this community last night,
due to the public's misinterpretation of the broadcast
through WABC at about 8:15, dramatizing H. G. Wells'
"War of the Worlds", which completely crippled communication facilities of our Police Department for
about three hours, I am requesting that you immediately make an investigation and do everything possible
to prevent a reoccurrence.

The situation was so acute that two thousand phone
calls were received in about two hours, all communication lines were paralyzed and voided normal municipal
functions. If we had had a large fire at this time it
could have easily caused a more serious situation.
Tremendous excitement existed among certain areas of
this community and we were receiving constantly long
distance phone calls from many states making inquiries
of relatives and families thought to have been killed
by the catastrophe that was included in the play.

I can conceive of no reason why the name of Trenton
and vicinity should have been used on this broadcast.
The State Police were equally handicapped and it is
indescribable the seriousness of this situation.

Your prompt attention will be appreciated.

Very truly yours,

PAUL MORTON
CITY MANAGER

PM/mlw

FILED IN
DEC 17 1938
D. M. & F. SEC.

City of Trenton manager Paul Morton's indignant letter of complaint to the FCC, detailing
the problems caused to the Trenton emergency services by the *War of the Worlds* broadcast
(Federal Communication Commission).

Department and, together with another professor named Harry H. Hess, they set out for Grover's Mill. As described by Judson, on arrival they found Grover's Mill to be perfectly calm,[6] though other accounts suggest that Judson may have arrived and departed before things began to get out of hand.

A witness who was living at the time in Grover's Mill can corroborate the presence of Judson and professors Buddington and Hess. Erving Press was resident at the time on Clarksville Road and vividly recalled the arrival of the Princeton delegation. He and his family had been in the fields husking corn, when "before it got dark this man came out; he was some sort of professor or something, and he wanted to know where the meteor fell."[7] So it looks like Press met Judson that night, though his recollection of the time must be faulty, as it would have been dark by the time Judson arrived with professors Buddington and Hess. Unfortunately (though not unexpectedly) Press does not offer any corroboration of the widely reported but surely exaggerated descriptions circulated in the press, that the professors spent their evening tapping rocks with a geologist's hammer in search of the meteor. This with absolute certainty must be an example of a reporter with too much imagination livening up the story.

Press also offers an extremely intriguing account of the activities around Grover's Mill that evening. "Meanwhile the cars is getting thicker. I guess we should've started chargin' admission to park there.... And everything was in real turmoil. People come all wavin' and hollerin'. They were all nuts."[8] All this may conceivably have happened after Judson left, but it is equally possible that Press might have been confused and was describing what he saw the following day, as the area did become a major sightseeing destination, with the owner of the local "Wilson" farm (note the similarity to the fictional Wilmuth farm) allegedly charging parking fees to people wanting to see the Martian landing site. However, when many years later Howard Koch made a pilgrimage to Grover's Mill and interviewed the farm owner, this story was hotly denied.

The *Seattle Star* of November 1 also records something of the turmoil that was allegedly engulfing the area surrounding Grover's Mill. William Wassun was a resident of Cranbury, located about five miles east of Grover's Mill, and recalled encountering a carload of state troopers out "looking for a fight." "They were all dressed up to kill. I couldn't convince them it must be a fake and two hours later I saw them, still riding around looking for whatever it was supposed to be." Other accounts have the area positively swarming with civilians keen to engage the Martians, and police trying to defuse the tension. Howard Koch on his visit to the area in 1969 was told by the retired local fire chief that he was kept busy most of the night looking for fires believed to have been set by Martian heat-rays, and that he encountered farmers on the prowl with shotguns. It has also been said that more than 100 state troopers were deployed to the area to restore calm.[9]

But not everyone in Grover's Mill seems to have been quite so ready to take up arms against the Martians. According to the *Seattle Star* on November 1, tenant farmer James Anderson was woken by his wife, who had just heard on CBS that her sleepy little neighborhood was at the center of a storm of activity. Mr. Anderson got up, crossed to the porch and looked out into the night. "Durn fools," he declared, and without further ado went straight back to bed.

Certainly the most famous story centered on Grover's Mill has residents mistaking a water tower for a Martian tripod and blasting it with shotguns and rifles. There is a famous and much reproduced picture, in which local resident William Dock (76 years of age at the time) stands before the mill with his rifle at the ready, eager to repel the invaders. In reality the picture was staged by a reporter and it is doubtful that old Bill was actually out tramping the woods the night before in search of Martians, though the *Seattle Star* of November 1st is quite certain he was, alleging that he had become convinced of the reality of the broadcast when the Martians emerged. "Then he got out his shotgun and went looking for them," the paper reported.

Quaint though it is to imagine the backwoods of New Jersey full of panicky, heavily armed farmers, the evidence is clearly contradictory, though if some of the wilder stories have to be called into question, it certainly does not discredit the presumption that people in general were in a state of great alarm. This is quite clear from Morton's letter to the FCC and one other highly convincing piece of documentation, the logbook of the Trenton State Police Headquarters. This makes for fascinating reading, though it is interesting to note that the number of calls is not in the volume suggested by newspaper reports, nor is there any corroboration that, as reported in the *Trenton Evening Times* of October 31, State Police Headquarters was so flooded with calls that a squad of troopers equipped with riot gear and gas masks was dispatched to Grover's Mill. It is also interesting to note the discrepancy between the 50 calls recorded in the police logbook and the 2,000 calls claimed by

Grover's Mill resident William "Bill" Dock stands ready to repel the Martian invaders. The picture was staged in the days following the broadcast by an enterprising reporter (Mary Evans Picture Library).

Trenton city manager Paul Morton, though it is possible that Morton provided a figure covering all the emergency services within his area of responsibility.

The logbook notes:

> Between 8:30 P.M. & 10 P.M. received numerous phone calls as result of WABC broadcast this evening re: Mars attacking this country. Calls included papers, police depts including NYC and private persons. No record kept of same due to working teletype and all three extensions ringing at same time. At least 50 calls were answered. Persons calling inquiring as to meteors, number of persons killed, gas attack, military being called out and fires. All were advised nothing unusual had occurred and that rumors were due to a radio dramatization of a play.[10]

Page from the station record of the Trenton Headquarters of the State Police, October 30, 1938 (New Jersey State Police).

So we are clearly faced with a great deal of contradictory evidence, but if we are struggling to identify exactly what people were doing, can we be any more certain of the geographic scale of events? The evidence certainly seems to point convincingly toward it touching every corner of the United States. Thousands of miles from New York on the West Coast, the same degree of concern was recorded by local newspapers. The switchboard of the *Seattle Daily News* was, according to the October 31 edition, "deluged for hours with calls from persons trying to learn whether the alarming 'news' was authentic." Local CBS affiliate stations carrying the broadcast were also overwhelmed with calls, with station KIRO receiving upwards of 250 calls in one hour. The *Newark Evening News* rounded up several reports from around the country for its edition of October 31, including accounts that newspaper and radio station switchboards in Toronto, Ontario, had seen a heavy load of calls from concerned citizens. Other reports came from San Francisco, Boston, Memphis and Detroit.

So if the newspaper accounts are to be believed there was a large countrywide (even international) reaction by the listening public, but do we have any way of estimating the actual number of persons involved? Luckily the answer is yes, thanks to the work of a Princeton University professor called Hadley Cantril. It is Cantril who has bequeathed us one of the best pieces of evidence for the effects of the broadcast in the form of an in-depth survey that he and his researchers carried out soon after the event. The book that resulted also gathers together stories as told directly to Cantril and his team and largely bypasses any suspect newspaper reports. In that regard, there is an interesting and perhaps telling comment by Cantril in his introduction. He informs us that much of the information for his study was derived from detailed interviews with 135 persons who had been located by his researchers. He goes on to explain, "The names of persons who were listed in the newspapers as having been frightened failed to produce more than a half dozen interviews."[11] Could this be a smoking gun proving that the newspapers fabricated or at least exaggerated some of their stories?

Perhaps so, but even if the newspapers did fake or least exaggerate some stories to bolster the traditionally slow news day of a Monday, then Cantril not only offers up witnesses whose provenance seems more reliable but, better still, provides a considered estimate on the scale and nature of the panic. He begins by calculating the total number of people who heard the broadcast at approximately 6 million. This was not mere guesswork. Cantril based this figure on the results of two surveys, one carried out by the Gallup organization (known then as the American Institute of Public Opinion, or AIPO) and the other by C. E. Cooper, Inc., a commercial research organization that was in the business of monitoring radio audiences.

Working from a sample of some 2,000 adults, AIPO asked, "Did you listen to the Orson Welles broadcast of the invasion from Mars?" to which 12 percent answered yes. To calculate a potential listening audience, Cantril turned to the census of 1930, and combines the voting-age population of 75 million persons with the number of children ten years and older to arrive at a total potential audience of 99 million persons. Twelve percent of this figure suggests that some 12 million individuals heard the broadcast. However, as Cantril concedes, this is a very high number. It is also fair to say that including children undoubtedly introduces an additional variable, since there is no way of saying how many were safely tucked up in bed at the time of broadcast, or for that matter how many families routinely listened together. The C. E. Cooper survey put the listening figure at a much lower 4 million, so to arrive at his final estimate of 6 million listeners, Cantril conservatively pooled the results of the two surveys.

More fascinating still, Cantril goes on to draw some conclusions about the actual number of listeners who were scared by the broadcast. Again he bases his core numbers on the AIPO survey, which indicated that 28 percent of respondents believed that the broadcast represented a real series of breaking news stories. Of these, 70 percent were willing to admit that they had been disturbed by the content of the broadcast. This, Cantril suggests, means that of 1,700,000 listeners who potentially took the broadcast to be real, 1,200,000 were upset to one degree or another. He also makes the interesting passing point that not every respondent may have been truthful, given that admitting you were taken in by a radio play is not the easiest thing to do. Of additional significance, Cantril documents a number of other supporting pieces of evidence that he and his team gathered personally. A postal survey of high school principals garnered 305 responses (from 1,044 sent) and indicated that, on average, 5 percent of their student bodies had been upset by the broadcast. From this Cantril extrapolates a figure of some 250,000 children adversely affected. Managers of radio stations reported on greatly increased volumes of mail in the days following, and the Mercury Theatre itself received a bursting postbag of 1,450 letters, though it is interesting to note in passing that 91 percent were congratulatory in nature.

That the telephone system was under immense strain that night is also strongly supported by Cantril's research. One of the more interesting statistics provided by Cantril comes from the American Telephone Company, which furnished him with data indicating a 39 percent increase in calls during the hour of the broadcast. Calls were said to have been made to friends and families, hospitals, newspapers, CBS and, of course, the police.

So what of the stories of the chaos within the CBS building that night and in particular the response of the New York Police Department? It is said the control booth of the studio was invaded by a sea of blue uniforms as the effect of the broadcast took hold, and that the building was convulsed with panic as network executives saw their careers flashing before their eyes, but if so, the effect seems to have been localized to the 20th-floor studio that Welles and his Mercury players regularly occupied. John Houseman alludes to the presence of "dark blue uniforms,"[12] yet Norman Corwin, who as we learned in the previous chapter was rehearsing a new program just one floor above, was completely oblivious to the momentous events unfolding just a short distance away.[13] Of course this is not to say that stories of the chaos in the CBS building should be dismissed out of hand, since the building was large and Corwin was otherwise occupied with his rehearsal.

So what are we to conclude? At the very least, all this contradictory evidence proves that we should not always believe what the papers tell us, yet documents such as the Trenton Police Headquarters log and the letter of city manager Paul Morton clearly prove that there is no smoke without fire, and this particular battlefield is an especially murky one. On consideration, it seems unreasonable to assume that many of the published stories in 1938 were essentially truthful, although their accuracy could well have been tainted by poor, not necessarily malicious, reporting practices. At the same time it is equally valid to propose that the idea of print media hostility toward radio has itself been subject to a certain amount of mythmaking, so that the suggestion of a seedily unprofessional (indeed corrupt) press has taken on something of a life of its own and has been repeated so many times that it has become an unchallenged historical "fact."

Certainly we should not discount out of hand the idea that there could very well have been some lingering resentment among newspaper reporters at the capitulation of their industry to the power of radio. *Variety* magazine certainly thought so, suggesting in an editorial in the days after the broadcast that "anti-radio press overplayed it, for its own reasons."[14] Nor is it unreasonable to assume that a number of attention seekers took advantage of reporters' willingness to paint events in the blackest and most sensational of lights, but newspaper journalism had clearly matured considerably by the late 1930s and was therefore capable of responsible reporting. It is also worth remembering that many of the stories recounted in the previous chapter were told years later on anniversaries of the broadcast, such as the 50th in 1988. There seems little reason for all these people to falsely claim they were taken in so thoroughly by something so pedestrian as a radio play. Nevertheless this must be tempered by the acknowledgment that memories are notoriously prone to error and there is therefore every chance that some of the stories told in later years have become contaminated by the more sensational aspects of the reporting.

Weighing all the evidence it is impossible to come to any conclusion but that there was indeed a widespread, sizable disturbance across the United States on the evening of October 30, 1938. It crossed all social, economic and geographical boundaries and was characterized by a great swell of fear and anxiety that saw people react in a wide variety of ways, from finding simple comfort in the company of friends and family, to alerting others to the danger in person and by telephone or, in extreme cases, taking flight by foot and automobile. The next intriguing question to answer is why such an unusual reaction occurred.

8

Smoke and Mirrors
Why the Panic?

Few of the great battles of history are recorded with anything like precision. The fog of war obscures facts and befuddles detail, and just as historians easily take issue with the cause of conflicts or the competence of generals, so too has *The War of the Worlds* become mired in controversy. What was going on in the minds of listeners that night? Why did they believe so ardently that the broadcast was the truth? And, most intriguing, of all, what was Orson Welles really thinking? Was he as much a victim of chance and circumstance as everyone else, or did this wily young maverick secretly plan to spring the ultimate Halloween prank on an unsuspecting public? If he did, it is fair to say he had allies, a potent mix of simmering political and social tensions, combined with a large dash of pure dumb luck.

"Dumb luck" is certainly an apt phrase to describe the improbable contribution of a ventriloquist's dummy to the pandemonium that night. It is hard to believe that a wooden puppet could have such a significant role in what has been described as the biggest mass panic in history (let alone be the star of a hugely popular radio variety show) yet if one commonly advanced theory is correct, then by an unfortunate convergence of the airwaves and the deleterious influence of an unpopular song, this is precisely what happened.

The Charlie McCarthy Show had started out on the Red Network of NBC radio just over a year prior to *The War of the Worlds* broadcast, but in that short time it had already established for itself a huge and appreciative audience, such that in terms of listeners it outperformed the Mercury Theatre by a staggering ratio of 34.7 percent to 3.6 percent of the listening audience.[1] Sponsored by the Chase and Sanborn coffee company, it was actually formally announced and promoted as *The Chase and Sanborn Hour*, but such has been the lasting popularity of its sawdust-headed star that it is now far more affectionately remembered as *The Charlie McCarthy Show*.

Somewhat eclipsed by the charismatic dummy on his arm was Edgar Bergen, a stalwart of the vaudeville tradition who had taught himself ventriloquism from a 25-cent pamphlet at the age of eleven. The top-hatted and monocle-wearing Charlie McCarthy started as a mischievous small boy, but by his radio debut he had evolved into a far more mature and edgy character. Bergen was not afraid to push the boundaries of prevailing public decency, and the show courted controversy on more than one occasion, none more so than in December 1937 when Charlie and guest Mae West scandalized the listening public with a (for the time) highly salacious routine set in the Garden of Eden. Such was the outcry that West was banned from radio for 14 years.

Broadcast weekly on NBC network opposite the second season of the Mercury Theatre on CBS, the format of *The Charlie McCarthy Show* varied little from week to week. Master of ceremonies Don Ameche would introduce Bergen and McCarthy, who would then talk about the forthcoming highlights of the show and engage in some witty banter. Then regular crooner and comic foil Nelson Eddy would sing. It was an innocuous musical interlude like this that is customarily said to have brought about the fateful collision with Orson Welles.

We are all familiar in this modern age with the phenomena of channel surfing on television, but it is really nothing new, and radio listeners in the 1930s were just as prone to "itchy finger syndrome" if something failed to hold their interest. It even had a name: dial surfing. Most people had every intention of turning back to their favored program after a few minutes, but on this particular evening it is thought that a considerable number deserted Charlie McCarthy and landed in the midst of *The War of the Worlds* on CBS. Many listeners abruptly forgot the puppet and left their dials in place, for the incredible news appeared to be that a military invasion of the United States was under way.

The prevailing opinion even in recent writings about the broadcast is that Nelson Eddy's rendition of "Neapolitan Love Song"[2] was to blame, with dial-twiddling listeners arriving at CBS at the very moment the Wilmuth farm was about to be obliterated

Edgar Bergen holds Charlie McCarthy in a lobby card from the 1939 movie *Charlie McCarthy, Detective* (Universal Pictures Company).

by a Martian heat-ray. Arriving in the middle of a furious battle would certainly have captured anyone's attention, but assigning the blame to Nelson Eddy does not hold up to analysis for a number of important reasons. First, Eddy never actually sang "Neapolitan Love Song" that evening, and secondly, his opening number, "Song of the Vagabonds," started at two minutes and seven seconds into the show, long before the Wilmuth farm sequence of *The War of the Worlds*.

Eddy did sing a second song immediately after the first, but the "Canadian Logging Song" finished some six minutes and 23 seconds into the show, so even this does not line up satisfactorily, since reporter Carl Phillips did not start his "outside broadcast" from the Wilmuth farm until 11 minutes into *The War of the Worlds*. Anyone tuning in at the approximate six-minute mark would therefore have chanced upon the scene in Princeton Observatory. For the scientifically inclined, this would have been quite interesting, but it seems unlikely that the average listener would have been much enamored of this and so would most likely have kept dial surfing or returned in due course to Bergen and McCarthy.

Immediately after Eddy's second song, Bergen, McCarthy, and show regular Dorothy Lamour launched straight into a long Halloween skit, which would certainly have held their core listeners' attention. So does this mean the central plank of the Charlie McCarthy theory is something of a fabrication, or could it be that the blame has been wrongly apportioned? Might poor Nelson Eddy be innocent and is the true culprit none other than Dorothy Lamour? At 15 minutes and 20 seconds into the show, Lamour launched into a soulful rendition of Hoagy Carmichael's "Two Sleepy People." This matches perfectly with the most terrifying moment of the Wilmuth farm scene, as Philips describes in horrified and panicked tones the emergence of the first Martian from the cylinder and the subsequent attack on Grover's Mill. If anything was likely to cause an intense reaction it was Philips' bravado performance at this moment, though as this timeline aptly demonstrates, there were several moments in the broadcast when unwary listeners could easily have stumbled on the broadcast with varying degrees of effect. But arriving at almost any moment between the Wilmuth farm scene and the mid-program break would have been extremely alarming.

Do we have any substantive proof at all that any listeners actually left the *Charlie McCarthy Show* at any time at all during the show and became riveted by *The War of the Worlds*? Thanks to the work of Hadley Cantril, we do. Cantril first offers up the finding that according to "restricted meter-checks" the average family heard 48 minutes out of 60 minutes of a *Charlie McCarthy Show*.[3] This certainly seems to imply the possibility that listener loyalty was not absolute, but in order to more precisely determine the influence of Charlie McCarthy on the panic, Cantril's team surveyed 846 persons who were known to have heard *The War of the Worlds*. They were asked, "if at any time during the hour they had heard the Charlie McCarthy program and, if so, had they tuned out when McCarthy had finished his first act." Respondents numbered 518, of which 18 percent admitted to have also heard something of *The Charlie McCarthy Show* that evening. Of those 93 respondents, 62 percent (or 58 persons) admitted to having switched over to *The War of the Worlds* and that they had not then returned to Charlie McCarthy.

So it seems that there was a significant migration of bored listeners from Charlie

McCarthy, and some 11 percent remained glued to *The War of the Worlds*, though it is worth noting several caveats. First, the wording of Cantril's question specified the first act of *The Charlie McCarthy Show* as the point of departure, and while he does propose the idea that listeners switched channels "when the dummy act was finished,"[4] this does not in itself pinpoint any one particular point of departure, nor does it lend support to any one particular song being to blame. It is also worth noting that just because a large number of people alighted on *The War of the Worlds*, this is not to say that all of them would have leapt to the conclusion that they were listening to a real news broadcast. It seems perfectly plausible that some simply thought it was superior entertainment and stayed put.

What we do know from the other surveys conducted in the days after the broadcast is that those who tuned in late were far more likely to have accepted the broadcast as real than those who heard it from the beginning—though, surprisingly, even a proportion of the latter group were fooled. In surveys conducted by CBS and the AIPO, respondents were asked if they had listened from the beginning or tuned in late. They were also asked if they had believed the program to be a real news story or a play. The results from both surveys reveal a marked disposition among latecomers to take the drama for real. The CBS survey put the figure at 63 percent, the AIPO survey at 35 percent.

Another important factor influencing the arrival of latecomers seems to have been the telephone and word of mouth. Turning again to the AIPO and CBS surveys, we find that when asked if they had tuned into *The War of the Worlds* late because someone had suggested it, 21 percent of AIPO respondents answered in the affirmative. This is aptly demonstrated by a story from the *Seattle Post-Intelligencer* of October 31, which describes how in Washington, "a near panic broke out at a religious revival meeting when an excited woman rushed in and told of 'an attack' on New Jersey in which forty or more persons were killed." When the parishioners turned on a radio to check what was happening, it was at a particularly alarming moment in the broadcast and many promptly rushed for the exits, although, the *Post-Intelligencer* added, "scores of women in the big tent tabernacle fell to knees in prayer."

The CBS survey also indicated that many people had received calls urging them to listen to the broadcast, with their findings putting the figure at 15 percent of respondents. Cantril quotes an increase of 39 percent recorded by the American Telephone Company as contrasted to the usual volume of that hour of the evening,[5] though there is some dissent among sociologists as to the precise meaning of this surge in telephone traffic. Sociologist Eric Goode promotes the view that there is little evidence to show that panicked individuals were responsible for all the calls,[6] and it is true to say that the Cantril summation does not quantify the reasons these people were urged to listen, or their reaction on tuning in. It is then perfectly reasonable to point out that there were reasons other than blind panic to pick up the phone during and after the broadcast. Some may simply have wanted to alert friends and family to a particularly good play on CBS, others to share in the excitement of the evening and swap stories of the antics of more credulous folk, but to the detriment of his argument, Goode takes no account of the very strong evidence that a high proportion of calls were made by extremely scared people.

We have already seen in Chapter 5 that several switchboard operators recalled the terrified nature of the calls they received, and Cantril also provides some striking firsthand accounts. "My sister called up and I immediately got scared," says one woman. Says another, "I was resting when an excited person phoned and told me to listen to the radio, that a big meteor had fallen. I was really worried."[7] Such calls, coming largely from trusted friends and relatives, would certainly have created heightened feelings of dread in the recipients, in effect priming them to believe that what they were hearing was a true reflection of events.

Yet not only those who tuned in late by accident or were urged to listen by those they trusted were susceptible to panic. A small but not insignificant number of listeners heard the broadcast from the very beginning, yet still took it to be a real news event. The CBS survey reported that 20 percent of those who had listened from the beginning thought it was news, while the AIPO put the figure at 11 percent. Cantril offers several convincing explanations for this, backing them up with testimony from those involved. One unidentified individual said, "My radio was tuned to the station but I wasn't paying attention to it." Said another, "My radio had been tuned to the station several hours. I heard loud talking and excitement and became interested." So some listeners were simply not paying attention, but another explanation is by far the most revealing, showing that the listening public was in a highly receptive mood to take seriously a dire message of doom and destruction. As one listener told Cantril, "I have heard other programs interrupted in the same way for news broadcasts."

This statement is not in the least bit surprising. As we established in the previous chapter, radio was then coming into its own as a provider of news, flexing newly discovered muscles and pushing the technical boundaries in exciting ways. The Lindbergh baby kidnapping and the attempted assassination of president-elect Franklin Roosevelt were just two examples of the sort of rapid, on-the-spot newsgathering that was now possible. Even more groundbreaking was foreign news, and this (and the urgent style of reporting) was fueling a growing sense of alarm among American listeners.

The news from Europe in 1938 was not good. On March 12, Adolf Hitler had declared the Anschluss (political union) that absorbed Austria into greater Germany, and thanks to radio news American listeners were able to follow this and subsequent events with an unprecedented degree of immediacy. The speeches of Hitler were carried into living rooms across the nation, and on September 30 America heard Chamberlain, after his disastrous appeasement of Germany at Munich, declare "peace for our time." Then, just weeks prior to *The War of the Worlds* broadcast, German troops occupied the Sudetenland, signaling the beginning of the end for Czechoslovakian independence and a now inevitable slide toward the horrors of a second world war.

CBS was at the forefront of this pioneering reporting, with reporters William L. Shirer and Edward R. Murrow broadcasting round the clock, live from London and other European locations as the crisis accelerated. Murrow was often introduced by H. V. Kaltenborn in New York, another figure of great importance to the development of radio news. It was Kaltenborn who in 1936 had made history by reporting live for the first time from a front line, crouched by a haystack outside the Spanish town of Irun as bullets and bombs fell around him. During the 18 days of the Munich Crisis, Kaltenborn made 102 broadcasts[8] and CBS is said to have lost $25,000 in advertising revenues because they constantly pre-empted commercial broadcasts. In the same period, NBC interrupted regular programming over 440 times.[9]

As Kaltenborn recalled, "The intensity with which America listened to the radio reports from the Munich crisis was without parallel in radio history. Portable radio sets which had just been developed had a tremendous sale. People carried them to wherever they went, to restaurants, offices, and on the streets. That was the day of the taxicab radios, and every standing cab was surrounded by crowds as on World Series days. Here was a world series with a vengeance! Never before had so many listened so long to so much. Millions of Americans concentrated intently as they heard the words: "America calling Prague ... London.... Come in, Paris.... Berlin ... Munich."[10]

In this heightened atmosphere of anticipation and tension, many of Cantril's respondents interpreted the events they heard on the radio as something other than a Martian invasion. Said one panic-stricken woman, "I kept saying over and over again to everybody I met: 'Don't you know New Jersey is destroyed by the Germans — It's on the radio.'"[11] Some went to great lengths to ponder the situation and construct carefully reasoned rationales: "I knew it was some Germans trying to gas all of us. When the announcer kept calling them people from Mars, I just thought he was ignorant and didn't know yet that Hitler had sent them all."[12] Said another, "The announcer said a meteor had fallen from Mars and I was sure he thought that, but in back of my head I had the idea that the meteor was just a camouflage. It was really an airplane like a Zeppelin that looked like a meteor and the Germans were attacking us with gas bombs."[13]

These last comments are particularly illuminating, as Cantril's interviewees often allude to their terror of the poison gas being spread by the invaders. But why focus on this particular element of the story? Gas is in itself of course a terrifyingly indiscriminate weapon, but there is some evidence to suggest that the threat of a gas attack would have some extra resonance in 1938. In August, newspapers had carried reports claiming that poison gas had been deployed in fighting between the Japanese and Chinese. A *New York Times* article of August 26 reported on a League of Nations protest note that had been delivered to Japan alleging that two Chinese battalions had perished in gas attacks in the Juichang sector, west of Kiukiang. The short piece is buried away on page 6, but the *Washington Post* also carried the same report, and on September 21, the *Times* reported on pleas from China to take action against Japan over gas attacks. No doubt radio news was also reporting on this, so it seems likely that some listeners to *The War of the Worlds* would have been aware of the Japanese attacks, adding greatly to their sense of alarm. Fear of gas and the approaching invaders was so intense that some people were reported to have actually witnessed the smoke and flames rising up from the fighting. The *Trenton Evening Times* of October 31 reported on one hysterical man who entered a police station with the alarming news that planes were bombing New Jersey. When the officer on duty asked how he knew this, the man replied that he had heard it on the radio, and then when he had gone to the roof of his building, he said, he could "see the smoke from the bombs." In the same article, a woman from Boston was reported to have called a switchboard with the news that "the flames of ravaged New Jersey were visible in Massachusetts."

Usefully, the many references to gas among Cantril's interviewees provide some additional evidence to help establish how long people remained panicked by the broadcast. The first reference to gas (other than the gaseous explosions from the surface of Mars) occurs 31 minutes into the broadcast, when army fieldpieces go up against the Martians and are choked into submission by the black smoke. This is also not long before one of the most terrifying moments in the entire play, when a lone reporter atop the "Broadcasting Building" in New York City describes the black gas rolling down the streets and people jumping "like rats" into the river. The moment the reporter falls silent and his microphone drops to the ground is scary enough now, but in 1938 it must have been chilling.

The destruction of New York occurred at about the 40-minute mark, at which point the first and only station break in the broadcast came. From this point onwards the story switched style completely to a conventional drama and so it is very likely that alert listeners would then have begun to realize their error. However, as we have already seen with the musical interludes, various inaccuracies have crept into the telling of the broadcast story over the intervening years, and the precise timing of this station break has itself become the subject of misinterpretation.

David Miller is a sociologist who has downplayed sensationalist reporting of the broadcast, but his argument that the effect on listeners was short-lived and localized to one key moment in the broadcast can be challenged on several important points. Miller writes of "the station break at the middle of the broadcast"[14] as if it were at the 30-minute point that the drama switched to a more conventional style, but he is off by ten crucial minutes. For listeners, these extra few minutes would have seemed like an eternity. Miller is also clearly mistaken to suggest as he has that the Wilmuth farm sequence represents the nexus of the panic and that everything else should be downplayed. This view fails to take into account the 40 minutes of broadcast without pause or intermission, and the predominance of listener stories that talk of a fear of gas. All this implies that the panic was longer, more sustained and intense that Miller suggests.

For those listeners better able to marshal their fears, there was of course much in the broadcast that could break the spell, most notably the rapid advance of the Martians over wide swaths of territory, the brevity of enormous battles and the incredibly fast response of the authorities in mustering resistance to the invasion. According to Cantril's analysis, 25 percent of listeners did indeed have the presence of mind to notice these impossibilities or took the trouble to make other calming checks,[15] but for the remainder, Miller offers up the theory that some listeners were blind to the obvious because they perceived the broadcast not as a sequential series of events, but as a hodgepodge of random reports from any number of battlefronts. This seems an eminently reasonable idea. As is well documented by Cantril, many people heard a portion of the broadcast, became alarmed and felt the need to pass on the news. They would have either telephoned someone and so stepped away from the radio momentarily, or even left the radio altogether and sought out company, perhaps dipping back into the broadcast a considerable number of minutes later, and in the process severely damaging their time sense.

It is also worth noting that scriptwriter Howard Koch was aware that the necessity of squeezing his invasion into such a short time frame would stretch the credulity of his listeners. To this end, the Martian tripods are described as "advancing at express-train speed," scouting planes keep the "speeding enemy in sight," and the Martian war machines are seen "kicking over trees and houses in their evident haste." While it is unlikely that this convinced a great many people that the invasion was real, it does seem likely that this clever acknowledgment of the problem would have had some impact at a subliminal level. To this, John Houseman adds the observation that in building the suspense so slowly at first, and then accelerating the story at a faster and faster pace, Welles was able to capture the attention of his audience so perfectly that they failed to notice when events that should have taken days flew by in minutes.[16]

But perhaps the most important factor that helped promote the reality of the broadcast was the trust that Americans held in the integrity of radio. This is amply indicated by a *Fortune* magazine survey quoted by Cantril, in which listeners were asked to state, "Which of the two — radio or newspaper — gives you news freer from prejudice?"[17] Only 17 percent rated newspapers. Newspapers had not always enjoyed an unblemished reputation with readers. The early 1900s had seen a circulation war between Joseph Pulitzer's *New York World* and William Randolph Hearst's *New York Journal* in which the first casualty had been truth. The term "yellow journalism"* was coined in this period to describe such sensationalist reporting, and it is likely that by 1938 some lingering mistrust existed. Nonetheless radio was not without its own brand of yellow journalism; it was just that most listeners had been seduced by the wonder of news delivered instantly into their homes. "We had so much faith in broadcasting,"[18] said one of Cantril's interviewees.

With such a trusting audience, and in using real place-names in the *War of the Worlds* broadcast, Welles only reinforced the feeling that the events coming across the airwaves were real. When Kenny Delmar did his uncanny impersonation of Roosevelt, the illusion was complete. The key question remaining is, how badly did people panic? This is a vexing question for sociologists like Miller and Goode, who are representative of a general consensus in their field that the broadcast was not a "panic" in the strict definition of the word, and that Cantril was in error for representing it as such in his book. The charge should be examined, but no discussion of this issue can truly be settled without first arriving at a satisfactory definition of a panic. This is where a lot of the trouble arises. Sociologists have been arguing over this question for decades, and *The War of the Worlds*, as one of the few well-documented instances of a so-called mass panic, has become something of a cause célèbre in their deliberations.

From a sociologist's perspective, there are several phrases that can be used to describe what happened on October 30, 1938, such as "mass panic" or "mass hysteria," but all come under the general heading of "collective behavior." Sociologist Neil Smelser defines a panic as "a collective flight based on a hysterical belief."[19] If we accept this definition, then the *War of the Worlds* broadcast cannot comfortably fit within this classification. There was no mass flight, no heading for the hills or jammed highways, but there was a great deal of fright. So does any other definition fit the bill? Miller provides a much more elastic definition for the term "mass hysteria," attributing to it anything from physical symptoms of nausea and fainting to widespread excitement and fear.[20] This seems like an excellent definition for the *War of the Worlds* broadcast, but Eric Goode is quite scathing of the entire concept and goes so far as to say that "mass hysteria is so rare as to be practically nonexistent."[21] Instead, he characterizes the events of that night as a "mass delu-

*The term "yellow journalism" is generally thought to have arisen when Pulitzer and Hearst fought over the rights to publish a comic strip by R.F. Outcault called the "Yellow Kid."

sion," distinct from a panic in that actual cases of flight were statistically tiny, and most listeners simply believed they were faced with what he calls a "threat from an unlikely, improbable source." Sociologist William Sims Bainbridge also took issue with Cantril because in "...quoting the stories of a few people who claimed to have been very frightened, he implies that there was a widespread panic. *There wasn't.*"[22]

Cantril's sample is indeed small, but rather than dwell on the number, it is instructive to remember what many of his survey respondents actually said in their interviews: "When I came out of the telephone booth, the store was filled with people in a rather high state of hysteria. I was already scared but this hysterical group convinced me that something was wrong."[23] Another story comes from a nurse who was having a party at her house. "Everybody was terribly frightened. Some of the women went almost crazy."[24] In fact, often Cantril's respondents indicate they were not alone in their fears and either shared in the terror with friends or family, or encountered others who were similarly panicked. This domino effect, as listeners infected others who had either not yet heard the broadcast, or reinforced the belief of those who had, implies a far larger number of disturbed persons than Bainbridge supposed. We should also not forget the huge number of calls said to have been received by various telephone switchboards across America.

Cantril's selection of witness accounts cannot then be so easily dismissed, and he was also more careful than modern sociologists give him credit for in making a distinction between "fright" and "panic." When Cantril estimates 1.2 million people were affected by the broadcast, he talks about them being "disturbed" or "frightened."[25] In the preface to his book, he suggests that "thousands of Americans became panic-stricken."[26] Note that he said *thousands*, not *millions*. These are not the words of a man intent on creating a sensationalist interpretation of events, nor indeed does it sound unreasonable to suggest thousands were "panic" stricken. In fact it seems clear the sociologists have seriously underestimated the extent and strength of the panic, relying as they did for their analysis entirely on a narrow review of the evidence presented in a single book. That they have in the process also unfairly maligned Cantril and his findings seems incontrovertible.

But while the sociologists may disagree over the strength of reaction to the broadcast and we can take issue with their interpretations, the field can offer intriguing insights into the forces at work that night. Seen in a purely sociological context, *The War of the Worlds* inadvertently included one particularly well-understood trigger for panic. Throughout the broadcast, listeners were told that the enemy was advancing across great swaths of territory, destroying familiar landmarks and place names as they went, cutting off possible escape routes. Name-checked among others are the Pulaski Skyway, Raymond Boulevard and the Hutchinson River Parkway. In doing this, the broadcast created a feeling in listeners that their possible escape routes were being cut off one by one. The possibility of escape still existed, but it was becoming ever more constricted. Smelser suggests that panics cannot occur if all the perceived escape routes are blocked, such as in mine or submarine disasters.[27] In these conditions the more likely response is mental incapacitation, but if people have any hope of escape, they seize on this and panic can ensue.

The War of the Worlds offered people the glimmer of hope that escape might still be possible, but was Goode right to maintain that few people actually took flight that night? Certainly people did not flee into the hills en masse, but there are enough stories available to suggest that many did begin frantic preparations to leave, and in some extreme cases, such as occurred in Newark, people were apparently discovered by the police loading furniture onto cars. It seems likely that had the broadcast lasted just a little longer, or had further stimulus occurred, the desire to flee would have become overwhelming, as may actually have happened in the town of Concrete in Skagit County, Washington. In the middle of the broadcast, the whole town was reported to have been plunged into darkness by a power failure, convincing the residents that the invasion was on their doorstep. According to the *Seattle Post-Intelligencer*, women fainted and some residents fled into the nearby mountains. Again, of course, we have to take the newspaper accounts at face value, but if they were true, we can only shudder at the thought of what would have happened if the lights of the New York skyline had gone out that night!

If Mars had risen that night over a darkened New York, it would have been a potent vindication of its continuing power over the public imagination. Scientists were making confident predictions that the planet lacked any appreciable atmosphere by the early 1930s.* Percival Lowell's canals may no longer have been in vogue in 1938 but the public's fascination with the Red Planet and the possibility of life there was an idea not so easily suppressed. In 1921, Marconi had made the amazing claim that he had received signals from Mars, and in 1924 a concerted effort was organized during a period of opposition to listen in on Mars for any sign of intelligent life striving to make contact. Science fiction too had continued to mine the rich vein of potential represented by the Red Planet, with Edgar Rice Burroughs beginning his John Carter of Mars series in 1912 and Stanley Weinbaum producing in 1934 one of the avowed classics of the genre, his marvelous short story *A Martian Odyssey*. But 1938 was also a banner year for Martian fiction. In Britain C. S. Lewis published his novel *Out of the Silent Planet*, set on an inhabited Mars, and just a few months prior to the Mercury Theatre broadcast, *Flash Gordon* had wowed American movie audiences with his own trip to Mars.† No wonder, then, that Mars was anything but a dead world to the average person in the street, providing yet one more incentive for listeners to take *The War of the Worlds* far more seriously than expected.

Of course we can look for and find any number of reasons why the broadcast had such a startling effect on its listeners, from wooden dummies to war jitters and even inexplicable power failures, but we should not lose site of one simple fact. Such was the realism of the broadcast that many people made a rational decision to believe what they were hearing. Welles and his Mercury players and staff are therefore deserving of credit for succeeding, as Miller succinctly puts it, "in scaring the hell out of 20% of the listening audience."[28] This is a sentiment to heartily endorse, for without Howard Koch's script or John Houseman's determination, without Bernard Herrmann's music and a talented company of actors and technicians who had honed their craft to perfection, the broadcast could not have been so devastatingly effective. And standing over all of them, supreme in the mastery of his craft, was Orson Welles, without whom none of it would have happened at all.

---

*A *New York Times* article published on July 31, 1938, considered the question of intelligent life on Mars and proclaimed, "No reputable astronomer believes in it."

†*Flash Gordon's Trip to Mars* was originally a 15-chapter serial that had begun showing in cinemas in March of 1938. Universal Pictures had planned a movie version adapted from the serial, but capitalized on *The War of the Worlds* furor by hastily renaming it *Mars Attacks the World* and rushing it out just a few days after the broadcast.

So what about Welles and the persistent rumor that he planned the whole dark deed himself? Certainly there is one person in particular who would have liked nothing better than for the finger of blame to be pointed in this direction. And that person is? Why, none other than Welles himself. In fact, he positively encouraged the belief, but the trouble is that Welles, genius or not, was also prone to a great deal of fabrication and frequently took great personal satisfaction in lying about his life to biographers and interviewers. According to Welles, he indeed planned it all, though this is not what he claimed in the days after the broadcast.

Appearing before the press the day after the broadcast, Welles was the very epitome of a contrite man, expressing profound surprise that the broadcast had such a terrible effect on his listeners, and admitting utter bafflement that anyone could have been so fooled. It was an extraordinary performance, as Welles, hemmed in by a large press pack, alone, unshaven and looking quite vulnerable and uncertain, attempted to defend himself. He began by reading a prepared statement in which he outlined four key reasons why he felt that the reaction of listeners had been entirely unexpected. First he explained that since the broadcast had been clearly set in the future (1939) this should have given the game away. That might have been true had many people

Illustration from a 1940 issue of the pulp science fiction magazine *Amazing Stories*, showing that in the popular imagination, the idea of Martian canals and a thriving civilization still held a powerful sway over the public (Mary Evans Picture Library).

actually heard that part, but of course we know a large number would have missed this fleeting clue, positioned as it was at the very beginning of the broadcast. In fact, Welles seems to be clutching at straws with this statement, since even had someone listened from the very beginning, the single reference to the year 1939 was hardly shouted from the rooftops.

Welles is more successful with his second reason, in which he points out that the Mercury Theatre was listed in all the newspaper

October 31, 1938: Hemmed in by reporters, Orson Welles explains that he was as surprised as anyone at the public reaction to his *War of the Worlds* broadcast (Mary Evans Picture Library).

radio schedules and had been on air for 17 consecutive weeks. It should therefore have been perfectly familiar to listeners, argued Welles, though his contention that the show had been on for 17 consecutive weeks was not strictly accurate, as the network had recently rescheduled the show from Monday to Sunday night. *The War of the Worlds* was therefore the eighth consecutive show broadcast at this new time and day. It is unlikely that this had anything but the most moderate of bearings on events, but it should be noted.

Welles' next statement offers an interesting insight into his thinking as to the relative attentiveness of his audience, and as such merits reproduction in full. "The third element was the fact that at the very outset of the broadcast, and twice during its enactment listeners were told that this was a play that it was an adaptation of an old novel by H. G. Wells. Furthermore, at the conclusion, a detailed statement to this effect was made."[29] So Welles was implying his listeners should have known better, though it does seem disingenuous of him to claim that the final closing statement would have been any use to listeners. One also cannot help but wonder if during the broadcast he had been aware of the efforts to reach him from the control room in order to issue earlier warnings.

Welles' fourth and final reason is an interesting one. He points out reasonably that fantasies concerning Mars were not at all new to the public, who were used to seeing and hearing them. Though he mentions nothing by name, it is fairly certain he was referring here to *Flash Gordon*. However, Welles does miss the point that for the public, fantasy had not yet been satisfactorily separated from fact, and as we have already seen earlier in this chapter, the average reader of *Flash Gordon* would not have considered the possibility of life on Mars entirely out of the question.

Welles then took questions from the assembled reporters. Asked if he now thought he should have toned down the language of the drama, he replied no, remarking, "You don't play murder in soft words." Asked then, "Were you aware of the terror such a broadcast would stir up?" he replied, "Definitely not. The technique I used was not original with me, or peculiar to the Mercury Theatre's presentation. It was not even new. I anticipated nothing unusual."[30]

It is certainly true that Welles was not the first to have used the technique of news reports to tell a story. We have already seen that he was perfectly aware of previous American broadcasts that were very close in style to his version of *The War of the Worlds*, but there was an even earlier precursor made in England, and it has been suggested that Welles might have been referring to this.

It is actually rather appropriate that England can claim (given the nationality of H. G. Wells) the dubious honor of being the first country on earth to be fooled by a radio invasion, though in this case there were no Martians involved. The effect on the listening public would, however, prove remarkably similar to the 1938 broadcast. The man responsible for this history-making event was a Catholic priest, Ronald Arbuthnott Knox. Like Orson Welles he was a man of many talents and a truly unorthodox character with a varied résumé, including a career as a broadcaster, a successful crime fiction writer, and a passionate religious commentator. He was also something of a practical joker, as the British public were to discover on the evening of Saturday, January 16, 1926. At the time, Knox was working for the fledgling British Broadcasting Company, which was then only some four years old. At 7:40 p.m., from cramped Edinburgh offices, located in the back premises of a music shop at 79 George Street, Knox began his one-man reading of a production he called *Broadcasting the Barricades*.

Crafted in a style prophetically similar to the 1938 *War of the Worlds* broadcast, it begins innocuously with a report on the latest cricket scores, segues into a banal news story, and then suddenly takes an ominous turn for the worse, reporting on a growing crowd of unruly demonstrators in the very heart of London at Trafalgar Square. The demonstrators, described as an anti-unemployment gathering, are reported to be led (in one of many blatant hints to the phony nature of the broadcast) by a Mr. Poppleberry, the secretary for the National Movement for the Abolishment of Theatre Queues. Exactly as in Welles' later broadcast, Knox next shifts to a musical number, leaving the audience with a sense of unease but the impression that normal life goes on. There follows a weather forecast, more on the cricket scores, then back to the demonstration, which is now pouring through Admiralty Arch in "a threatening manner."

Again and again, Knox deftly switches back and forth between outrageous humor and quite disturbing imagery. One moment he has the unruly crowd attacking waterfowl on a lake with bottles, the next "roasting alive" a dignitary who was on his way to the radio studio. Knox observes in deadpan style, "He will therefore be unable to deliver his lecture to you." More run-of-the-mill interludes follow, then comes the menacing announcement that the crowd is preparing to demolish the houses of Parliament with trench mortars. Knox follows with a description of the Big Ben clock tower crashing to the ground, a hugely iconic image that has since been repeated time and time again in modern films. Comically pricking the grandiosity of the moment, Knox says of this disaster, "Greenwich Time will not be given this evening by Big Ben, but will be given from Edinburgh on Uncle Leslie's repeating watch."* As the broadcast nears its end, the minister of traffic is hung from a lamppost in the Vauxhall Bridge Road before the demonstrators enter the BBC broadcasting building and Knox draws proceedings to a close after just over seventeen minutes of simulated mayhem.

The Knox broadcast certainly can't boast the terrifying verisimilitude of *The War of the Worlds*, peppered as it is with mischievous observations on the unlikely nature and progress of the rioters, but it is unquestionably a very clever and amusing piece of theater. Listening to a reconstruction of the broadcast produced by the BBC (the original is tragically lost) it is hard to believe that anyone could have taken it entirely seriously, yet according to reports at the time, women fainted, mayors dusted off emergency plans and one listener even called the Admiralty and demanded that the navy be dispatched up the Thames to deal with the rioters.†

So given the undoubted similarities between the two, could Welles or someone else connected with the 1938 broadcast conceivably have heard of the Knox production and then used it as a template for *The War of the Worlds*? Certainly the similarities to the Welles broadcast are quite astounding. Not only are there sudden interruptions of what appear to be regularly scheduled programs in the style of breaking news reports, but even innocuous interludes of music, in Knox's case from the Savoy Hotel in London. Not only this, but it has even been suggested that Knox was motivated to produce his broadcast by a desire to give a warning to radio listeners that they should not believe everything they heard on the radio, an alibi that Welles would himself use to justify his *War of the Worlds* broadcast.

But if we are to seriously entertain the notion that Welles was influenced by the Knox broadcast, we have to take into account the fact that in 1926 he was only 10 years old. This is not to say that he did not read about it in the newspapers at the time and file it away in his remarkably able memory for later use. The American press did carry the story, reporting on it in slightly bemused, moderately condescending and (in hindsight) extraordinarily embarrassing terms. The *New York Times* ran a regular opinion piece called "Topic of the Times" and it was here in the January 19, 1926, edition that it proclaimed confidently, "Such a thing as that could not happen in this country." The writer elaborated, stating; "...or at any rate its harm would be confined to those who were listening to one of the 600 broadcasting stations which we — for our sins, doubtless — are as radio fans afflicted. The situation in Great Britain is different. There all broadcasting is done by or through a single company, and it is responsible for everything that goes out." Of course the colum-

---

*This refers to a character in the popular juvenile program *Children's Hour*, which was a mainstay of BBC broadcasts at the time.

†Just as Welles had tapped into the fears of the average American that their country might become involved in a new world war, so Britain in 1926 had its own problems to worry about. In late 1925, the government had arrested members of the Communist Party (formed only five years previously) on charges of committing seditious conspiracy, and a mass strike of workers was brewing, such that there were serious concerns among the ruling class that the country might suffer a revolution as had befallen Russia in 1917.

nist could not have imagined the changes that would take place in the years to come and that by 1938 the CBS network would be affiliating its programs all across the nation.

So what of Houseman? Could he have used the Knox broadcast as inspiration? There is an interesting reference in the BBC *Radio Times* magazine of June 29, 1967, that argues for just such a substantive connection, but alas this does not stand up to analysis. Prompted by the BBC broadcast that year of a dramatization of *The War of the Worlds* novel, a BBC correspondent in America called Leonard Miall suggests that John Houseman had heard the Knox broadcast as a schoolboy while living in England. It's an entertaining thought, but unfortunately the dates simply do not fit. Houseman did indeed live in England for a time, but sailed as an adult for America in 1925, arriving in New York aboard the liner *Mauretania* on October 3 of that year. Paperwork on file at Ellis Island confirms this date beyond any shadow of a doubt, so he clearly could not have heard the Knox broadcast.

It is conceivable that Houseman may have read the *New York Times* stories of 1926 (he was certainly in a better position than Welles to remember it later) or acquaintances back in England had corresponded with him and told him of the Knox broadcast, but it again seems unlikely that a relatively minor story should have so thoroughly impressed itself upon him that he would have recalled it in 1938. This is not to say that that it would have been entirely beyond Welles' own innate sense of self-aggrandizement to have conveniently forgotten his debt to the earlier broadcast, but Houseman was patently a man of clearer conscience and would surely have made at least passing reference to the connection in later years. Of course none of this speculation entirely discounts the possibility that there was at the very least some subconscious influence at play in one or the other man, and for there to be a connection of sorts, no matter how tenuous, certainly adds spice to an already astounding story.

To seriously entertain the possibility that Welles had in fact anticipated the response to his broadcast, then we must also consider a motive. Barbara Leaming repeats speculation in her Welles biography that it was all a clever ruse to create publicity for the ill-fated *Danton's Death*,[31] and certainly Welles was acutely aware that the production was in trouble, and that it could do with all the help it could get. Oddly, a similar charge would be leveled at H. G. Wells over the timing of the broadcast, for on October 27, stores across America put on sale his new novel, *Apropos of Doloros*. It was an allegation that his publisher, Charles Scribner's Sons, flatly denied, and indeed, Wells, via his New York spokesman, had issued an angry condemnation of the broadcast.

On the face of it neither theory sounds convincing, but there is an additional motive that carries more weight. It is often forgotten that Welles was very politically aware and during the Second World War would become a tireless champion of Roosevelt and his policies, putting much time and effort into various propaganda activities. In particular Welles had a keen understanding of the dangers of fascism. He was especially incensed by the inflammatory radio broadcasts of Father Charles Coughlin, an anti–Semite and hatemonger who at the height of his popularity could be heard all across America. Might this have been the catalyst that drove Welles to terrify a nation? In later interviews, he himself candidly asserts as much.

Interviewed in 1982 for *Arena*, a prestigious BBC arts program, Welles amplified on this idea, saying, "...we had a lot of real radio nuts on as commentators in this period.

People who wanted to keep us out of European entanglements, and fascist priests called Father Coughlin. People believed anything they heard on the radio, and I said let's do something impossible and make them believe it and tell them, show them, it's only radio." But Welles is also on record as saying that the extent of the panic took him by surprise. In *This Is Orson Welles*, a collection of conversations recorded by his friend and fellow film director Peter Bogdanovich, Welles was asked if he had anticipated the reaction. "The *kind* of response, yes — that was merrily anticipated by us all. The *size* of it, of course, was flabbergasting.... We began to realize, as we plowed on with the destruction of New Jersey, that the extent of our American lunatic fringe had been underestimated." Asked why he had pleaded innocence in the days after, Welles replied, "There were headlines about lawsuits totaling some $12 million. Should I have pleaded guilty?"[32]

It did not take him long to change his plea. In 1955, Welles was in England, where he produced two series for the BBC, one of which was the six-part *Orson Welles Sketchbook*. Welles spoke directly to the camera with the same kind of intimacy he had employed in his radio broadcasts. (This being television, Welles added the novel twist of sketched illustrations.) For the fifth episode he chose as his subject *The War of the Worlds*, giving a fascinating and beautifully illustrated talk in which he told several unique stories about the broadcast and pointedly claimed, "we weren't as innocent as we meant to be." He goes on to explain, "People, you know, do suspect what they read in the newspapers and what people tell them, but when the radio came, and I suppose now television, anything that came through that new machine was believed. So in a way our broadcast was an assault on the credibility of that machine; we wanted people to understand that they shouldn't take any opinion pre-digested, and they shouldn't swallow everything that came through the tap, whether it was radio or not." Welles tempers the claim of premeditation by saying the broadcast was a "partial experiment" and that "we had no idea of the extent of the thing."

To illustrate his own shock at the extent of the public reaction, he then goes on to tell that in the aftermath of the broadcast he received repeated death threats from one outraged individual, with the very specific assurance that he would be killed at the opening of his new play. The play in question was *Danton's Death* and the opening night the very next day. To make matters worse, Welles, who was not acting in *Danton's Death*, was scheduled to take the stage after the final curtain to deliver a speech, and describes his terror at standing in a spotlight waiting for the assassin to strike from the audience.

Welles continued to have fun with the claim over the years, even lampooning the whole suggestion himself when he appeared on an early 1970s episode of the *Dean Martin Show*, when he claimed, tongue firmly in cheek, "Now, it's been pointed out that various flying saucer scares all over the world have taken place since that broadcast ... everyone doesn't laugh any more. But most people do. And there's a theory this is my doing. That my job was to soften you up ... ladies and gentlemen, go on laughing. You'll be happier that way. Stay happy as long as you can. And until the day when our new masters choose to announce the conquest of the earth is completed, I remain as always, obediently yours."[33] Asked on the *Today* show in 1978, "Did you get a laugh out of it, Orson?" He admitted, "Huge, huge, yes, a huge laugh. I never thought it was anything but funny."[34]

Sadly, Welles was to endure a lifetime of mean-spirited interviews in which he was baited about his perceived failure to live up to the promise of *Citizen Kane* and constantly asked to relive the infamy of *The War of the Worlds*. Perhaps it was simply a desire to salvage some dignity that caused him to claim the entire event was premeditated, for to have to admit that one of his greatest achievements was a fluke would have been particularly galling and demeaning. Welles was also in great demand in his later years to appear on chat shows, so here, too, perhaps is a reason for him to come up with an entertaining story.

So what firm evidence can we find that Welles was guilty of planning the scare? On the face of it, there seems to be little that can be described as conclusive. For one thing, Welles was scarcely connected with the planning stages of the broadcast, though it is interesting to note that he talked on more than one occasion as if others were in on the scheme. Yet John Houseman, who would surely have known better than anyone else if it were premeditated, never so much as hinted at the possibility in all the interviews he gave, nor in his autobiography. The closest he came was to describe Delmar's impersonation of Roosevelt as "the only naughty thing we did that night. Everything else was just good radio."[35] Slightly more damning, Delmar himself has been quoted as saying that when Welles came in to direct the dress rehearsal, he told him "Oh, Kenny, you know what I want."[36]

Another glimmer of proof comes from Howard Koch. Interestingly, he waited until 1988 to make the claim. Perhaps he felt that Welles' death in 1985 made it safe to let the cat out of the bag, though his evidence is rather thin. Writing in an essay for the New York Museum of Broadcasting, Koch explains that he was at the press conference held by Welles the day after the broadcast. Koch is circumspect in his speculation, but offers the opinion that the contrite Welles on display struck him as unconvincing, and that as the press conference broke up, he witnessed Welles and Houseman exchange a congratulatory gesture. It "spoke volumes,"[37] says Koch.

The same year, Koch was interviewed for a radio documentary celebrating the 50th anniversary of the broadcast and, though he does not repeat the claim, it is interesting to note that he, too, was angry at the trusting nature of his listeners. "I am disappointed in the gullibility of the American people politically as well as in this instance, that they accept [the] most outrageous things as truths. There are good schools in our country, but I guess there a lot of schools that don't teach the fundamental things of how to think for yourself. In that aspect it was a warning."[38]

It is certainly fun to speculate that Welles and his collaborators planned the entire thing. There is no smoking gun per se, but there is at least a faint whiff of cordite. The most compelling evidence in this regard is the final page of Koch's script. If indeed there was no intent to scare listeners, why are Welles' closing remarks set in type? If he had no preconception that it would scare listeners, he would hardly have needed to prepare in advance a text that assures listeners that, "*The War of the Worlds* has no further significance than as the holiday offering it was intended to be." Equally suggestive of premeditation is the line, "...and remember, please, for the next day or so, the terrible lesson you learned tonight."

There are other tantalizing clues that point to the guilt of Welles and his collaborators. Why for instance, as the pandemonium visibly built up in the control booth, did

Welles not attempt to find out what was happening, for we have testimony that the booth was filling with Police, and so surely he must have known something unprecedented was happening. Why also did John Houseman physically prevent CBS producer Davidson Taylor from entering the studio to interrupt the broadcast? Of course these are not necessarily the acts of men complicit in a conspiracy. Both were fiercely proud of their show and would have deeply resented interference of an kind, and even if it were an entirely inadvertent accident, both Welles and Houseman must have suspected they were making history that night. To stop the show would have been anathema to them. They may also have realized that even if they earned an infamous reputation for their night's work, the eventual benefit to their careers would likely outweigh any short-term harm.

If truth be told, we are probably never going to know for sure what Welles intended that night, so instead let's leave the last word to Alexander Woollcott, the famous critic and commentator for the *New Yorker* magazine. In a telegram he sent to his close friend Welles the day after the broadcast (and which Welles gleefully pinned on his office door) he slyly observed, "This only goes to show, my beamish boy, that the intelligent people were all listening to a dummy, and all the dummies were listening to you."[39]

9

ANIMOSITIES AND RAPPROCHEMENTS
The Aftermath of War

With no shattered cities to rebuild and no war dead to identify or grieve over, *The War of the Worlds* might have been a flash in the pan, limited to a few days' worth of sensational news stories and a rather sheepish desire by all involved to forget the whole embarrassing episode. But the ramifications of the broadcast were considerably more far-reaching, triggering a vigorous debate on the nature and responsibilities of radio, and for one person in particular, setting his life on a whole new course. Yes, Orson Welles was about to confound his critics and continue his meteoric rise to stardom, but it was a lucky escape.

In the days immediately following the broadcast, there were rumors that criminal charges might be leveled against Welles, and the specter of crippling lawsuits hung over him, CBS and the Mercury Theatre. The actual amount in claims filed varies: John Houseman put the figure at a hefty but not unbelievable $750,000,[1] and by the 1970s Welles had inflated the figure to a dizzying (and much more impressive) $12 million. It seems fairly certain that there were indeed attempts to take legal action by a variety of people who alleged they had been injured during the course of the broadcast, with claims ranging in severity from simple distress to broken bones and heart attacks. A William A. Decker of 249 South Arlington Avenue, East Orange, New Jersey, was reported by the *Newark Evening News* of November 1 to be planning a lawsuit because his wife had suffered a heart attack while listening to the broadcast, but actual specific instances of injuries are surprisingly rare among the hundreds of individual stories that were published in the immediate aftermath of the broadcast. Perhaps the closest thing we have to an actual confirmed instance of an injury is that of the actress Caroline Cantlon, who was pictured with her arm in a sling in a number of newspapers, including on the front page of the *New York Daily News* of October 31. Cantlon reportedly panicked at the reports of gas in the city and, rushing into the street, fell and broke her arm. The cynical observer will note Cantlon's profession and suggest that in her case the adage "no publicity is bad publicity" is perhaps particularly apt.

Welles might have become personally liable for any injuries sustained by his listeners but for the foresight of his attorney L. Arnold Weissberger, who in vetting the contract between Welles and CBS had insisted a clause be amended that would have seen his client responsible for any legal action taken against the network. The revised clause simply made Welles accountable for libel and plagiarism, but as it happened, it seems unlikely any of the claims reached court, though Welles biographer Frank Brady suggests that CBS may have quietly settled a few cases to a total value of several thousand dollars.[2]

John Houseman in his autobiography makes plain that all the claims were dismissed, though he does disclose that he and Welles made personal restitution to one unfortunate victim of the broadcast. A pitiful letter was apparently received at the Mercury office* from a man in Massachusetts, who wrote: "I thought the best thing to do was to go away. So I took my $3.75 out of my savings and bought a ticket. After I had gone 60 miles I knew it was a play. Now I don't have money left for the shoes I was saving up for. Will you please have someone send me a pair of black shoes size 9B!" Houseman wryly explains, "We did. And the lawyers were very angry with us."[3]

Also very angry was the head of CBS, William Paley. He was at home that evening playing cards and so was not amused when he started to receive irate phone calls from the public. "I remember very well I was annoyed by it," said Paley, who recalls that he was often plagued by complaining calls, but this evening they were coming in so thick and fast that at first he couldn't make head or tail of it. Then a call from his office came through to tell him that "...a terrible thing has happened." As Paley describes it, "the whole country was bursting wide open."[4]

Paley and the network were naturally horrified at the situation, and the public relations department quickly swung into action, issuing an apology the next day. "Naturally it was neither Columbia's nor the Mercury Theatre's intention to mislead any one, and when it became evident that a part of the audience had been disturbed by the performance five announcements were read over the network later in the evening to reassure those listeners." But it wasn't their audience that most concerned CBS; it was the Federal Communications Commission (FCC).

The FCC had been established by the communications act of 1934 to oversee all extra-governmental use of the radio spectrum, so it seemed logical that it would have something to say to CBS about the *War of the Worlds* broadcast. FCC chairman Frank P. McNinch issued a widely reported statement to the press on October 31 in which he announced, "I have this morning requested the Columbia Broadcasting Company by telegraph to forward to the commission at once a copy of the script and also an electrical transcription of "The War of the Worlds" which was broadcast last night and which the press indicates caused widespread excitement, terror and fright. I shall request prompt consideration of the matter by the commission." He went on to conclude, "I withhold final judgment until later, but any broadcast that creates such general panic and fear as this one is to have done, is to say the least, regrettable."

McNinch's cautious tone was intentional. The FCC found itself caught between a rock and a hard place. There was clearly a desire for some form of action to be taken against those responsible for the broadcast, but what could they be charged with? Indeed, what laws had they actually broken? The FCC was empowered to prevent station interference and investigate monopoly ownerships, but punishing the purveyors of fake news broadcasts went far beyond its authority. T. A. M. Craven, a New Jersey member of the FCC, went further than his boss; while agreeing an investigation should be conducted,

---

*Almost the exact same story is recounted in Hadley Cantril's book, but in this case a letter was sent directly to him by one George Bates, who is identified as an unskilled laborer. Three questions arise: Did Houseman borrow the story from Cantril? Did Cantril get it from Houseman? Or did the enterprising gentleman from Massachusetts perhaps hedge his bets and write to both?

he was quoted in the *New York Times* of November 1 that "utmost caution" was required to avoid censorship and that the public "does not want a spineless radio."

This was a sentiment shared by many members of the public. We have already seen that the Mercury Theatre received a very supportive postbag, as did the *New York Times*, but the FCC also appears to have received letters urging that it take no action against Welles and his colleagues. J. V. Yaukey of Aberdeen, South Dakota, wrote an impassioned letter to the FCC in which he sarcastically mocked the reaction of his fellow listeners: "I was one of the thousands who heard this program and did not jump out of the window, did not attempt suicide, did not break my arm while beating a hasty retreat from my apartment ... but sat serenely entertained no end by the fine portrayal of a fine play." Yaukey went on to urge the FCC to consider asking for a repeat of the program before contemplating any action.

However, there were some in positions of authority who were less inclined to take a relaxed view of the situation. Senator Clyde L. Herring of Des Moines, Iowa, pronounced his displeasure, and was quoted in the *Seattle Post-Intelligencer* of November 1, 1938, as saying, "Some of the bedtime stories which are supposed to put children to sleep — but involve murder and violence — are an outrage and should be stopped." He pledged to bring a bill before Congress to restrict the ability of radio to perpetrate such abuses. Declared Herring, "Radio has no more right to present programs like that than someone has in knocking on your door and screaming."[5] A comment attributed to FCC commissioner George Henry Payne in the *Seattle Star* of November 1 also indicates the pressures radio was under: "Ministers throughout the country have protested that radio programs are frightening children."

Meanwhile, CBS was desperate to avoid the imposition of any sort of legislation or censure, and so bent over backwards to prove that they were keeping their own house in order. W. B. Lewis, vice president in charge of programs at CBS, was reported by the *New York Times* of November 1 as making the following pledge: "In order that this may not happen again the program department hereafter will not use the technique of a simulated news broadcast within a dramatization when the circumstances of the broadcast could cause alarm to numbers of listeners."

But it seemed that the reaction was getting out of hand, and ironically the "panic broadcast" was actually causing a second panic among broadcasters. Writing in the March 1939 issue of *AM Magazine*, Earl Sparling summed up the growing paranoia of the situation when he warned, "On guard against government censorship, radio has clamped its own hand over its mouth in a self-censorship as rigid as, if not more rigid than, anything the government could order. The jitters began with Mae West's burlesque of the Garden of Eden, and reached chronic proportions with Orson Welles's recent 'War of the Worlds' debacle. Today broadcasters are scared silly. Their every decision is dictated by fear — fear of a club held over their heads by a handful of political appointees in Washington, the FCC, who, in turn, are at the whim of any Nice Nelly in the country."[6]

The censorship was indeed becoming pervasive. Comedian Fred Allen was a hugely popular radio star whose material was generally very topical and satirical. He was renowned as someone who enjoyed battling against censorship, but even he couldn't get a *War of the Worlds* skit past a nervous censor on his NBC show *Town Hall Tonight*. Luckily the very funny text of his original introduction survives and is well worth reproducing here:

> In view of the recent happenings in radio, I think it would be better, before we start, if I made a sort of announcement.... Ladies and Gentlemen, before this radio presentation starts, I would like to announce that this is a comedy program. Any dialogue or sound-

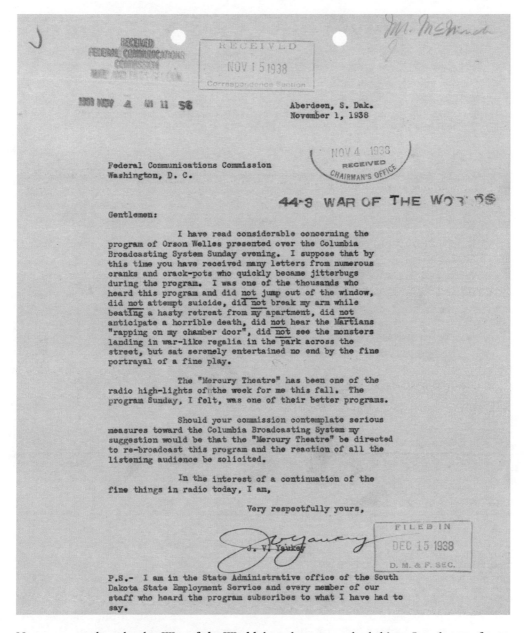

Not everyone thought the *War of the Worlds* broadcast was a bad thing. In a letter of support to the FCC, this listener urged restraint. A considerable number of letters received by the FCC were supportive of Welles (Federal Communications Commission).

effects heard during the next hour will be purely imaginary and will have no relation to any living sounds. If you hear a phone ringing, like this (telephone rings), do not pick up your receiver. If you hear a knock, like this (door knock), do not run to open your door. Ignore everything you hear on this program. Just sit back and relax. Nothing is going to happen. And to prove that the offering is positively crammed with nothing, we plunge instantly into the latest news of the week.[7]

The situation was certainly tense, but then on December 5, 1938, came the news that everyone had been waiting for. The FCC had reached a decision on *The War of the Worlds* and, to the relief of all involved, its conclusion was the mildest possible form of rebuke. The FCC distanced itself from any punitive action and placed the responsibility for the prevention of any repetition firmly with the networks. Welles and CBS no doubt felt a great weight lifted from their shoulders as they read the FCC press release:

> The FCC announced today that in its judgment steps taken by CBS since the Orson Welles "Mercury Theatre on the Air" program on October 30 are sufficient to protect the public interest. Accordingly complaints received regarding this program will not be taken into account in considering the renewals of licenses of stations which carried the broadcast. The FCC stated that, while it was regrettable that the broadcast alarmed a substantial number of people, there appeared to be no likelihood of a repetition of the incident and no occasion for action by the FCC.
>
> In reaching this determination, the FCC had before it a statement by W. B. Lewis, CBS vice president in charge of programs, expressing regret that some listeners "mistook fantasy for fact" and saying in part, "In order that this may not happen again, the Program Department hereafter will not use the technique of a simulated news broadcast within a dramatization when the circumstances of the broadcast could cause immediate alarm to numbers of listeners."
>
> The FCC had also heard a transcript of the program and had been informed regarding a number of communications about it. It was made known that the FCC received 372 protests against the broadcast and 255 letters and petitions favoring it. Counting those who signed petitions, those who expressed themselves as favorable to the broadcast numbered approximately 350.[8]

So the threat of punishment had passed, though if anyone had cared to check, the FCC response would have come as no surprise at all. The commission was bound by its own rules in the matter, which explicitly prohibited it from regulating program content. Section 326 of the 1934 Communications Act states, "Nothing in this Act shall be understood or construed to give the FCC the power of censorship over the radio communications or signals transmitted by any radio station, and no regulation or condition shall be promulgated or fixed by the FCC which shall interfere with the right of free speech by means of radio communication."[9]

This was not the only fallout that Welles had to contend with. From England came word that H. G. Wells had heard of the broadcast and was furious that his story had been so freely adapted. Wells' representative in New York, Jacques Chambrum, who had sold the rights to CBS on his client's behalf, issued a strongly worded protest in the days following the broadcast. "In the name of Mr. H. G. Wells, I granted the Columbia Broadcasting System the right to dramatize Mr. H. G. Wells's novel *The War of the Worlds* for one performance over radio. It was not explained to me that this dramatization would be made with a liberty that amounts to a complete rewriting of *The War of the Worlds* and renders it into an entirely different story. Mr. Wells and I consider that by so doing the Columbia Broadcasting System should make a full retraction. Mr. H. G. Wells personally is deeply concerned that any work of his should be used in this way, and with a totally unwarranted liberty, to cause deep distress and alarm throughout the United States."[10] Strong words but, as with the FCC, the bark would prove stronger than the bite, and the desired restitution was never pursued. In fact, as we will see later in this chapter, there was something of a surprising postscript to this story.

Welles may have succeeded spectacularly in annoying a great many people, but some in the press were of the opinion that he had done the country a great service. One of his biggest defenders was the influential journalist and commentator Dorothy Thompson.* Her article in the November 2 edition of the *New York Tribune* is credited with helping to save Welles from a far worse drubbing than he received. Thompson heaps praise on Welles, while directing withering criticism at her fellow citizens and warning her readers that the broadcast exposed serious dangers to their democracy. Lamenting, "...the incredible stupidity, lack of nerve and ignorance of thousands" she cautions that Welles had proven, "...how easy it is to start a mass delusion." But Thompson is no soapbox haranguer; she had serious points to make about the state of American politics and notes that it would be frighteningly easy for an American Hitler to arise should any one political body gain a controlling monopoly of radio. She reserves her most rapturous praise for Welles, suggesting that, if anything, he deserved a congressional medal for alerting the country to the power of radio.

So Welles was both hero and villain in the days after the broadcast, but as he was soon to discover, notoriety had its benefits. Where before sponsorship had proved maddeningly elusive, suddenly the Mercury Theatre was a hot property, and so it was that on December 9, 1938, the series was graced with a new name: *The Campbell Playhouse.* With a sponsor came money and the ability to attract big-name stars to the show. The very first Campbell Playhouse broadcast featured Margaret Sullavan in an adaptation of Daphne du Maurier's *Rebecca*, but with Campbell holding the purse strings came new responsibilities and after the high principles of the first season it was a shock to hear Welles extolling the virtues of a soup. So the first tangible benefit from *The War of the Worlds* might be described as something of a double-edged sword for Welles, who had always fiercely resisted any kind of creative interference in his projects.

Perhaps the most curious outcome from *The War of the Worlds* broadcast was a rather one-sided row that erupted over the authorship of the play. When Hadley Cantril came to write his account of the broadcast and its effect, he sought to include the original script and quite naturally credited Howard Koch as the playwright. He then innocently sent the galley proofs of the book to Welles for his approval, but was unprepared for the furious response that came forth. Welles claimed the book contained "an error so grave, and in my opinion so detrimental to my own reputation that I cannot in all fairness speak well of it until some reparation is made."[11]

---

*Thompson was described by *Time* magazine in 1939 as one of the two most influential women in America, an accolade previously conferred on Welles' sound person Ora Nichols.

He was referring to Howard Koch's credited authorship of the play, which he refuted strongly, saying, "Now it's perfectly true that Mr. Koch worked on *The War of the Worlds* since he was at the time a regular member of my writing staff. To credit the broadcast version to him, with the implication that its conception as well as its execution was his, is a gross mistake."[12] On the one hand, and given the strength of his personality, one would be forgiven for thinking that vanity or hubris drove Welles to react so forcibly to this perceived slight, but as always with Welles, the truth is never quite so easy to untangle. Welles went on to assert that many others had contributed to the play, including John Houseman, actor Paul Stewart and sound engineer John Dietz. Welles was saying that it was a collaborative effort and to single out one person as the author was a slight to all those who had worked on the production.

This was an extraordinary and uncharacteristically noble position for Welles to take, defending the rights of his hardworking team to share the credit for the broadcast, but throughout the correspondence, a sense of great personal injury is never far away, none more obviously than in an explosively angry telegram to Cantril which fully revealed his motives. "Think how much more unfavorable an impression your book will make as it now stands and try to conceive the effect on my professional prestige and standing in the theatre world. Can see no conceivable reason for your steadfast refusal to believe *The War of the Worlds* was not only my conception but also, properly and exactly speaking, my creation. Once again, finally, and I promise for the last time, Howard Koch did not write *The War of the Worlds*. Any statement to this effect is untrue and immeasurably detrimental to me. I fail to see how I can put this more strongly."[13]

As it happened, it wouldn't be the last time. Cantril responded with affidavits from Koch and a telegram from Houseman's secretary Ann Froelisch that Koch had dictated the script to her from a manuscript in his own handwriting and that Houseman and Paul Stewart had had little to do with any subsequent revisions. To this Welles responded in a churlishly high-handed manner that surely Cantril should take the word of the producer, director and star of the Mercury Theatre over that an author in his employ. The authorship of the script was no longer quite so collaborative as he had implied.

During their lengthy correspondence, both men attempted to engineer a compromise. Welles suggested an erratum slip be included to clarify his authorship in future editions. Cantril responded with the suggestion that a more fulsome and descriptive credit be employed, which would read (rather reasonably) "Script idea and development by Orson Welles assisted by John Houseman and Mercury Theatre staff and written by Howard Koch under the direction of Mr. Welles."[14] But Welles was having none of this and, further sullying his initial egalitarianism, wrote back, "Your suggested revision for the second printing is far too elaborate and incorrect a statement. Repeat *War of the Worlds* was not written by Howard Koch."[15]

The whole affair had become distinctly unpleasant, but as Welles biographer Simon Callow has observed, this was a time of great personal anxiety for Welles. He was working at the time on *Citizen Kane*, the movie that would be considered by many the high point of his career, but it was yet in a very early and uncertain stage of development. For now, *The War of the Worlds* was his greatest claim to fame and it was partly upon the strength of this that he had negotiated the extraordinary contract with RKO that would launch his film career. Welles had sold himself as a man who needed no help. He was writer, actor, and director all rolled into one, and to have his authorship questioned could be a potentially mortal blow to his reputation, a fear that Welles made plain in his correspondence with Cantril. "I'm sure you can appreciate the untold damage done to my professional reputation [that] the publication of this book in its present form will create. I know you will understand that I cannot permit this to occur."[16]

Welles seems to be implying that he would take legal steps to prevent further printings of the book, having already failed to stop the book's first printing. But perhaps Welles knew that in truth he was powerless and so simply hoped that he could intimidate Cantril by the sheer force of his personality. After all, how could a lowly university professor hope to prevail against a man of Welles' stature and importance?

As it happened, Cantril did prevail and the book was published with Koch duly listed as sole author of the script, but Welles need not have worried; no one called attention to the crediting of Howard Koch as writer of *The War of the Worlds*. Indeed, such was Welles' ability as a blatant self-publicist that as the years went by the broadcast and his name became so synonymous that Koch's vital contribution was frequently sidelined or, in extreme cases, criminally omitted.* Of course the irony is that if only Welles had had the courage of his convictions and continued to argue (perfectly correctly) that the Mercury Theatre had always been a fusion of many talents, he might have emerged from this rather farcical imbroglio with his reputation enhanced. Unfortunately, by acting in the way he did, he simply confirmed himself as a man unwilling to share the limelight with others. Arch Oboler was a contemporary of Welles. It was he who had written the infamous Mae West "Adam and Eve" sketch for *The Charlie McCarthy Show*, and his show *Lights Out* was renowned for its fantastic themes. He and Welles would work together on a number of occasions, but Oboler was cool toward his colleague. "I didn't particularly like Orson. He is a great actor and a fine director, but he didn't know how to give credit to the people around him who did the work. He had nothing to do with the writing of [the script]. He simply did not admit that in co-operative business — the entertainment business — that anybody does anything, including sweep the floor, but Orson Welles. During the war we had a series. I was given a network time-slot to do a series called *Plays for Americans*, where I turned to any in the writing industry and said, 'write something for the war effort.' He knew that I knew that he's not a writer. Yet he sat at that table and played beautifully. He played the part so well that I thought I was with the Bard. But I knew darn well the minute I left that he'd call up Koch and say, 'Hey, can you write this for me?'"[17]

That's actually an extremely tainted judgment, but Welles brought such sentiments upon himself. John Houseman put it less abrasively but just as clearly when he talked about a similar dispute that broke out a few years later between Welles and Herman Mankiewicz, the scriptwriter of *Citizen Kane*. Houseman wrote, "*Citizen Kane* is Welles' film. The dramatic genius that animates it and the creative personality with which it is imbued are wholly and undeniably Orson's — just as, in another medium, *The War of the*

---

*Howard Koch stayed with the Mercury Theatre for a short while and then moved on to Hollywood, as did Welles. Like Welles, Koch hit the ground running. In 1942 Koch won an Oscar for his screenplay for the classic film *Casablanca*.

Worlds owed its final impact to his miraculous touch. But he did not write either of them."[18] This is actually a very fair judgment; it mirrors closely the creative process on *The War of the Worlds* and does Welles no disservice at all.

Cantril's book was not the only awkwardness to arise from the ashes of *The War of the Worlds*. A few days after the broadcast, Welles received a very unexpected letter bringing news of his estranged brother Richard. The story of Richard Welles is a very sad one and something of a black mark against the Welles family in general. Richard Welles, Jr., had never found favor with his parents. His father — partly motivated, it seems, by simple disappointment in his son — had had him committed in 1927 to the Kankakee State Institution for the insane. The pretext was that he was suffering from advanced schizophrenia and dementia simplex, whose symptoms include an aversion to going out, the tendency to sleep all day and a general detachment from reality. But by 1938, Richard, Jr., had been released and appeared to have been making a living as a social worker, though Orson claimed he was fired from this job for locking himself in his room with a prostitute.

The letter that Orson Welles received alluding to his brother came from a Miss Azzie Ireland of Marin County, with the surprising information that his brother Richard was "planning to put on a presentation of '*The War of the Worlds*,' which he wrote for you."[19] Suffice to say, nothing further seems to have been heard of this extraordinary project, though interestingly the 1939–1940 and 1942–1943 telephone directories for Marin County do list an Eldred Ellis Ireland and his wife, Azzie M. Ireland, as living in Belvedere, a town in Marin County. There is, however, no news story to be found in the local paper, the *Marin Journal*.

Despite his best efforts to forget it, the public fascination with *The War of the Worlds* would continue to vex Welles, and on more than one occasion he had to resist invitations to revisit his greatest triumph. One such incident occurred in June 1939, when he embarked on a futile and short-lived attempt to reinvigorate the vaudeville tradition that he loved so much. The original suggestion was for Welles to present a 30-minute condensed version of *The War of the Worlds* without scenery or costumes; essentially a retelling of the staging of the broadcast, with actors appearing to read into microphones from scripts. It would have surely been a smash, but Welles refused, opting instead to stage a play called *The Green Goddess* and to resurrect the dubious idea of combining filmed interludes with live stage actors that had so befuddled the production of *Too Much Johnson*.

True to form, on the opening night the ghost of *Too Much Johnson* would return to haunt Welles, when a film of a plane crash in *The Green Goddess* was accidentally threaded into the projector backwards to unwanted comic effect. The production limped on for a while before it was unceremoniously shut down, but one can't help wonder if the most annoying thing for Welles was not that his play was cancelled, but that on the promotional posters he was billed as "the man who scared the world, then charmed it." It must have been galling, yet it is surely a testament to Welles that years later the broadcast was still fresh in people's minds. On the March 24, 1940, episode of *The Jack Benny Show*, Orson was welcomed by announcer Phil Harris with the greeting, "Hi Orson! Still scaring people?"[20]

Toward the end of that same year, Welles was putting the finishing touches to *Citizen Kane*, but with only six weeks of work remaining he had found himself running low on personal funds. RKO was not scheduled to advance him any more money until the film was completed, so Welles reluctantly departed Hollywood for a two-week whistle-stop lecture tour, fetching up on October 28 in San Antonio. By pure chance, H. G. Wells was in town on the same day, there to address the United States Brewers Association. Charles C. Shaw, an enterprising reporter at local radio station KTSA, realized that here was an opportunity not to be missed.* For the first and only time, the two men were interviewed together. Not unnaturally the *War of the Worlds* broadcast was the first thing raised. Welles must have felt a degree of trepidation to be seated with the author of *The War of the Worlds*; especially as just a few years previously Wells had condemned the broadcast. But in fact the two men were remarkably polite, positively vying with each other to say the nicest thing about the other.

> WELLS: Well, I've had a series of the most delightful experiences since I came to America, but the best thing that has happened so far is meeting my little namesake here, Orson. I find him the most delightful carrier, who carries my name with an extra e, which I hope he'll drop sooner or later.† I see no sense in it. And, I've known his work before he made this sensational Halloween spree. Are you sure there was such a panic in America, or wasn't it just your Halloween fun?
>
> WELLES: I think that's the nicest thing that a man from England could possibly say about the man from Mars. Mr. Hitler made a good deal of sport of it you know, he actually spoke of it in the great Munich speech, you know. There were floats in Nazi parades.
>
> WELLS: (Interjecting) Nothing much else to say.
>
> WELLES: (Laughs) Nothing much else to say. It was supposed to show the corrupt condition and decadent state of affairs in democracies that *The War of the Worlds* went over as well as it did. I think it's very nice of Mr. Wells to say that not only I didn't mean it, but the American people didn't mean it.
>
> WELLS: Well, that was our impression. We had articles about it and people said, have you never heard of Halloween in America, when everyone pretends to see ghosts?
>
> SHAW: Well, there was some excitement caused. I really can't belittle the amount that was caused, but I think people got over it very quickly, don't you...?
>
> WELLES: (Interjecting) What kind of excitement? Mr. H. G. Wells wants to know if the excitement wasn't the same kind of excitement that we extract from a practical joke in which somebody puts a sheet over his head and says "Boo!" I don't think anybody believes that that individual is a ghost, but we do scream and yell and rush down the hall, and that's just about what happened.
>
> SHAW: That's a very excellent description.
>
> WELLS: You aren't quite serious in America yet. You haven't got the war right under your chins and in consequence you can still play with ideas of terror and conflict.
>
> SHAW: You think that's good or bad?
>
> WELLS: It's a natural thing to do until you're right up against it.
>
> WELLES: 'Til it ceases to be a game.
>
> WELLES: And then it ceases to be a game.

*An alternative account of the meeting (emanating from Welles) has it that H. G. Wells was lost in San Antonio and stopped to ask for directions from none other than Orson Welles.

†In fact it appears that the addition of the "e" had only occurred recently. Orson Welles' father was born with the surname Wells but on leaving home had changed it slightly, adding the extra *e* to become Welles.

This portion of the interview ends on a distinctly melancholy note, both men acutely aware that a very real world war was under way. It is also interesting to note that this interview represents the only time Orson Welles was recorded as downplaying the effect of the broadcast on his listeners, though one will notice that the great showman still couldn't but help inject a colorful embellishment into the story. Claiming that his exploits caught the ear of Adolf Hitler is particularly impressive even for Welles, but there is (possibly inadvertently) an element of truth to the claim.

The *Völkischer Beobachter* (The People's Observer) was the official Nazi Party newspaper in Germany. Its edition of November 1, 1938, carried (as did many German newspapers of the day) a substantial article on the broadcast. Not unsurprisingly, the opportunity was seized upon to mount a propaganda coup against the Americans, and to tie in some Nazi philosophy. "As a result of the terror-psychosis that has now been spread for five years by Jewish circles, for many hours, countless Americans seriously believed an enemy invasion from the planet Mars was taking place." The paper goes on to lambast the American press for its coverage of recent events in Czechoslovakia, accusing it of fostering "an artificial war mentality," and further attempts to show that in whipping up hostility to German foreign policy, the Americans had brought mat-

VÖLKISCHER BEOBACHTER

Die Folgen der dauernden Kriegshetze:

Mars alarmiert Amerika

Massenpanik in USA. über Rundfunkvortrag — Bombenangst und Greuelpsychose

The Nazi newspaper *Völkischer Beobachter* of November 1, 1938, makes propaganda from *The War of the Worlds* broadcast with the headline "The Results of Continuous War Propaganda: Mars Alarms America."

ters upon themselves by creating such a tense atmosphere that a panic was the inevitable result.

Claiming that he had made a splash in Nazi Germany was not the last time Welles would work the growing myth of *The War of the Worlds* into his life. In typical tall tale fashion, Welles recounted that on the very day of the Pearl Harbor attack, December 7, 1941, "We were doing a patriotic broadcast, with excerpts from Walt Whitman, and I don't know what else, Norman Corwin and all the rest of it. Choirs humming melodically and so on, and I was in the midst of some hymn of praise to the American cornfields or something of the kind, when suddenly, a gentleman darted into the radio studio, held up his hand, and said 'We interrupt this broadcast to bring you an announcement: Pearl Harbor has just been attacked.' And of course this very serious and terrible news was never believed. Not for hours, by anybody in America, because they all said 'Well, there he goes again, really, rather bad taste, it was funny once, but not a second time.'"[21]

So is this another case of Welles with tongue firmly in cheek? Some facts can be verified. Welles delivered numerous propaganda programs on the radio at that time and he was on the air that very day, reading, as he claimed, from the work of Norman Corwin. The show was *The Gulf Screen Guild Theater* and Welles was narrating Corwin's paean to the United States, "Between Americans." Unfortunately for Welles, the attack on Pearl Harbor had already taken place, grimly described by the show's announcer as "the tragic and foreboding news that came today." So Welles could not have been preempted by the news of the attack while performing on *The Gulf Screen Guild Theater.* The reference in his anecdote to reading from work by Walt Whitman seems to be a genuine mix-up with dates, for it was the next day, December 8, that Welles read from Whitman's "Leaves of Grass," on his very own *Orson Welles Show.* Thus, either by design or accident, Welles is not in this case a reliable witness. Regardless, it remains a great story and Welles would go on to embellish it further in conversation with Peter Bogdanovich, declaring that he subsequently received a telegram from Roosevelt in which the president mentioned the perils of "crying Wolf."[22]

In June 1944 Welles was producing a series of patriotic radio programs that took him from Texas to Los Angeles and finally Chicago. It was grueling and exhausting work. Returning from Chicago, Welles' business manager Jackson Leighter suggested they stop off in Kansas City for the night. It was to prove an unpleasant detour. Entering the lobby of their hotel, Welles suddenly found himself under vicious attack by an enraged man, who pounded Welles with his fists, screaming, "I'm going to kill you, I'm going to kill you! I promised I'd kill you if I saw you!"[23] Leighter eventually pulled the man away, and a bruised and confused Welles was bundled into an elevator. An incredible story then emerged. The distraught attacker claimed that his wife had committed suicide on the night of *The War of the Worlds* broadcast, and he had vowed ever since to exact his revenge on Welles. There was no way to be sure the story was true, but after hearing his explanation, Leighter had him released without charge.

Welles was to be reminded of the broadcast yet again in 1956, when he was approached by producer Walter Wanger to film an introduction to Wanger's classic science fiction movie *Invasion of the Body Snatchers.* The idea never came to fruition, but the final film is probably all the better for the absence of the rather hokey dialogue Welles was asked to deliver:

> I am Orson Welles. A few years ago, people were frightened by my *War of the Worlds* broadcast which, I must say, seems pretty tame considering what has happened to our world since. When I think of the A-bombs, the H-bombs, the fall-outs, the changing climates, the unprecedented number of earthquakes, cyclones, tornadoes, and the floods that have occurred all over the world; and the space ships, the "flying saucers," the supersonic flights, and more flaming volcanoes than ever, surely even Nature is behaving strangely, and no phenomenon seems impossible today. Strange things are happening all around us, some visible, and some not. I'm not sure that Dr. Bennell didn't recognize what he was about to encounter when he was called back to Santa Mira, that small town in California, which surely, was the last place he would expect to discover what he did. But there is no doubt our world was in danger![24]

In 1958 Welles became involved in the final legal tussle over the authorship of *The War of the Worlds* script, when the renowned television drama series *Studio One* retold the story of the broadcast. Welles filed suit for $375,000 and duly lost again, though it seems likely that the perennially insolvent Welles was less concerned with any lingering sense of injustice than the chance to finance one of his many cash-starved pet projects.

It is of course a matter of record that Welles was to spend much of the rest of his life trying and more often than not failing to get his film and stage projects realized, with the shadow of early triumphs like *The War of the Worlds* hanging over him. In later years he seemed to come to terms with this and would happily regale chat show audiences with the tale. He even mentioned the broadcast in his film about fakery, *F for Fake*, in which he told a reasonably accurate version of the story, though he could not resist adding one of his classic flights of fancy. He explained with not a hint of subterfuge, "I met a welfare worker years later who told me that he spent weeks trying to woo some of the refugees back to civilization." Perhaps they had been residents of the town of Concrete, Washington, convinced by a power outrage that the Martians were on their doorstep.

No one but Welles himself could ever really say for sure if he regretted making *The War of the Worlds*, and that was something he kept to himself, the truth shrouded in his trademark mystery and evasion. That in his closing years he was reduced to working the chat show circuit making a living from past glories would be galling to most men, but Welles was patently not most men, and to the very end the mischievous twinkle in his eye never quite faded. He must have also drawn some satisfaction from the knowledge that others had followed in his footsteps, having mentioned in *F for Fake* that "somebody down in South America" had reproduced the 1938 broadcast, though it is interesting to speculate if Welles was entirely aware of just what kind of Pandora's box he had opened, for as we will discover in the following chapters, the South American invasions were a whole different ball game.

10

THE LATIN AMERICAN FRONT
The Martians Return

One would think that the terrible lessons learned from the Orson Welles broadcast would dissuade anyone of sound mind from repeating the same mistake twice, but in 1944 a second *War of the Worlds* scare was unleashed on an unsuspecting listening public. At 9:30 P.M. on November 12 residents of a number of Chilean towns and cities were convulsed with alarm when a radio station in Santiago staged its own invasion from Mars. This was actually the first of two productions made in Latin America in the 1940s that borrowed heavily on the central conceit of fake "breaking news" stories utilized by the Mercury Theatre, though it is a considerable testament to the power of the original idea that the effect on listeners was much the same and, in one particularly tragic case, far worse.

Ironically, it is remotely possible that the instigator of the Chilean scare had crossed paths with Orson Welles. According to the *Newsweek* magazine of November 27, 1944, the script was cowritten by an American — "William Steele, former writer for Mutual's *The Shadow* series."[1] Welles had starred in *The Shadow* in 1937–38, but unfortunately there seems to be no record that a William Steele ever wrote for the show during this period, or indeed for American radio at any time.

There was, however, a Bob Steel who was a director and (under the name of his wife Catherine B. Stemler) an occasional writer on *The Shadow* during the 1944–45 season. John Archer, who assumed the role of the Shadow in 1944, recalls auditioning for Steel in September of that year,[2] but since this was the same year as the Chilean scare, it seems highly unlikely Steel was also moonlighting in Santiago at the same time.

So the precise identity of William Steele, if indeed such a person even existed, remains a tantalizing mystery, though we do know something of his partner in crime, one Raúl Zenteno. Zenteno seems to have occupied a pivotal role in the history of Chilean radio, having been involved in its formative years of radio. He was a principal writer for Radio Hucke (now Radio New World), which was one of the earliest stations in Chile, and by 1944 he was a writer for the Cooperative Vitalicia Network based in Santiago. The station was quite a powerful one, with long- and shortwave transmitters operating out of the cities of Santiago and Valparaíso. It is even said to have reached abroad, styling itself "The voice of Chile for all America."[3]

Given the relative remoteness of these events at the time, piecing together exactly what happened that night is fraught with difficulties, but turning back to the *Newsweek* article we are told that Steele and Zenteno did exactly as Howard Koch had done and decided to plot the conquest of Chile using familiar place-names. The initial "landing

The Plaza de Orenas in Santiago photographed sometime between 1908 and 1919. The Cooperative Vitalicia Network broadcast its version of *The War of the Worlds* from Santiago (Library of Congress, Prints & Photographs Division).

site" they chose was some 15 miles south of Santiago in the town of Puente Alto. Now the thriving capital city of the Cordillera province, in 1944 Puente Alto was a sleepy little rural backwater, not unlike Grover's Mill and just as blissfully unaware of the role it was about to play in a second Martian invasion of the Earth.

In a further nod to Howard Koch, the action was relayed to listeners as a series of news flashes, beginning with reports that Martian forces were landing with the aid of giant parachutes. Realistic references to people and organizations that would have been familiar to Chilean listeners peppered the broadcast, adding to the growing mood of disquiet among listeners. An actor impersonated the voice of the interior minister, the Red Cross was mentioned and the Santiago Civic Center reported destroyed, as were air bases and army barracks. As the play fictitiously reported roads jammed with refugees, in reality listeners apparently fled into the streets or barricaded themselves in their homes as word came from the radio that 400 policemen had been injured in Puente Alto and that the minister of defense was mobilizing troops. It is even said that the governor of one province telegrammed the actual minister to tell him that he had placed his troops and artillery on alert to repel the invaders.

The broadcast appears to have laid considerable emphasis on the destruction meted out by the Martians and the overwhelming nature of the attack. "The Air Force is fleeing..." reported the radio; and "the firefighters are incapable of containing the flames that have left the following cities in ruins: Rancagua, Temuco, Cautín Concepción, Talca and San Bernardo." A reporter announced, "There are many dead and the invasion is approaching Santiago."[4] A military weapons depot was also said to have been destroyed. Embroidering the story further, the radio fabricated a live link with the Palacio de La Moneda (the Government Palace) in Santiago.

On the streets of Santiago, the situation was getting out of hand. Believing everything they had heard, up to thirty service personnel reported for duty at the Maturana artillery group, the telephone systems collapsed under the strain of numerous calls made to hospitals and newspapers, and there were reports of minor injuries received as people fled their homes, many making their way to the downtown areas of the city in search of safety. Journalists who arrived quickly on the scene found large, agitated crowds thronging the streets of Santiago. The next day the newspaper *La Opinión* (The Opinion) described the scene: "The alarm was indescribable. People had flooded the streets, and when we arrived, *Carabineros* were trying to calm the crowd down." Said resident Jorge Balmaceda, "Everyone in my house was petrified."[5]

But of course none of this should have happened. Not wanting a repeat of the 1938 events in America, the broadcasters had taken care to give one-week on-air notice of their

The first recorded victim of a Martian invasion lived in Valparaíso, Chile. José Villarroel died of a heart attack on hearing that the Martians were invading (Library of Congress, Prints & Photographs Division).

intentions, as well as placing a prominent ad in the local newspaper. The fictional nature of the drama was also reported twice during its proceedings and once again at the end, yet this proved insufficient to prevent a panic of such intensity that according to *Newsweek*, an electrician named José Villarroel was so frightened that he died of a heart attack. If this is true, the unfortunate Villarroel (who was a resident of Valparaíso, 70 miles northwest of Santiago) seems to have earned the dubious honor of becoming the first person on Earth to be killed in an alien invasion, something that even Welles' Martians conspicuously failed to do. On first impressions, one might think that the death of Villarroel is a tall tale concocted to spice up the story, but there is additional corroboration from an article published by the Santiago newspaper *El Mercurio*, which further identifies Villarroel as an official of the Chilean Electric Company from its mountain campsite Los Maitenes, and even quotes an official apology for his death by the radio station.[6]

But what of the reasons for this new scare? In 1938 Orson Welles had tapped into growing feelings of dread and uncertainty plaguing his listeners; war jitters were amplified, and a number of other social and political factors intensified the effect on listeners. It would therefore be remiss not to examine the situation in Chile in 1944 and ask if there was anything politically or socially contentious occurring in the country that mirrored the situation in America in 1938.

On the social and economic front, Chile was still recovering from a shocking earthquake that on January 24, 1939, killed upwards of 30,000 people and devastated 40,000 square miles. The cost of the damage was enormous and squabbling between elements on the left and right of the political spectrum marred the reconstruction efforts. Politically, the country was also in a state of tension over its neutral position in the Second World War. Despite great pressure from both sides, it was only in April of 1945 that Chile entered the war on the side of the Allies, but both the Allies and Axis powers had been extremely active in Chile beforehand, such that all foreigners suspected of involvement in local politics had been expelled, including a German national accused of distributing 100,000 anti–Jewish pamphlets and a Briton who had produced leaflets that attacked Hitler and recommended a boycott of German commercial concerns. In this already complex and destabilizing situation, rumors were also rife that President Juan Antonio Rios was suffering an incurable disease.

Clearly, then, this was another situation where, just as in America in 1938, the populace was feeling a great deal of unease. In such a high-pressure situation an explosive release of tension was likely. The authorities had even thought to legislate against the possibility of panic being triggered by irresponsible journalism, though when they drafted the law, those responsible can hardly have imagined it would one day apply in such outlandish circumstances. Passed only a year earlier, it stated, "The transmission of sensational programs that can produce alarm among the public is strictly prohibited."[7] Several radio employees were briefly arrested by police, including the well-known announcer Renato Deformes, but no one was actually charged.

No doubt deeply concerned by what might happen next, the radio station issued an explanation and apology to the press, in which they argued that they were "trying to present a universally known play, demonstrating the talent and technical capacity Chilean radiotelephony has, and, knowing the sensational nature of the play, had previously and repeatedly announced it a month earlier. Moreover, it was announced that it was a play before, in the middle and at the end of the transmission. Those advertisements warned about the 'imaginative and fantastic character of the work,' recommending that people with an impressionable temperament not listen to the transmission."[8]

But the press was incensed, and in the following days, a great many newspapers demanded that the station be soundly punished. They suggested that the public should bring pressure to bear on the government to have Cooperative Vitalicia shut down, though the station claimed that the broadcast had "earned the applause of thousands of listeners."[9] The clamor became particularly strong when the death of José Villarroel became widely known, but in the final event, the station escaped any sanction, and this particular instance of a *War of the Worlds*–inspired scare was quickly and unfairly consigned to a dusty footnote in the history books.

However, with one death recorded in Chile the stakes in this dangerous game had been significantly increased. Anyone electing to spin this particular wheel of fortune was clearly taking an awful chance, but perhaps it was the very thrill of that risk that inspired yet another *War of the Worlds* broadcast, this time in Ecuador. Suffice to say, it was a very bad wager. On the night of Saturday, February 12, 1949, an appalling series of events unfolded in Quito, the capital city of Ecuador, culminating in a riot, a hugely destructive blaze that would level the offices of a major newspaper, and a significant loss of life. Yet again the Martians were on the march, but unfortunately it seems that some of the more impressionable inhabitants of Quito (the population then standing at some 250,000) were caught unawares by the realism of the broadcast. It has even been suggested that forces within the radio station had intended creating a panic by keeping their plans to themselves. Even if there is any truth in this accusation, it is very doubtful that anyone actually intended events to spiral out of control the way they did.

The two men behind the Quito *War of the Worlds* broadcast were named Leonardo Páez and Eduardo Alcaraz. Alcaraz (whose real name was Alfredo Vergara Morales) was Chilean born, which certainly dangles the intriguing possibility of a direct lineage to the events there in 1944. Though there is no specific

Leonardo Páez, photographed circa 1950. His production of *The War of the Worlds* in Quito, Ecuador, caused a riot and resulted in the death of at least six people (courtesy of Ximena Páez).

evidence he personally had a hand in the earlier Latin American "invasion," in correspondence with the author, Ximena Páez (the daughter of Leonardo Páez) has provided categorical assurances that Alcaraz did actually bring with him a copy of the 1944 script to Ecuador, and that this was then freely adapted for the Quito broadcast.

Described as a portly, balding, mustachioed character actor,[10] Alcaraz was born in Santiago on April 13, 1915, and forged a successful career in film in the early 1950s, working mostly in comedies where he was frequently cast as a pompous banker or businessman. But in 1949 he was working as the dramatic director for Radio Quito alongside Páez, who was the artistic director and seems to have been the senior partner of the pair. Having worked at Radio Quito since at least 1943, Páez had established a comedy program about everyday life in Ecuador called *La Familia Luna* (The Luna Family), which aired on Thursday nights, and the weekly drama *Theater on Sunday*.[11] It would not be entirely presumptuous to call him a Latin American Orson Welles, for clearly Páez was an important pioneer of Ecuadorian radio, as well as an accomplished journalist, songwriter and poet.

Leonardo Páez's greatest claim to fame began innocuously enough in the studios of Radio Quito, located on the third floor of the office of the *El Comercio* newspaper, which owned the station. At 9 P.M., largely unsuspecting listeners were told that they were to be treated to a special program featuring the music of Luis Alberto "Potolo" Valencia and Gonzalo Benítez. This guitar-playing duo was immensely popular in Ecuador and would doubtless have drawn a large and appreciative audience. They had just reached their second song of the evening, "For Me Your Memory," when they were interrupted by the sudden arrival of a station reporter, who announced without preamble, "We are being invaded by Martians. They are invading us."[12]

The reporter goes on to describe the landing of a fleet of flying saucers in Cotocollao, a northwest-

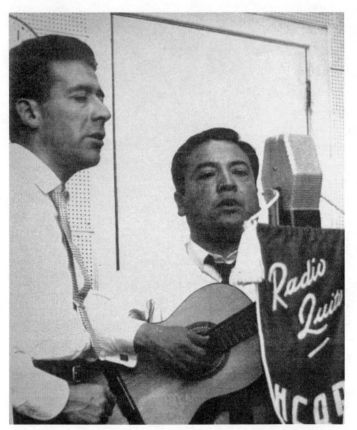

Gonzalo Benítez (left) and Luis Alberto "Potolo" Valencia at the microphone of Radio Quito. Both men would be caught up in the disastrous 1949 broadcast of *The War of the Worlds*.

ern parish of Quito near a military air base. With other voices in the studio appearing to confirm his words, the reporter, who now sounds like he is on the verge of tears, adds, "The incredible news report comes from qualified international agencies and the city's main newspaper, *El Comercio*. Important: The news flash you are listening to, ladies and gentlemen, is sponsored exclusively by Orangine, the unbeatable orange refreshment."[13]

It is sobering to ponder what the people behind Orangine, "the unbeatable orange refreshment," must have thought the next morning as dazed spectators surveyed the smoldering remains of the *El Comercio* building, but as the city became gripped by the unfolding drama, they must have been congratulating themselves on what seemed like a very shrewd investment. Having secured Cotocollao, the Martians swiftly advance on the parish of Chaupicruz and the military air base located there. It is efficiently and mercilessly swept aside. The *New York Times* of February 14, 1949, "The air base of Mariscal Sucre has been taken by the enemy and it is being destroyed. There are many dead and wounded. It is about to be wiped out."

It was very definitely beginning to sound like a rout of civilization as other areas in and around Quito were swiftly added to the tally of those fallen or about to be destroyed by the Martians. Latacunga City was reported smothered with a lethal gas, while in the south the Martians were said to be moving toward the city of Tambillo, and in the north they had already taken Otavalo. Extraordinarily, other radio stations now fell for the deception. Radio Continental from the city of Ambato, The Voice of Cochabamba from Cuenca and Radio Zenith from Guayaquil all announced that they were trying to reach Radio Quito to learn more about the danger to the nation.[14] It is easy to suppose that the phone lines into Radio Quito must have been hopelessly jammed, so lacking any means of independent corroboration, these other stations could only repeat and amplify that which they themselves were hearing. Listeners with the presence of mind to try tuning into another station must have been shocked to discover the story was not restricted to Radio Quito. Disquiet was rapidly turning to dread.

Once again, a *War of the Worlds* broadcast was following closely the template set down by the Mercury Theatre, but far more effectively. The renowned Ecuadorian journalist and novelist Nicolás Kingman recalls the astonishing intensity of the broadcast. "Soon detonations, machine gun fire and howls were heard in the middle of the extraordinary confusion and daze. It was thought that the combat was heavy between the extraterrestrials and our heroic defenders, but it seemed that no human force could stop them. It was a slaughter!"[15] Familiar voices (impersonated by actors) added to the panic. The *New York Times* of February 14, 1949, reported that the interior minister was heard urging citizens to be calm, "in order to be able to organize the defense and evacuation of the city," and the mayor announced, "people of Quito, let us defend our city. Our women and children must go out into the surrounding heights to leave the men free for action and combat." A priest asked for divine forgiveness as church bells tolled, and then from atop the La Previsora tower (the highest point in Quito) came a terrifying description of a monster engulfed in plumes of fire and smoke that was advancing from the north.

When the reporter (played by Páez) transmitting from Cotocollao was suddenly cut off as if killed by a Martian weapon, frantic crowds rushed into the streets. In the excitement, agitated imaginations transformed ordinary clouds into ominous alien objects.

Chaos began to engulf the streets of Quito and other cities thought to be in the path of the Martians. Journalist Tony Fields, investigating *War of the Worlds* panics, spoke to residents of Quito for a WNYC Radiolab program on March 7, 2008, and was told that many people had congregated in churches and that whole crowds were absolved en masse of their sins by priests. By now news of the terror sweeping Quito was filtering through to the station. Realizing that the situation was totally out of hand, the station announced to its listeners that they were hearing nothing but a play and transmitted urgent pleas for calm. But the effect was anything but calming — the very opposite, in fact.

Furious that they had been so thoroughly and humiliatingly fooled, a crowd of some 300 people began to mass and march on the *El Comercio* building. On arrival they found the doors locked against them, so they began to hurl stones at the windows. If matters had only been left at a few broken windows it would not have been so bad, but the mob had other ideas. Some had brought gasoline, others found copies of the latest edition of *El Comercio*, and with these materials improvised firebombs were constructed.

One of the most reliable sources of information we have on what happened next is the autobiography of César Larrea Velásquez, a reporter for over 30 years with *El Comercio*. His account of the events of that night and in particular the attack on the newspaper office paints a grim picture. "Furious people, some frightened and others just curious, attacked the building. At that moment, a mysterious truck loaded with stones arrived, and the doors and windows were destroyed by stone missiles. Soon, several individuals arrived with torches. They managed to force open the iron curtains and toss their torches into the basement where the rotary press was, along with ink and paper. The combustion was violent. While that was going on, others managed to get inside the building. They removed typewriters, destroyed registers and stole valuables and papers."[16]

A station DJ named Luis Beltrán who had been assisting in the broadcast broke character and pleaded on air for help from the authorities, but with no way to know when or even if they might be rescued, some 60 to 100 staff and performers, many located on the upper floors of the building, were faced with a terrifying dilemma: to brave the fire below or to try and escape through windows or across the fragile adjoining rooftops. As the flames edged closer, decisions were made. Some people scrambled down a half-completed wall at an adjacent building site; others clambered through windows and attempted to form human chains which then collapsed, tumbling people to the ground below. Still others made the dangerous jump to other buildings.

Gonzalo Benítez was one of those who elected to brave the rooftops. As he recalls, he was on the floor above the studio enjoying a glass of wine with his collaborator Luis "Potolo" Valencia, when they became aware of the commotion outside. "That's what we were doing when I heard something bang against the windows. I told Potolo to go see what was going on. He returned worried. 'I think we're in trouble. There's a lot of people outside throwing stones and shouting against the radio.' When we wanted to go down to leave, a whole bunch of employees were coming up."[17] Unable to get down the stairs, Benítez had a lucky recollection. "I remembered a skylight in the men's room. I ran to it. I didn't even think about Potolo. The jump was onto a metal roof. The dear Lord gave me strength and I managed to open the skylight and get out. From there, I had to jump onto the roof of another house. That one was made of clay, and my feet fell through."[18]

Those who did make it to street level with life and limb intact still had to run the gauntlet of the mob, which had blocked Chile Street and was now apparently stopping and interrogating everyone in search of Páez and Alcaraz. There is no record of Alcaraz's escape, but Benítez was witness to the flight of Páez from the roof of the studio. The frightened Páez told Benítez that he thought the mob was going to immolate him if he were caught. "I advised him to go by roof to La Providencia; that's what he did and got to the old Conservatory. There he got down and a truck saved him. They say he was taken to a hacienda near Ibarra* to hide him." Ximena Páez also confirms that her father had fled that night across the rooftops, finally reaching street level where sympathetic bystanders helped him to escape the mob.

Also in the studio that night was 18-year-old actress Blanca Salazar Bautista. Born on August 21, 1930, she had begun performing on radio as a child, and in 1943 Páez cast her in the play *House of Dolls*.† So impressed was he by her performance that he promptly offered her 100 sucres a month to become a regular on his *Teatro en Domingo* [*Theatre on Sunday*] program. (If we allow ourselves the indulgence of thinking of Páez as the Ecuadorian Welles, then Bautista would be his Agnes Moorhead.) When the fire began, she was trapped with the other performers on the upper floors of the building, but made a miraculous escape. This particular account would seem to place her with the group that Benítez had seen on the roof with Páez, though the story of her escape is slightly different. A biographer wrote, "With the help of ropes they managed to cross onto the roof of a neighboring convent and escape through a back door that led to García Moreno Street."[19]

The situation on the streets surrounding the *El Comercio* building was turning ever more ugly. Elements of the mob reportedly removed fire hydrants to prevent firefighters from tackling the blaze, and the first police on the scene came under attack, with one singled out for a savage beating. Unfortunately, police reinforcements were slow to arrive, as the majority of the force had set out for Cotocollao to fight the Martians, an extraordinary development which seems to be confirmed by Tony Field of WNYC, who interviewed a witness who claimed to have seen a large column of police and troops heading in that direction. The *El Día* newspaper of February 15 could not help but take a sarcastic swipe at the expense of the police and their rather embarrassing blunder. "With the fire of *El Comercio*, it has been proven that the Civil Guard [police] are identical to national brand matches: they are missing when you need them the most."

As the fire raged out of control, it even began to threaten the adjoining Government Communication Building, which according to the *New York Times* of February 14 was slightly damaged. In the end it fell to the army to clear the way with tanks and tear gas for the fire services to reach the blazing *El Comercio* building, which they finally did at three in the morning. By then the damage was done, and in the cold light of day all that remained standing was the front wall. But there was a far worse reality to digest than the loss of the building and presses. At least six people were dead and many others injured, including a young lady described as Páez's girlfriend and his 15-year-old niece. Ximena Páez confirms the loss of someone close to her father, but describes her as more a friend

*The capital of the province of Imbabura, located 115 kilometers north of Quito.
†Possibly an adaptation of the 1943 film *Casa de Muñecas*, written by Alejandro Casona.

and fan rather than a girlfriend. She also adds that the young woman's nephew was among the casualties. The *New York Times* of February 15 put the death toll much higher, reporting that up to 20 were dead, with 12 bodies thus far identified by relatives, though this figure seems to have been an exaggeration and the figure of six dead is by far the more reliable. Additionally confirmed as dead was a pianist named Molestina and counted among the injured was the announcer Luis Beltrán.[20] He had been the last man in the building that night, and suffered considerably for his bravery in remaining behind to help save his colleagues. Jumping from the window, he landed awkwardly on a second-floor balcony. In attempting to save himself from falling to the pavement below, he grabbed onto a metal railing which was red hot from the fire now raging all around him. As he dangled from the searing hot railing, he pleaded fruitlessly with the crowd below to catch him. With flames all around him he finally had no choice but to let go. He left the skin of his hands on the railing and landed heavily on the concrete pavement, breaking numerous bones. Lying on the pavement with terrible burns and other appalling injuries, Beltrán later recalled to his daughter Maria Beltrán Testagrossa that as he slipped into unconsciousness he thought he had heard someone saying "let him die in peace,"[21] though Maria believes that others in the crowd may have tried to throw him back into the blazing building. Luckily one Samaritan took pity, bundling Beltrán into a jeep and rushing him to the hospital. Doubtless this brave act of charity saved his life.

So the question once again arises: How could this have happened? And more to the point, how could this particular broadcast escalate like no other into a truly cataclysmic outpouring of anger? In fact, in a rather morbid way, the Quito riot is an even better candidate for analysis than the 1938 event, as it has far fewer of the ambiguities that plague the Orson Welles broadcast. The precise scope and nature of the terror sparked by the Welles broadcast is still a matter of conjecture, but in Quito there is a horrible and unassailable fact: the offices of *El Comercio* were burned down by a furious mob incited by a broadcast of *The War of the Worlds*, and people died. Of this there is simply no doubt.

But why was the reaction so ferocious? The trite response would be to blame the stereotypical passionate Latin American temperament, and there might just be a glimmer of truth in that statement, but then why was the Chilean broadcast so moderately received in comparison? There must be more to it than a fiery disposition, and there is indeed one generally held theory, though unfortunately it is not at all kind to the memory of Leonardo Páez. In hindsight, it does not seem unreasonable to suggest that a lack of understanding (even naivety) of the inherent dangers of this kind of broadcast had led to a fatal lack of urgency in preparing listeners for what they were to hear that night. Advertisements were apparently placed in *El Comercio* and *Últimas Noticias* newspapers several days before the broadcast, but these were crucially lacking in detail. They merely asked cryptically, "What will happen on February 12?" The question of just how much advance warning the population received or how explicitly it was expressed has stoked theories that Páez had in fact neglected to inform the station management of his plans and in reality was hell bent on creating a great sensation with his play, regardless of the danger. This shocking idea is passionately refuted by his daughter Ximena Páez.

As related by Ximena, it was in fact the station manager, a Mr. Mantilla, who had asked Páez to organize the creative side of the production, but the actual idea for the broadcast, along with the 1944 script, had indeed been brought to the station by none other than Eduardo Alcaraz. The contract to create the program was therefore made between Alcaraz and the station manager. From an artistic perspective, Páez had simply set about creating on their behalf as realistic a drama as possible, but had emphatically not been party to any deception. However, this does not entirely remove the suspicion that there was a curiously secretive aspect to the production. Though it would be cavalier to suggest with absolute certainty that someone on the station staff had harbored a sinister motive in this regard, it has been suggested that some members of the cast were not entirely certain what was going on that night.

Reminiscing to the newspaper *La Hora* in 2002, the singer Gonzalo Benítez insists he and his singing partner were as much in the dark about the intention of their hosts that night as were the listeners. They knew the title of the program, but that

Leonardo Páez, photographed circa 1980. Páez spent his later years in Venezuela, returning often to Ecuador where he is considered something of a national treasure (courtesy of Ximena Páez).

seems to have been the entire extent of their knowledge. "As the Benítez and Valencia Duet, we were invited to sing three songs to launch the first chapter of a new Radio Quito novel. It was an adaptation of *The War of the Worlds* by the writer H. G. Wells. We had no idea what it was about. We went to the station the evening before, and the only thing they told us was not to get upset if they were to interrupt us, that it was to promote the novel. February 12, 1949. I remember every detail. Potolo Valencia and I arrived feeling very happy. It was unusual for us to be presented on air on Saturday. We had a contract with the radio to sing on Mondays, Wednesdays and Fridays on the program called *Songs from the Soul*, but since they asked us to come in on Saturday as a favor, there we were."[22]

Were they then just a pair of unsuspecting worms on the hook, dangled before listeners to reel in a big fat juicy audience, who were to be then lulled into a false sense of complacency by their two favorite singers? This is one interpretation, but another equally valid view is that no one had thought to adequately explain the story to them, not through any desire to deceive, but for no more complex reason than it was considered unimportant to their performance. However, in the immediate aftermath, Eduardo Alcaraz certainly seemed keen to promote Páez as the villain and himself as the innocent bystander who had tried to restrain his colleague. Interviewed on the radio program *El Día* (The

Day) he claimed that he had insisted on Páez previously making an announcement about the radio play, just as had been done in Chile.* Páez had refused, claimed Alcaraz, arguing that this "would only make people lose interest in the play and that he had a better idea.'"[23] That better idea, asserted Alcaraz, was to plant fake stories in the *El Comercio* newspaper (and possibly the *Últimas Noticias* newspaper as well) about the appearance of flying saucers in the northern region of the country and to send a reporter to talk to the director of the Quito Observatory on the Avenida Colombia, though the account suggests that this approach was very sensibly rebuffed. Ximena Páez is however absolutely certain of her father's innocence in this regard, stating that he had no authority to do any such thing and besides which he would never have thought to stoop to such a deception.

But even if there had been any intent to deceive, would this and a few crudely planted stories about UFOs be enough in itself to elicit a reaction on this scale? What then of the realism of the broadcast itself? Alas, the fire destroyed any recording that might have been made that night, and we have only a few scraps of handed-down dialogue that may or may not be accurate, so we cannot be sure just how good a job Páez and his actors made of bringing the story to life. But assuming for a moment it was even half as good as the Mercury Theatre broadcast, and given that listeners in this case quite likely lacked any means at all of independent corroboration, we can safely assume they succeeded in delivering a very frightening experience. These factors alone would seem cause enough for the scare that ensued, but just as in America in 1938, there is yet another reason that listeners took for real what they heard on their radios, and the parallels are quite eerie.

Ecuador in common with many Latin American countries has suffered a long and troubled past characterized by civil war, periods of dictatorship and meddling in civilian affairs by the military. In 1949, the country was, however, ruled by a democratically elected president called Galo Plaza Lasso. He had assumed power in September of 1948 but had inherited some serious problems from earlier administrations. Economically the country was in a bad way, with high inflation and the foreign currency reserves at dangerously low levels, while militarily the nation was still reeling from a recent traumatic defeat. On July 5, 1941, neighboring Peru had launched an invasion over a border dispute. The war ended badly in 1942 with Ecuador signing a humiliating peace treaty that lost the country some 200,000 square kilometers of territory. The wounds of this defeat were still raw in 1949, as was the fear that the conflict might reignite, so it is no surprise that in exactly the same way as had happened in America, rattled listeners dismissed the improbable idea of a Martian invasion and substituted instead a renewal of hostilities with Peru; others thought it might be the Soviet Union. The level of tension felt in Quito that year was succinctly summed up by the newspaper *Hoy*, which observed, "The truth is that this was simply a reaction of a city on the verge of a nervous breakdown."[24]

In the days that followed the broadcast, as the city tried to get back on its feet, the police set about hunting down the perpetrators. Diaz Granados, the minister of defense, was appointed in charge of the investigation. On February 15 the *New York Times* reported that 15 people had been arrested, though Páez and Alcaraz were still missing. Others,

---

*An interesting choice of words, which adds additional credence to the idea that Alcaraz had some intimate knowledge of the 1944 broadcast in Chile.

too, were lying low. Blanca Salazar Bautista was in hiding for several weeks and was out of work for a year afterward. She appears to have avoided arrest, but was unable to act and had to take up typing and shorthand. Alcaraz was not so lucky. On February 16, the *Times* reported that he too had been captured, along with his wife Maya Wong. Also arrested the same day was José Alfredo Llerena, the editor of *El Comercio*. But of the elusive Páez, nothing had yet been found.

Facing the prospect of jail, Alcaraz continued to point the finger of blame at his absent colleague, claiming that Páez had actually enjoyed the panic he set in motion and had even ordered the doors to the studio locked,[25] ostensibly so that the actors would not be disturbed, but clearly hoping to imply that his colleague wanted nothing less than to maximize the damage. This vilification of Páez must, however, be balanced against the very real possibility that Alcaraz was out to paint his colleague in as black a light as possible, with the aim of getting himself off the hook. Certainly Alcaraz seems to have spent little or no time in jail, for in 1950, having clearly worn out his welcome in Ecuador he surfaced a free man in Mexico, where he began a highly successful film career.* He even provided the voice of the villainous Doctor Smith in the Spanish dub of the television series *Lost in Space*. As for Páez, the last confirmed sighting we have of him that night is atop the roof of the *El Comercio* building. Conventional wisdom relating to this tale has it that Páez then slipped away, never to be seen again, and this certainly suits the popular idea that he was guilty of a diabolical criminal act and knew it, but the disappearance of Leonardo Páez seems to have been greatly exaggerated.

Ximena Páez offers a much less mysterious explanation of her father's movements in the aftermath of the Quito disaster. Far from fleeing the country, Páez simply and sensibly laid low for four months until a writ of habeas corpus could be obtained, protecting him from arrest. Ximena describes her father as a cautious man, such that he had the forethought to retain a copy of the contract arranged between Alcaraz and Radio Quito. As he was able to produce this document in court, he was able to prove to the satisfaction of a judge that the station management was fully aware of the broadcast and hence he could not be held accountable for the damage and loss of life. Thus, far from spending the rest of his days on the run from a vengeful judiciary, Páez returned quietly to public life, working for other radio stations and newspapers in Ecuador. Six years later he moved to Venezuela where he continued to work in radio and newspapers for several more decades. He passed away in 1991 in Venezuela.

It is one of the more curious aspects of this tale that in all the English-language accounts of his role in the 1949 broadcast, Leonardo Páez has been cast without question as the villain of the piece, and his activities before and after the broadcast entirely overlooked. Yet evidence exists that clearly contradicts these accounts. Páez even wrote a novel about his fateful experience at Radio Quito, called *Los que Siembran el Viento* (Those That Seed the Wind). He also penned over 20 popular Ecuadorian songs, including "La Tuna Quiteña" (The Fiesta of Quito), which has become a perennial national favorite. History has certainly judged him harshly, but was he really guilty of anything? Ximena Páez recalls that her father was hoping for good reviews the following day (certainly not

---

*His first role was in the highly regarded *El Rey del Barrio* (The King of the Block).

a mass panic), so perhaps the answer is that in the same way that Orson Welles and his colleagues were swept along by the passion of the moment, so Páez and his colleagues were seduced by the excitement of the story and lost some perspective on what they were doing. But of course this is hardly a crime. In the final analysis, it is highly instructive to ask: Would a man who was allegedly held responsible for the cold-blooded death of six of his compatriots at Radio Quito later be given the keys to that very same city, as indeed he was during his last visit to his hometown in 1985?

Yet regardless of what internal machinations had produced this disaster, there was undoubtedly complete outrage in the press concerning the activities of the mob. This was summed up in no uncertain terms on the front page of next morning's *El Día*, with an editorial comment lamenting, "*El Comercio* has been the victim of an aggression in which all primitive impulses have become evident, demonstrating the capability of the forces of resistance against any means that strive for the benefit of culture."[26]

Nicolás Kingman arrived in Quito a few days after the broadcast to attend a political event and found a surreal situation, the city still reeling from the chaos that had engulfed it. "Days after that hallucinating night, a congress of the Confederation of Workers of Ecuador met. When 'we' the delegates arrived, we found a practically deserted city. We had lodging problems in the hotels, receiving a series of excuses[;] they refused to receive us and even to get food was difficult. The village folk watched us with distrust, the children ran away upon seeing us, and the nuns blessed themselves when they passed us. They exorcised us. In addition, almost all the businesses were closed, the cinemas did not work and there was a sensation of neglect, sorrow and melancholy. The place was full of omens."[27]

No doubt badly rattled by events, the Ecuadorian government lost no time in putting in place safeguards against another panic broadcast. On February 15 *El Día* reported in a front page article, "In order to avoid future imprudent radio broadcasts that could be the source of fatal events, it has been brought to our attention that at today's session of Government Council, the Ministry of Defense in charge of government communications will propose that adequate regulations should be dictated with the purpose of reviewing in advance any radio program that hopes to be presented. A new position will be created: An artistic and cultural inspector for the radio, whose obligation will be to read beforehand the theatre scripts that will be broadcast."[28]

But what of *El Comercio*, now a blackened and twisted pile of rubble, its records, offices and machinery razed to the ground? In fact the paper was swiftly back in production thanks to the solidarity of *El Día*. In an extraordinary gesture, *El Día* gave over four columns of its front page to its rival, so that on February 15, just three days after the disaster, a special joint edition was issued. Further good luck blessed *El Comercio*, for on examination of the ruins of their building it was found that not everything was destroyed as first thought. Thanks to the actions of a quick-thinking employee who had opened all the water taps to hold back the fire, the entire basement linotype workshop had survived intact. This was an especially lucky break, since had the fire only advanced a little further, it would have reached large stocks of acids, gasoline, nitroglycerine, paper, ink and oils. The resulting explosion could well have elevated the situation into a disaster of simply unimaginable proportions.

With nine machines recovered from the workshop, the staff of *El Comercio* were able to make makeshift arrangements to start reprinting the paper, doing what work they could with salvaged equipment, and then transporting the half-finished pages to *El Día* offices where they would be printed. As César Larrea Velásquez recalls in his autobiography, "Reporters and workers labored without rest day in and day out, manufacturing the newspaper, every dawn transporting its pages by truck to 'El Día'; suffering the repeated risks that during the trip they would be ruined or that the lead pages disintegrate, subjected to an irregular printing schedule, but with everlasting faith in their work and with minds saturated with the director-founder's words: 'It's the forces of evil; we must begin anew.'"[29]

The arrangement with *El Día* lasted until November 3, 1949, when *El Comercio* was able to restore full production with a triumphant 36-page edition, the top of the front page aptly emblazoned with the figure of a phoenix. An editorial had these words to say:

> Saturday night was a night of adversity and also shame for the good standing of the city. The flames indiscriminately attacked everything inside the building and took the lives of persons that were doing their jobs. In the street, before the stoic attitude of the authorities, were the instigators of hate, hurting without any risk, killing without mercy. But the newspaper is not a material organization that one can kill: the newspaper is another flame that lights, that serves, that discusses and takes an interest in the nation's well being. We are appointed a role to serve the country, and that is where we are again. And now, readers, we continue the dialogue that, with you, has gone on for 43 years. We continue at our country's service and its legitimate interests.[30]

El Comercio is still in existence, but clearly the events of that night are not something that Ecuadorians are keen to relive, such that in a 1980 article on the 40th anniversary of Radio Quito, *El Comercio* omitted any mention of *The War of the Worlds* broadcast.[31] Yet while the torching of the *El Comercio* building was unquestionably an act of unspeakable violence, there are still moments of dark humor to be found, and even human kindness. Recounted in the pages of *La Hora* are tales of adulterers asking their wives and God to forgive their indiscretions and misers who suddenly became spendthrifts.[32] Small comfort, perhaps, to the people of Quito, who have never quite lived down the indignity of losing their heads in such spectacular fashion, but they should take comfort from the fact they would not be the last to suffer the embarrassment of succumbing to a Martian invasion.

11

SOS FROM CARATINGA
Brazil Battles the Martians

His name was Anor Ferreira da Silva, a bored but highly imaginative 25-year-old telegraph operator from the city of Caratinga in the Minas Gerais state of eastern Brazil. For a few days in 1954 he would become the most infamous person in the country, thanks to a prank that went horribly and spectacularly wrong. Yet his only crime was to transmit a fake message to a fellow telegraph operator announcing that a Martian flying saucer had descended on Caratinga. It should have stopped there, a joke between friends, but to his horror and the fury of his employer, the nation's press mobilized to cover the news and the Brazilian air force scrambled over the city in search of the invaders.

It was on November 22, 1954, that da Silva hatched his unfortunate plan, little knowing that he was about to cause a massive commotion in the country. During a lull in regular communications, he allegedly transmitted a Morse code message to a colleague named Geraldo Bastos in the state capital of Belo Horizonte, some 180 miles west of Caratinga. The message he transmitted was preserved for posterity by the newspaper *Estado de Minas* (State of Minas) in their edition of November 24. "My dear Friend, the city here is in turmoil, busier then ever with the unexpected events this morning: A flying saucer has fallen at the Quarry, a few kilometers from here, causing incalculable emotion in the entire population."

Da Silva went on to color his message with some elaborate detail, claiming that two airline pilots flying near the city of Juiz de Fora had first spotted a fleet of 15 flying saucers. One of these saucers landed near Caratinga, but onlookers were prevented from getting a closer look because it was emitting choking gases and fumes as well as a very bright light. They were, however, able to observe from a distance that the occupants resembled short human beings.

Exactly how long da Silva continued to broadcast his extraordinary fantasy is uncertain, but there are suggestions that the messages continued for the best part of an hour, with repeated requests that the authorities send "urgent forces"[1] to defend the city from the Martian invaders. Unfortunately Bastos appears to have swallowed his friend's story hook, line and sinker, and the situation escalated quickly out of hand when a colleague looking over Bastos' shoulder also took the messages to be real and dashed out to the nearest Belo Horizonte newspaper office to spread the news. Extraordinarily, the story of a Martian invasion then took on a life of its own, spreading from the telegraph office to newspapers and radio stations, before finally coming to the attention of the authorities.

The confusion seems to have been pervasive, with attempts to confirm the landing over the telegraph bringing an apparent confirmation at midday, only for this to be contradicted by long distance telephone calls made to Caratinga by newspapers and radio stations. Other contradictory rumors spoke of the saucer beaming out light signals and of police converging on the landing site. As the telephone system in Caratinga imploded under the strain, the city was effectively cut off from the rest of the country for several hours. Into this vacuum stepped the *Esso Reporter*, which at the time was the most widely listened to and respected radio news program in Brazil. It began transmitting regular updates, spreading the story as far afield as São Paulo and Rio de Janeiro.

Such was the conviction of the media that they were sitting on the story of the century that many Belo Horizonte air taxi companies were allegedly chartered to fly hordes of reporters and photographers to Caratinga, though this is almost certainly an exaggeration. Popular versions of the story also have it that at 4 P.M. a storm broke out over the city, preventing several planes from landing and further isolating Caratinga. Those reporters able to reach Caratinga apparently found a city under a pall, with the population clearly alarmed but strangely reticent to speak to reporters about the drama apparently unfolding just on their doorstep. Reported the *Estado de Minas* of November 24, "Nobody wished to speak up on the strange phenomenon, yet all were talking about it. The fact is that nobody had seen a thing, neither saucers nor Martians, and all knew about the rumor through word of mouth begun by the telegraph operator but they would not say a word."

The press and citizens of Caratinga were not the only victims of this amazing hoax. The Brazilian military also found itself caught up in the drama. One brigade leader was on his bike to the south of Rio de Janeiro in the beachside town of Leblón when he received word of the invasion. He immediately returned to his base to organize the defense of Caratinga. Incredibly, C-47 planes took to the air on a photoreconnaissance mission and other aircraft were idling on the runway, their motors ready for a rapid takeoff. Eventually the reconnaissance planes returned with nothing to show for their trouble, and a message was received from Caratinga saying, "Here, there are no flying saucers. The city is in perfect calm."[2] This began to defuse the situation, but poor Anor Ferreira da Silva's troubles were only just beginning.

Speaking to the press in the days after his hoax, da Silva expressed the earnest belief that he would likely escape punishment for his indiscretion, but in hindsight this seems utterly naïve. Quoted on the front page of the newspaper *Estado de Minas* of November 24, he said incredulously, "I did not expect the case to take such serious proportions." His superiors were anything but amused. "The National Telegraph is nobody's joke," fumed Venero Caetano da Fonseca, the director of the Mailing and Telegraph Department, on the front page of the November 23 edition of *Diário da Tarde* (Afternoon Diary). In the immediate aftermath of the hugely embarrassing misappropriation of government communication channels, *Diário da Tarde* further reported that da Fonseca had assigned a colleague named Gil João de Lima to travel to Caratinga and interview da Silva, with the ominous aim of deciding what "applicable administrative measures can be taken."

There seems to be no record of what, if any, "administrative measures" da Silva eventually faced, but if the newspaper accounts of the time are to be believed, he certainly deserves some credit for mounting a hugely successful one-man invasion from Mars, but what could have possessed people to believe his story? The newspaper *Estado de Minas* offers an interesting opinion in its edition of November 24, suggesting that the city of Caratinga was prone to losing its head over improbable stories. In support of this assertion, the story is told that a doctor leaving the city hospital one day had jokingly told a group of children, "Be quiet because a man has just given birth and he is not feeling well." The story then spread like wildfire and the hospital was besieged by curious onlookers. It sounds like a highly apocryphal tale, and the cynical may just detect a hint of face-saving in this story, with the big city mocking their unsophisticated country cousins for having fallen for so spectacular a lie.

But perhaps they had good reason to lose their heads. Though now a thriving modern nation, Brazil has undergone any number of upheavals in its recent history, seesawing uneasily between nascent experiments in democracy and outright dictatorship. The year 1954 had its fair share of trouble, and at the heart of this was a war fought between rival factions in the media, a conflict characterized by salacious muckraking, outright lies and, eventually, murder.

It was the political machinations of President Getulio Dornelles Vargas and his opponents that had brought the Brazilian media to such a lamentable nadir. Vargas had been president once before, between 1930 and 1945, presiding over an extremely authoritarian regime, but after a period in the political wilderness he had returned to power in 1950 on a large popular mandate. On reassuming the presidency Vargas poured a great deal of dubiously obtained money into a new newspaper called *Ultima Hora*, with the purpose of exercising control over the media. Edited by a crony named Samuel Wainer, it drew the ire of the opposition, who used their own media connections to fight back. Globo Radio was one such organ of the opposition, and several of its programs paint an interesting picture, not only of the limited respect of the broadcasters for the truth, but also of the extremely unsophisticated nature of the listeners. A program called *Family Conversation* purported to listen in on a family around a kitchen table (actually a group of journalists) as they discussed important matters of the day; another program called *Congress in Action* was a mixture of interviews and commentary. However, as Colin MacLachlan observes in his book *A History of Modern Brazil*, "Both programs blurred the lines between hard news, rumor, and opinion. A relatively unsophisticated audience could not separate fabrications from actual events."[3]

The intense rivalry came to a head on August 24, just a few months before da Silva made his hoax transmissions. Vargas committed suicide after the botched assassination attempt of a radio commentator named Carlos Lacerda was revealed to have connections to Vargas' bodyguard. Lacerda was a firebrand commentator of extremely dubious ethics who was a major thorn in the side of the Vargas regime, and while there was no direct evidence that the president had known of the plot, an air force officer died in the crossfire. The powerful military, which had already forced Vargas to step aside once before, was incensed and again demanded that he be removed. On failing to negotiate a compromise deal with the military, Vargas shot himself. Yet despite his unpopularity and having presided over an economy in total freefall, Vargas' dramatic suicide note was read out repeatedly on radio, thousands attended his funeral and riots had to be put down by the armed forces.

But radio at this time in Brazil was not only flexible with the truth, it was also dumbing down in other ways. When radio first arrived in Brazil in the early 1920s it produced some incredibly sophisticated programming with the aim of educating its listeners in any number of cultural and scientific fields. By the early 1950s, however, the commercialization of Brazilian radio was almost complete and the airwaves were dominated by soap operas, beauty advice and cooking programs. Even the *Esso Reporter* (sponsored by a petroleum company) provided little more than a verbatim regurgitation of newswire reports, with no real comment or insight provided on the events it was reporting.

Clearly, in this chaotic atmosphere of political chicanery and with a media beholden to advertisers and driven by its own private agendas, there was plenty of scope in early 1950s Brazil for a wily hoaxer to make mischief, but if there is one aspect of the story that demands attention, it is the assertion that the Brazilian air force scrambled aircraft to seek out the Martians. It is an extraordinary claim, and the immediate inclination is to dismiss it as a circulation-boosting fabrication of the newspapers, but — incredibly — it may just be true. For other than suicidal presidents, a broken economy and a corrupt media, Brazil in 1954 had something else to contend with, something that was truly out this world.

Just seven years previously in America, a pilot named Kenneth Arnold had reported seeing a number of curious flying objects near Mount Rainer. He described them as saucerlike, and thus was born the term "flying saucer."* It was the beginning of the UFO age, and sightings would come thick and fast in the years that followed, not just in America, but all over the world. Brazil was no exception, and in October and November of 1954 the country was awash in stories of UFO sightings, some of them extremely compelling and many including the direct involvement of the Brazilian air force. This unprecedented surge in sightings began on October 12, 1954, when the pilot of a T-6 Texan fighter plane making a night training flight over the cities of São Leopoldo and Nova Hamburgo reported seeing a glowing orange object. Two other pilots flying in the area corroborated the sighting. That same night, members of the fire department of the city of Pelotas, Rio Grande do Sul, claimed to have witnessed a disc-shaped object moving silently at great speed in the sky, and on October 15 several witnesses spotted what seemed to be the same object over Pelotas again. There followed a brief lull in sightings, but then on October 24 the air force was forced to sit up and take notice.

In what would become known as the "Gravataí incident," personnel at Gravataí air force base in Porto Alegre, Rio Grande do Sul, watched two UFOs perform a series of astounding aerial maneuvers for two hours. The UFOs were said to be a dull white aluminum in color and were seen to zigzag through the sky and make fast, tight circular turns.[4] The sighting had an impact at a very high level in the military. Just over a week later, on November 2, Brigadier General João Adil Oliveira, chief of the Air Force General Staff Information Service, spoke in surprisingly candid terms about the UFO problem, telling a meeting at the Army War College, "The problem of 'flying discs' has polarized the attention of the whole world, but it's serious and it deserves to be treated

---

*The precise origin of the term "flying saucer" is shrouded in some controversy. Arnold made his sighting on June 24, 1947, and subsequently described the objects in a number of different ways, but primarily as saucer-like or resembling a pie plate. The term "flying saucer" entered the popular parlance a few days later, but was very likely the invention of a newspaper editor rather than something directly attributable to Arnold.

seriously. Almost all the governments of the great powers are interested in it, dealing with it in a serious and confidential manner, due to its military interest."[5]

In fact, the level of anxiety in the Brazilian military in 1954 seems to have bordered on outright paranoia. There were allegedly attempts made to cover up sightings, and the Air Defense Command supposedly started a twenty-four-hour air patrol over all military installations in the state of Rio Grande do Sul. Most tellingly, and though it was not reported in the press at the time, just two days prior to the Caratinga hoax the air force was confronted with yet another close encounter between its personnel and an object of seemingly unearthly origin. On November 20 a military plane on a regularly scheduled flight to deliver mail departed its base near the city of Uberaba, in the state of Minas Gerais destined for São Paulo. At the controls were Lieutenant A. Sobral and his copilot Lieutenant Francisco Hardy. As the plane approached the Rio Grande, Hardy's attention was drawn to a strange glow coming from an island. Lieutenant Hardy later made the following report to the São Paulo air force base command.

> I kept my eyes on the spot and watched the glow growing steadily in size as the plane closed in. Soon I saw it as a round light apparently attached to the ground, or a little above it. But a few minutes later, I realized that this light — now ten to fifteen meters in diameter — was being emitted by a glowing object landed in the island, or hovering in the air near the ground. As the plane came nearer it, I could see better through the luminous halo surrounding entirely the object. This glowing halo was chrome-yellow in color, at the center; and silvery-white at the extremities.[6]

Having become alarmed at the sight of this object, Hardy alerted Sobral, who immediately took his aircraft down in a dive toward the UFO. As if sensing their approach, the object immediately shot upwards at a steep angle, the glow about it intensifying as it launched itself into the air before disappearing rapidly toward the East. Landing an hour later at São Paulo airport, the two airmen reported their story and written accounts were sent on to Air Defense Command Headquarters at Rio, but the air force had no intention of publicizing this incendiary event, and the story only came to light several weeks later when a nosy reporter heard rumors about the encounter.

While it would be foolhardy to assume that Brigadier Oliveira spoke with authority for the very highest levels of government, a subsequent statement that he made in 1958 offers further confirmation of the military mindset on UFOs during the 1950s. Oliveira had gone on to lead the first official investigation into UFOs in Brazil, and on February 28 told the *O Globo* newspaper, "The flying saucer is not a ghost from another dimension, or a mysterious dragon. It is a fact confirmed by material evidence. There are thousands of documents, photos, and sighting reports demonstrating its existence. For instance, when I went to the AF High Command to discuss the flying saucers I called for ten witnesses — military (AF officers) and civilians — to report their evidence about the presence of flying saucers in the skies of Rio Grande do Sul, and over Gravataí AFB; some of them had seen UFOs with the naked eye, others with high powered optical instruments. For more than two hours the phenomenon was present in the sky, impressing the selected audience: officers, engineers, technicians, etc."[7]

The close involvement of the Brazilian military in responding to the hoax of 1954 is of considerable significance. We have already seen how in Ecuador, UFO stories were allegedly planted in the press to whip up hysteria prior to a broadcast of *The War of the Worlds*, but here in Brazil we are confronted with a situation in which a national government appeared in all seriousness to believe itself threatened by alien invaders, and even went so far as to take the necessary steps to confront them.* With the Rio Grande incident coming so close to the events of November 22 it seems very likely that the Brazilian air force would have been at a hair trigger to respond to any other sightings, and in these circumstances, sending planes aloft to investigate the Caratinga incident seems not only plausible but also perfectly understandable.

Pity, then, the poor civilian population. In this rarefied atmosphere of rumor, speculation and official obfuscation, they too must have been left in a state of considerable agitation, so is it really any wonder that da Silva came up with his tall tale, and that so many were willing to believe it? However, in all fairness, it must be observed in the interests of balanced analysis that the events in Caratinga are much harder to quantify than is the case with the 1938 U.S. broadcast. Who was scared, how many reacted and what exactly they did as a result cannot be easily verified. There are several contemporary newspaper accounts, one scholarly article and a lot of hearsay available to the researcher, though it is at least telling that Anor Ferreira da Silva is still known affectionately in Caratinga as "Disco Volador" (Flying Saucer).

One other crucial fact we cannot establish with any certainty is whether there was a direct connection between the events of November 22 and *The War of the Worlds*, be it the original novel or any version on radio. The novel of *The War of the Worlds* does not seem to have been available in Portuguese in the early 1950s, and it seems unlikely that anyone in Caratinga would have known of the 1938 broadcast, given that in the 1930s the town was extremely small, poor and isolated, with very little access to news from outside Brazil. It is just possible that da Silva was aware of one or more of the previous South American broadcasts, but nothing is mentioned in newspaper reports of his prank to suggest that his motivation was anything more sophisticated than boredom and a desire to have some fun. Certainly it is noteworthy that the press reported the invaders to be Martian, which if nothing else proves that Mars even in the early 1950s was still exerting a powerful influence on the public imagination.

But all this happened a long time ago and so one might be forgiven for thinking that with each passing year it would become more and more difficult to convince people to believe the impossible. Better educational standards and a greater understanding of the power of the media should make it all but impossible for such events to be triggered, yet against all common sense *The War of the Worlds* continues to challenge this presumption. It is as if the very idea of Martians taps a primordial fear deep in the human heart, triggering an instinctive reaction that bypasses all our acquired knowledge and learning, and indeed the 1950s were not yet over before the invaders would return, just as bold and just as terrifying, but this time with their sights set firmly on western Europe.

---

*The Brazilian government has not shied away from the subject of UFOs in subsequent years, and as recently as May 20, 2005, met with prominent UFO researchers to discuss a number of sightings and allowed access to formally secret files, including the events experienced in 1954.

12

THE EUROPEAN THEATER
OF OPERATIONS
Paralysis in Portugal

With a contemptuous shove in the back from a secret police inspector, Matos Maia was unceremoniously deposited back onto the streets of Lisbon. The hapless radio producer had been held for over seven hours and subjected to the sort of psychological pressures and stress techniques that are perhaps more correctly described as torture. Kicked, locked up alone, and marched relentlessly from subterranean cell to cell by implacably silent agents of the state, he had finally emerged from the gloom of the Polícia Internacional e de Defesa do Estado (PIDE, or International and State Defense Police) headquarters, frightened and relatively unscathed, though with a dire warning ringing in his ears. "If the day comes that you do something else that's 'over the Moon' you might come back here and not leave."[1]

But what precisely had Maia done to earn the ire of the infamous Portuguese secret police, the PIDE? Quite simply, he had obliterated the town of Carcavelos. Located some 12 kilometers west of Lisbon at the mouth of the Tagus River, Carcavelos is now a popular destination for surfers, but it was once a famous wine-growing region and served as an important landing point for various undersea telegraph cables. The town is still dominated by a huge 16th-century fortification, Forte de São Julião da Barra, that was originally built to defend the river mouth from enemy ships, but unfortunately on the night of June 25, 1958, the invaders came not from the sea but the sky.

Matos Maia (born 1932, died March 4, 2005) is an extremely well-regarded figure in the history of Portuguese radio. While still a 15-year-old student at a Lisbon business school he had begun writing for radio, and he was just 18 when he made his debut before the microphone at Lisbon's Rádio Peninsular. In subsequent years he went on to work at other notable stations such as Voice of Lisbon and Radiofónico Club of Portugal, making his name as a producer and director of considerable talent. Maia had a passion for police drama and procedure and produced a number of programs in this field that are considered classics of their type in Portugal, but it was his association with the Catholic broadcaster Rádio Renascença (Radio Renaissance) and his own version of *The War of the Worlds* that would be regarded as one of the defining achievements of his career.

Rádio Renascença began broadcasting from Lisbon in June 1936 and is still widely listened to today, having endured many turbulent times to become one of the most lasting and popular independent stations in Portugal.* Maia had been invited to join in 1956, and he would spend four highly successful years there, working on popular programs such as *Things That the Night Brings*, *Courtyard of Songs* and *The 23rd Hour*. In addition to police procedurals, Maia also enjoyed science fiction, and so when he came across an article about *The War of the Worlds* that included a few lines of the Howard Koch script, he was naturally inspired to emulate it in Portugal. First, though, he had to get the idea past the censors.

Getting anything creative made in 1950s Portugal was no easy matter. The country was under a brutal dictatorship, and censorship of the arts was a pervasive feature of daily life, such that Maia had to go through a number of strict bureaucratic processes to get his program on the air. First he approached the head of the station, who saw no problem with the idea but passed the question to the stations' internal state-appointed censor for a second opinion. The internal censor proved equally accommodating, but felt it prudent to let a government official give the green light. Amazingly, this hurdle was overcome, with not one iota of concern expressed as to the inherent dangers of the idea. Maia was now free to begin the work of adapting the story to suit the Portugal of 1958 and to assemble his cast, which (unusually) was not drawn exclusively from the ranks of professional radio broadcasters. Instead he cast his net wide, asking friends and colleagues if they could recommend relatives with the right kind of voices for the roles: loud commanding tones for the army personnel, and slower, more authoritative ones for members of the government.

Luckily the broadcast and script has survived in its entirety, and it is a very close adaptation of the Howard Koch script. In fact, it is almost identical in most respects, with just the names of places and characters changed in many instances. The program began at approximately 8:05 P.M. with a clear announcement of the station's intentions. The *Diário de Lisboa* newspaper of June 26 reported the opening words. "Dear listeners, we will now transmit a radio adaptation of the famous play *The War of the Worlds*, by none other than the famous English novelist Herbert George Wells. We ask that you remain calm, lend us your ear and your understanding." There follows a jaunty recording of the German violinist Helmut Zacharias playing his composition *China Boogie*, which is pre-empted at the approximate halfway point by an announcement that a Dr. Jorge da Fonseca of the observatory at Braga has witnessed a series of explosions on the surface of Mars, which he describes as looking like "a jet of blue flame fired by a weapon." It should be noted that an observatory at Braga was a complete fabrication by Maia, though the city itself is real, located some 230 miles north of Lisbon.

After this alarming announcement there is a rather long musical interlude, beginning with the well-known song "Petticoats of Portugal" by the Dick Jacobs Orchestra, followed by "O, Mein Papa," performed by the Harry James Orchestra. At just under six minutes into the broadcast, the music is interrupted by a report purporting to come from

*Rádio Renascença was closely involved in the army-led insurrection of April 25, 1974, that toppled the dictatorship in Portugal and set the country on the road to democracy. At 25 minutes past midnight, the station transmitted the song "Grandola Vila Morena," which was the cue to launch the coup.

the town of Cascais,* where Maia had located another fictional observatory. The scene now delivered from this observatory is virtually a word-for-word reenactment of the dialogue written by Howard Koch, with the reporter on the scene, here played by a friend and colleague of Maia named Alvaro de Lemos, describing the interior of the observatory and introducing a Professor Manuel Franco. Franco is of course Professor Pierson, the role taken in the original 1938 version by Orson Welles, but here played by Artur Mourato. Adding to the sense of déjà vu, the scene even retains the "tick-tock" sound of the telescope mechanism.

The sequence of events continues to follow closely those laid out by Howard Koch, with further bulletins arriving about a meteor that has crashed near Carcavelos. Also as was done in 1938, the passage of time is severely compacted, with de Lemos and the professor improbably on the scene at Carcavelos in a matter of moments, though the trip is claimed to have taken seven minutes. Here at just over 12 minutes into the broadcast, de Lemos and the professor discover a throng of excited onlookers, and we are provided with the first description of a Martian cylinder, which, mimicking the Koch script, has come to rest on a farm. The owner, a Mr. Jacinto Simões, is brought before the microphone and gives his nervous account of the impact, but then the plot deviates slightly from the Koch version with the arrival of another professor. Maia plays this new character, though the role is slim and adds nothing new of significance to the plot, so it should probably

Carcavelos in Portugal, the landing site of the Martians in 1958 (from the collection of Celestino Domingos).

*Cascais has been a popular beach resort for many years, and since Portugal was neutral during World War II, the town became a refuge for many European exiles. The town boasts several churches, a museum housed in the ornate Palácio de Conde de Castro Guimarães and a 16th-century fortress that was built to defend the bay of Cascais against invasion.

Cascais. Vista Parcial.

Cascais, where the writer Matos Maia located a fictional observatory for his Portuguese version of *The War of the Worlds* (from the collection of Celestino Domingos).

be thought of as a Hitchcock-like cameo. After some updated references to the arrival of a television crew, the narrative again picks up the Koch story line with the terrifying emergence of the Martians and their first use of the "heat-ray" to incinerate a peace delegation. In the confusion of exploding petrol tanks and panicked onlookers, the connection with Carcavelos is broken and listeners are left to agonize over the implications. Have they just heard the beginning of the end of the world?

It is now some 21 minutes into the broadcast, and while attempts are made to reconnect to Carcavelos, a news story is received from America, reporting that a Professor Carl Pierson of the Astronomical Society of California has dismissed the explosions on Mars as nothing more than volcanic eruptions. Much the same report was featured in the 1938 version of the broadcast, though in a polite nod to the source material, the professor's name is of course an amalgamation of Professor Pierson and Carl Phillips, the characters played by Orson Welles and Frank Readick.

With the grim news arriving from Carcavelos that there have been some 40 fatalities at the hands of the heat-ray, the station turns the microphone over to Colonel Brás da Cunha, the commanding general responsible for the defense of the area. Wasting no time, he informs the listening public that the army is mobilizing and that the towns of Carcavelos, Oeiras, Santo Amaro and Parede are now under martial law. Hot on the heels of this news comes word that communications have been restored with Professor Franco, who delivers his judgment on the armaments of the Martians. At this point it is announced that the charred body of Alvaro de Lemos has been discovered and that the station is turning over its broadcasting facilities to the authorities.

Some 35 minutes into the broadcast, an intriguing divergence from the Koch script comes about. In the original script, listeners are next patched into army communications as the first attack by a Martian tripod is mounted, but before Portuguese listeners can hear this, Maia inserts a rather clever sequence completely unique to his script. A report purporting to be from Britain is relayed to listeners. It seems likely that the intention was to make it seem as if it were from the BBC, though the script refers to the sender as the BCC. It is impossible to tell if this was an error in the script, or intentional. Perhaps, as with CBS in 1938, there was concern that a real institution like the BBC might have taken offense at having its good name used without permission. The dialogue is delivered in quaintly broken English and is heavily interrupted by faux interference so bad that at times the dialogue becomes almost unintelligible.

> London calling. London calling. This is BCC speaking in direct transmission through the broadcasting station Rádio Renascença. During the last 24 hours, many strange incidents of unknown and unidentified origin have taken place in different parts of Great Britain. Strange cylindrical machines have fallen in different parts of the country spreading terror and desolation and causing a great number of deaths. According to official statistics, more than 5,000 persons have succumbed, victims of a strange and deathly smoke expelled by these machines. The situation in the whole country is terribly serious and the Government is elaborating a detailed program of defense, and the areas attacked by the strange enemies are being isolated from the territories. Martial law was proclaimed in the country. Many of these strange machines were noted in the different parts of London. The enemy has practically conquered the regions of Essex and Kent. On its way the enemy has razed almost everything to the ground including houses and fields and caused a considerable number of deaths. The general situation in England is one of authentic terror. Many pathetic scenes were evidenced and numerous cases of suicides were recorded on account of the fear, which these machines have spread. Here, Portuguese listeners, we end our news program. Finally, there is nothing that we can do except follow the situation with the greatest possible calm and place our entire trust in His Divine Mercy. Let us place our faith in God. In Him lies our only possible salvation. Have mercy on us. Good night ladies and gentlemen. BCC calling from London. Attention, Lisbon! Attention Rádio Renascença! Attention Lisbon.[2]

Transmitting a long report in English shows a deft touch by Maia, as to hear something from faraway England and from a broadcaster seemingly posing as the BBC imparted an element of trustworthiness to the statement. One can also easily imagine many listeners straining to understand and perhaps picking out a few frighteningly familiar words or phrases, but for those unable to understand completely, Maia then cleverly follows up with a summary of the report in Portuguese.

With this remarkable detour complete Maia returns again to the Koch script, picking up proceedings some 41 minutes into the broadcast with the news of a terrible massacre at Carcavelos. Up to 2,000 men lie dead at the hands of the Martians, who are now cutting off lines of communication and cementing their control of the region. The roads from Lisbon are said to be choked with hysterical refugees, and with civil order at risk, the station transmits an urgent call for calm. In the original broadcast in 1938 this was one of the key flashpoints, as the actor Kenny Delmar circumnavigated the instructions of the censor to change his character from the president of the United States to a fictional secretary of the interior. Delmar did as he was told, though no one told him he couldn't make his secretary of the interior sound just like Roosevelt. Given that Portugal was in the grip of a brutal dictatorship at the time, it would probably have been nothing short of suicidal to try the same thing and mimic the voice of the dictator, President António de Oliveira Salazar. Even so, in a severely oppressed and controlled society used to taking seriously any pronouncement from the authorities, it is likely that the words of the fictional Secretário das Relações Interiores (secretary of interior relations) would have carried considerable weight with listeners.

The remainder of the script deviates very little from the Howard Koch version, except for the further localization of place-names. For instance, at the culmination of their attack on Lisbon, the Martian tripods wade across the Tagus River rather than the Hudson. Just as in the original 1938 version, this is a particularly harrowing sequence, as the reporter describes the drama and panic on Marquês de Pombal Square. Sirens wail, boat whistles hoot, and faintly heard in the background are the words of a hymn being sung by the huddled masses awaiting their fate. As the Martians' black poison gas sweeps through the streets, the reporter's words are abruptly choked off 55 minutes into the broadcast. The script then switches perspective as did the Howard Koch version to a far more conventional drama, with Professor Franco traveling across the devastated countryside in search of survivors. The story concludes with the Martians succumbing to the bacteria of the Earth, and a calmer professor Franco reflecting wistfully on events, though Maia does add one rather intriguing final line that was not in the original. What was he thinking, one can only wonder, when he wrote, "And strange to think that all this can happen ... can happen again!"

As it transpired, this was a somewhat prophetic thing to say, because on the night of June 25, 1958, it really was happening all over again, as seems clear from the avalanche of indignant front-page headlines and editorials published in newspapers the following morning. Typical was the *Jornal de Notícias*, which proclaimed the program "diabolical." And under the headline "A PROGRAM THAT CAUSED ALARM" the *Diário de Lisboa* went on to describe in positively poetic detail the reaction of listeners:

> We are at war!—A pale villager cried with emotion.
> No! It's worse than that ... it's the end of the world! ... The end of everything and everyone! Earth is being invaded by Martians.

Alas, these wonderfully colorful quotes are unattributed, and one can detect a degree of artistic license in the reporting, though the sentiment seems perfectly sound. Lisbon does indeed appear to have been in a veritable uproar that night. The *Diário de Lisboa* of June 26 spoke of emergency services swamped with calls, with police and firefighters on the receiving end of many frantic inquiries, while "courageous men rushed to offer to help the Red Cross." The Rádio Renascença switchboard was under no less a strain, with calls coming in from all quarters, including one from the French Press Agency (Agence France-Presse) asking where Quinta das Conchas was (a suburb of Lisbon where professor Franco seeks refuge) as they had dispatched a reporter there. Meanwhile, from the Public Security Police (PSP) and National Republican Guard (who have a civilian police role) came calls demanding an explanation, but what happened next is truly unique in the history of these broadcasts. As the broadcast continued and the calls mounted up, Maia was summoned twice to the phone to speak to an angry individual who claimed to be a captain of the PSP. The captain ordered that the transmission be halted or he would put Maia in prison, but Maia and his colleagues were not sure the caller was genuine, so they decided to call his bluff. This would prove a grave mistake. A commanding officer and three subordinates armed with guns were duly dispatched to the station and Maia was summarily detained. The broadcast, which had been scheduled to end at 11:15 P.M., was according to the *Diário de Lisboa* abruptly terminated at 9:45 P.M. "The infernal noise of the machines stopped suddenly" to be replaced by recorded music. Of course in reality, the noise of the "infernal machines" had long since stopped and the worst of the damage had been done, since the first and by far the most disturbing "act" of the play had already concluded. As for the unfortunate Maia, he was, in his own words, "...locked in a cell like a vulgar vagabond for about 3 hours."[3]

Maia had suffered badly for his art, but he had undoubtedly created an extraordinary production, as the heated response of the public, newspapers and authorities aptly demonstrates. This is hardly surprising, as Maia and his colleagues went to great lengths to fashion the perfect aural experience. That process took just over 11 months, from the moment Maia first put pen to paper to the night of transmission, with the search for exactly the right sounds and ambience taking them all over Lisbon. On one memorable occasion, burdened down with a portable recorder weighing some 50 pounds, Maia and his team took a late-night trip to the famous Lisbon park known as the Parque Florestal de Monsanto. Here they were able to give full fury to the dialogue needed for the dramatic scene in which the Martians are confronted by artillery defending the city of Vila Nova da Gaia. This is a particularly effective sequence, actually sounding much more raw and visceral than the rather unemotional delivery of the lines in the 1938 version. It is not hard to imagine Maia and his colleagues shouting out the dialogue with great gusto and abandon in the middle of the empty park.

On another occasion, showing a distinct flair for original thinking, Maia threw a New Year's Eve party at Casa do Algarve, a famous nightspot that happened to be just yards away from the Rádio Renascença studios. Maia recorded the boisterous crowd there and incorporated the recordings into his production, though it must be said that these crowd scenes are perhaps the weakest aspect of the production. It is perhaps easy to say this in hindsight, but the venue of the recording is betrayed by its tinny and echoing nature, and the tedious looping of the recording is monotonously irritating. In truth, the partygoers never sound particularly terrified, even when the Martian heat-ray lashes out.

Most bizarrely of all in his search for suitable sound effects, Maia and his soundman Moreno Pinto inveigled an invitation from Paramount Films to attend a screening of its stunning 1953 version of *The War of the Worlds*, taking along a tape recorder! This is the sort of thing that would get a person arrested in this day and age, and it is certainly interesting to speculate whether Paramount was aware of Maia's intentions, but he and Pinto somehow came away with a sound recording of the film. Amazingly, some of this material seems to have made its way into the recording, for the distinctive sound of the Martian war machines (created for the movie by manipulating feedback from electric guitars) can be clearly heard in Maia's broadcast.

So how did a radio play with sound effects borrowed from a movie cause listeners to react with terror? According to the *Diário de Lisboa* of June 26, the broadcast was repeatedly interrupted with disclaimers as to the nature of the program; upwards of once every 10 minutes, so there should have been little excuse for listeners to have taken the story at face value, though it should be noted that no such comments can be heard in the surviving recording until the very closing minutes. Perhaps they were issued originally but have since been lost, though their absence certainly calls into question the accuracy of *Diário de Lisboa* in this regard and how much was actually done during the broadcast to limit misunderstandings. However, it should be noted that apart from the key locations and street names, Maia had fictionalized names and institutions, so in that sense he had tried his best to ensure that the story had the clear trappings of a drama. There also seems to be no indication that people tuned in late in great numbers, nor was the country facing any particular external threats at the time. As to the broadcast itself, while it is difficult for this writer to judge the relative merits of a production delivered in Portuguese and how closely Maia succeeded in duplicating the prevailing style of news broadcasts at the time, the production values are clearly not quite as polished as the 1938 version and for the most part the dialogue is delivered in a noticeably unemotional tone. It is however important to emphasize that Maia may have succeeded all too well in mirroring the style of delivery then in vogue, which would have been diconcerting to listeners. But if we are unable to positively pinpoint one of the more generally accepted reasons behind a scare of this nature, can we, as in Brazil in 1954, find some specific localized reason to explain the extreme reaction of listeners?

The answer this time may lie primarily with religion. As has already been noted, Rádio Renascença was owned and operated by the Catholic Church. At the time Catholicism was enjoying a considerable resurgence in power and influence in Brazil, but it had not always enjoyed the protection and support of the state. In 1834 and again in 1908, monasteries throughout the country were closed, held to account for perceived abuses of power by successive liberal and republican governments with a strong anticlerical agenda. But with the rise to power of the dictator António de Oliveira Salazar, the Church once again found itself in the ascendancy. Salazar had trained for the priesthood, even sharing lodgings with Dom Manuel Cerejeira, who would later become cardinal-patriarch of Lisbon, but the lure of politics proved too much for Salazar and in 1928 he assumed control of a regime that would endure for 40 years.

Salazar was a shrewd politician, and with the full cooperation of the Church he set out to maintain a harsh and disciplinary control of the peasant population. Most tellingly, both church and state (though equally wary of each other) seized on an event with enormous religious resonance to help cement the control they both craved. This has become known throughout the world as the miracle at Fátima, and it seems entirely likely that in promoting this event and the apocalyptic connotations that went with it, Salazar and the church inadvertently sowed the seeds for the terror that would engulf Lisbon in 1958.

Fátima is itself a textbook example of a mass delusion, and has even been co-opted by some in the UFO movement as an example of an alien visitation rather than a religious experience. The controversial events began on May 13, 1917, in the town of Fátima, located some 80 miles north of Lisbon. Three young children claimed to have witnessed a vision of the Virgin Mary who revealed to them three secrets, one of which was mysteriously kept under lock and key by the Vatican until June 2000.* The third secret turned out to be a rather mundane call for religious devotion, though the first was a typically lurid vision of hell, replete with fire and brimstone. Others have reinterpreted the children's vision of the Virgin Mary as, not a religious figure, but an alien being suspended in a beam of light beneath a flying saucer, and while this is a fairly recent invention by some UFO investigators, it is not hard to see how Maia's *War of the Worlds* could have tapped into the cult that grew around Fátima. This seems especially likely when one considers what is said to have happened at Fátima on the afternoon of October 13, 1917, when, as apparently predicted by the children and promised by the apparitition of the Virgin Mary, a miracle was performed. In front of a crowd variously estimated as between 40,000 and 100,000 persons, the Sun was seen to dance in the sky, change color and rotate like a wheel. Photographs famously show the crowd staring up at this terrifying spectacle, though there is little in the way of quantifiable evidence to explain what people saw, or thought they saw, that afternoon.

But be it mass delusion, freak atmospheric effect or even genuine religious experience, the fact remains that Fátima was a state-sanctioned miracle, as David Birmingham commented in his book *A Concise History of Portugal*: "The church encouraged the hysterical dimensions of religious practice to the detriment of more thoughtful forms of worship and the regime adopted Fátima as its own national shrine with a huge basilica."[4] Imagine a typically pious parishioner tuning into Maia's drama and hearing that the world was coming to an end, and that, worse still, the news was being delivered by a Catholic radio station! For some, it must have seemed like a direct radio message from the almighty. This connection between religious fervor and Maia's *War of the Worlds* is no better illustrated than by the choice of words used by the *Diário de Lisboa* of June 26 to describe a listener's feelings. "Was Rádio Renascença transmitting the Apocalypse, with cries of terror and monstrous visions?"

Arriving under arrest that evening at the National Guard office, Maia witnessed the chaos he had caused. The office was completely jammed with long lines of people, some of whom he overheard saying they had seen the fires in Carvavelos. It was the beginning of a very unpleasant week for Maia, culminating in his summons by the Polícia Internacional e de Defesa do Estado (PIDE). The next morning, many newspapers denounced Rádio Renascença. Calls continued to be received for several days (some, at least, were congratulatory in nature), and there was even an attempt to organize a listener boycott of the station. Rádio Renascença duly issued a rather sullen apology, reported in *Diário de Lisboa* of June 26. The station complained to those who had been frightened that their "distress was just as unreasonable as it was unpredictable." For Maia the worst was yet to come.

The PIDE was created under the direct orders of Salazar and was the main tool of repression in Portugal for almost 30 years. It was headquartered in a building on António Maria Cardoso Street, a place with a horrifying reputation as a torture center. About

---

*Conspiracy theorists maintain that the Vatican has not actually released the real text of the third secret, as it contains portents thought too dangerous for public consumption.

a week after the broadcast, Maia found himself seated before an unsmiling PIDE agent called Ferreira da Costa. It must have been an incredibly unnerving experience. Da Costa was well briefed, even producing documents detailing the story of the 1938 *War of the Worlds* broadcast, but though after an intensive interrogation Maia was eventually released unharmed, there was a price to pay. He was given two days to produce a detailed list of all those who had taken part in the broadcast: their names, addresses, home and work phone numbers. Fearing for their safety, Maia reluctantly handed over the list, but time passed and no further retribution was forthcoming. Maia and his colleagues had dodged the bullet, figuratively and perhaps literally, though Maia was convinced that if not for the fact that the broadcast had emanated from a Catholic station, the situation would have been far grimmer. Certainly he had attracted some very unwelcome attention, for a few weeks later Maia was to learn from reliable sources that it was none other than Salazar himself who had given the order for his arrest.

13

"IT'S NOT A METEOR, HENRY"

The Second American Campaign

America, October 1968. Three decades have passed since the original *War of the Worlds* broadcast, plenty of time for memories to fade, bruised egos to heal and complacency to grow. After all, how could it possibly happen again? People are not nearly so naive and America is a superpower, well able to defend itself against any foreign invaders, no matter how real or imaginary they might be. Though if the evidence is to be believed, imaginary is precisely what the Martians have always been. In 1965 *Mariner 4* had hurtled past Mars, a fleeting encounter that returned 22 grainy black-and-white pictures, dispelling at a stroke the romantic notion of a world criss-crossed with canals. Mars was finally losing its luster in the public imagination, but radio too had slipped from its throne, elbowed brusquely aside by a brash new interloper.

That usurper was of course, television. By 1968,[1] 95 percent of American homes owned at least one TV set. Radio had endured a long period of painful change and retrenchment. The great radio stars either switched successfully to television or faded into obscurity, while radio drama, that theatre of the imagination and experimental wonderland for so many great talents, was virtually extinct. As the historian, actor, and broadcaster Studs Turkel lamented, "There were never couch potatoes in radio, only television. TV feeds the viewer everything. There is no need to engage the mind. Radio piqued the imagination. It was far more challenging and full of discovery. The wonderful world was lost when television ambled in."[2] Yet perhaps it was precisely because imaginations had become dulled that Americans in October 1968 were ready to believe again in Martian invaders. What Welles had mischievously called "that grinning, glowing, globular invader" was poised once more to leap from the pumpkin patch.

The station behind this latest Halloween scare was called WKBW.* Located in Buffalo, New York, in the county of Erie, it was founded in 1926 by Dr. Clinton H. Churchill as a broadcaster of religious programming. In 1968 WKBW was a powerful 24-hour AM station playing rock and roll and other popular music across Buffalo and a huge swath of America and Canada, such that it could boast to serving 17 states and two countries. In the right atmospheric conditions, the 50,000-watt signal had even been said to travel as far afield as Ireland and Morocco.

WKBW was not at all averse to playing practical jokes on its listeners. The previous year the entire on-air staff had secretly changed places with their counterparts at

---

*Founder Dr. Churchill is said to have proclaimed that the station call sign WKBW should stand for Well Known Bible Works (or alternatively Well Known Bible Witness), but as the station reinvented itself, the letters KB later came to stand for King of Buffalo, in reference to its powerful 50,000-watt transmitter.

WPOP as an April Fools' Day prank, and in 1969 WKBW would run an hour-long Halloween program that capitalized on the infamous urban legend that Beatle member Paul McCartney had died and been replaced by a lookalike. For the 30th anniversary of the Mercury Theatre broadcast in 1968 it seemed like a sure-fire idea to reimagine *The War of the Worlds*, updating the story with modern music and utilizing WKBW's patented "rock and roll radio news" format of bombastic, fast-paced delivery. Though the station transmitter was located in Buffalo, the majority of the events portrayed in the broadcast were to take place northwest of the city, primarily in and around Grand Island. It is here that the Niagara River splits in two to form a large island of some 33 square miles in area, before flowing west to Niagara Falls. The population at the time was some 10,000 persons* but with the immense broadcasting power and range of WKBW, the shock waves from this latest invasion would reverberate far beyond their shores.

It all began at 11 P.M. on Thursday, October 31, with a dramatic announcement from morning show regular Dan Neaverth. "Ladies and gentlemen of eastern America and Canada, WKBW Radio in Buffalo presents our adaptation of H. G. Wells' *War of the Worlds*, a dramatization." This was followed immediately by a real news report from Joe Downey at the WKBW Total News Department, with nothing obviously phony that might tip off unwary listeners. This is hardly surprising, as Downey was a familiar news

Grand Island was the location of the second Martian invasion of the United States (Grand Island Chamber of Commerce).

*Census figures put the 1960 population of Grand Island at 9,607. The 1970 population was 13,977.

personality, as in fact were all the reporters conspicuously mentioned throughout the drama. Not only is Downey a thoroughly trusted voice, he is also reading the real regularly scheduled 11 P.M. news bulletin. The top story of the night was the announcement by President Johnson of a cessation of the Vietnam bombing campaign known as Operation Rolling Thunder.

Local stories follow, with several minor holdups reported at service stations and a police raid on a local taxi firm where arrests were made for illegal gambling but, as in every news program the world over, the final minutes are reserved for something lighthearted and frivolous. It is therefore unlikely that anyone would have been particularly perturbed at the last item in Downey's report, as without the slightest hint of pretense he explains that for the past two nights astronomers at the Palomar Observatory have been observing enormous explosions on the surface of Mars. He further notes that observatory director Benjamin Spencer (a fictional character) has described the blasts as looking like "tremendous jets of blue flame shooting out into space"; but though they appear to have "as much energy as hydrogen bomb blasts," the professor has assured the public that "they are undoubtedly of natural origin" and therefore "not likely to have any effect on the earth."

Following an ad for the Peace Corps and a weather forecast, listeners are handed over to DJ Sandy Beach, another WKBW stalwart, who makes a disarming wisecrack that perhaps the "blue flames" are a publicity stunt by the gas company. He then spins his first song of the evening, "Eleanor" by the Turtles.* (In a significant deviation from the snippets of music used on the Mercury Theatre broadcast, the song is played in its entirety.) So far this *War of the Worlds* broadcast couldn't be more laid back. Some eight minutes into the drama comes an advertisement for the One Stop Tape Center. For those listening attentively the dramatic nature of the story is clearly signposted, as the store is credited as a sponsor of the show, but then another piece of unusual news intrudes.

Beach is handed a news flash, which he casually reads. "NASA tonight alerted all space watch facilities to expect unusual observations and communications difficulties." Nothing very alarming, it seems, so Beach makes another comic quip and without further preamble plays "White Room" by Cream. But this next song doesn't make it all the way through. A few minutes later it is interrupted by a dramatic piece of breaking news. "KB Commuter Call. Traffic condition red. All available firefighting equipment is rushing to Grand Island, where an explosion has set off a series of fires. Traffic on the Grand Island bridges has been halted. All onlookers and motorists are asked to stay clear of the area. That's traffic condition red on Grand Island."

Despite this rather ominous news Beach plays the remainder of "White Room" and his mood remains lighthearted when he returns to the mike, with no comment on the Grand Island fire, which must have been particularly frustrating to listeners. After another advertisement and a further prominent announcement that people are listening to a dramatization, Beach asks that listeners please stop calling the news department about the "Mars thing and the sunspots" as the phones can't handle the load. Of course, no such calls were arriving and this was just a clever part of the subterfuge, though given human nature, it

---

*Can it be entirely coincidental that the Turtles started out as a band called "Crossfires from the Planet Mars"?

wouldn't be at all surprising if an entreaty not to call had the exact opposite effect. The next song is "Hey Jude" by the Beatles, but the pace of events is quickening and at just under 16 minutes into the broadcast the newsroom breaks in with an earth-shattering announcement. "It has been reported that a large meteor has smashed into the ground along the East River Road on Grand Island setting off a series of fires. Several lives have been lost. KB Total News director Don Lanser on the way to the scene. Repeating, a large meteor is reported to have smashed into the ground on Grand Island killing several people and touching off several fires."

After a brief reprise of "Hey Jude," Beach returns to the mike and, sounding slightly rattled, now urges listeners to stay away from Grand Island, as spectators will only hinder the emergency services. His show is now suffering one spectacular interruption after another, but he does a superb job of appearing to be coping valiantly with each unexpected turn of events. Reporter Henry Brock is next on the air with a brief report that a meteor may indeed have struck in the vicinity of Grand Island Boulevard and that Don Lancer will be reporting from the scene. With a masterful use of understatement, Beach observes that playing another song, "seems a little frivolous at this time" and indeed Buffy Saint-Marie has barely begun to sing "I'm Gonna Be a Country Girl Again" before Lancer is piped in. He is still on his way to the scene, but reports massive traffic jams around the South Grand Island Bridge. Again listeners are urged to stay clear of the area and Lancer reports that an orange glow is visible on the island.

This is clearly developing into a crisis of unprecedented proportions, such that Beach is interrupted with the announcement that from this moment onwards the newsroom will be providing continuous coverage of events. On that alarming note he signs off to the sound of chaotic preparations in the newsroom. Someone is heard to call, "Are you ready with that mike for the newsroom? You all set? Communications hot." With more hectic activity audible in the background, Joe Downey reports that the entire news department has been mobilized to report on the unfolding drama.

Contact is briefly established with the Erie County Sheriff's Office, which can add no new information. Mobile reporter Jim Fagan is next to call in. He had been at Niagara University to interview Professor Robert Moore of the astronomy department (a fictional character) about the explosions on Mars, but with the situation developing on Grand Island, he and the professor are now en route to the island, presently heading south on the Robert Moses Parkway. Fagan asks the professor if there might be a link between what has been happening on Mars and the meteor impact on Grand Island, but the professor offers his firm opinion that there is no such connection.

Listeners must have been thoroughly caught up in events by this stage. The news is delivered raw and uncensored: reports are miscued, connections are filled with static and the reporters seem to be struggling to comprehend what is happening. Grand Island is virtually cut off and mobile news teams are having trouble penetrating to the center of the disturbance. In a simple but brilliant touch, the radio mikes appear to have been left open and listeners hear the private discussions of the reporters as they try to work out the best approach to reach the island. News comes in that Governor Nelson Rockefeller is mobilizing the National Guard, and then Jim Fagan calls in with a report from much closer to the epicenter. Houses have been leveled, and there is a huge hubbub as survivors and rescue workers mill about. Fagan describes a large hole in the ground but says the police are not letting him any closer. As Jeff Kaye in the newsroom tries to summarize the situation for listeners, we can hear a clearly agitated Don Lancer calling in and insisting he be put on the air. His next words, perfectly delivered with a hesitant undertone of uncertainty, must have put a chill down the back of many listeners. "It's not a meteor, Henry."

If not a meteor, then what? Lancer tries to explain what he can see from the edge of the crater and is able to describe a huge cylindrical object wreathed in clouds of steam before words fail him. But he doesn't need to describe everything in detail to alarm his listeners, because they can hear something too, a steady high-pitched whine emanating from the crater that will become the signature note of events for the next half hour. It is now some 33 minutes into the broadcast, and as Lancer retreats from the crater an ominous crash is heard and his signal is abruptly cut off. Frantic attempts to reconnect him fail, nor can the newsroom reach Jim Fagan, who has also arrived in the vicinity of the crater. Now, at this most inopportune of times, the sponsors must be acknowledged.

The jarring intrusion of commerce at this vital juncture could so easily have shattered the carefully built illusion, but in a clever piece of scripting we hear a frantic voice call out, "Take a spot." WKBW may have just lost one or more of its reporters, and what the newsroom desperately needs now is time to catch its breath and find out what has happened. In that context, any pretext to get off the air makes perfect sense, and the tension is ratcheted up another excruciating notch as listeners are forced to endure the maddening banality of another advertisement for the One Stop Tape Center.

Back on the air finally and an anxious voice from the newsroom demands, "What the hell happened to Don?" doubtless articulating a question that must have been on many minds that night. Thankfully, contact is reestablished with Jim Fagan and the answer is soon forthcoming. Looking across the crater he is able to report that he can see his colleague. The unstable crater edge had collapsed and Lancer had simply toppled over the side, but he has managed to clamber out safely and, except for some burns, is otherwise unhurt. Listening in on the conversation between Fagan and a somewhat shaken Lancer, we begin to build a clearer picture of the object in the crater, a great curved projectile with a silvery sheen that continues to emit that unearthly ear-piercing shriek. Fagan has the better view of the object and is the first to spot the crack in the hull. Then pandemonium breaks out, as what he first mistakes as cables spilling from the crack are revealed as living, moving tentacles.

Closely mirroring the description of the Martians in the original novel, the first hideous creature clambers slowly into view as Fagan and Lancer report on events in increasingly hysterical terms. As Fagan describes events, Professor Moore and an army lieutenant approach the crater with a white flag, but to his horror they are both struck by a red heat-ray and burst instantly into flames. The ray now sweeps out across the scene, striking down dozens of people. From the opposite side of the crater, Don Lancer can only report with horror that the fleeing figure of Fagan has also been cut down.

Back in the shell-shocked newsroom, word is starting to come in of other landings both in the United States and Canada, with rumored impacts in Toronto, Oshawa, Erie, Pittsburgh, the Finger Lakes area, Bradford and Dunkirk. Meanwhile Don Lancer has retreated to a sheriff's command post that he hopes is out of range of the heat-ray and is witness to a dramatic missile attack by air force jets. It's a bravado piece of radio, with Lancer competing to be heard over the sound of passing jet aircraft and the violent concussion of the explosions. But the attack has no effect other than to stir up a hornet's nest in the crater, as from the midst of the smoke and flame strides a Martian tripod.

Within seconds the Martian war machine has nonchalantly swatted aside everything in the air with its heat-ray, and Lancer hastily abandons his position as the tripod moves rapidly in his direction. In the newsroom, voices now betray a palpable edge of fear and helplessness as news continues to flood in and a definite connection is established between the explosions on Mars and the invaders. Quite closely following the Howard Koch script at this point, it is reported that over 1,000 service personnel have been wiped out by the Martians, either incinerated by the heat-ray or trampled underfoot by the tripod. The news that the charred body of Jim Fagan has been found among the dead is simply one more terrifying statistic to be added to the tally. There is no time to mourn as reports of death and destruction overwhelm the newsroom.

John Irvine, a reporter from WKBW-TV, next makes contact. He has reached the river but is unable to cross over to Grand Island as the bridges have been sealed off by the military. Irvine reports a huge influx of artillery pieces massing around River Road, and that soldiers appear to be mining the closest bridge. What follows next paints a breathtaking sound picture. Irvine plays his part with heart-rending believability, his voice trembling with terror and disbelief, as first one and then another of the bridges to Grand Island is demolished by the military. Many helpless civilians are either tossed into the raging waters or choose to jump, and Irvine struggles to maintain his composure as he describes the terrible calamity and desperation unfolding before his eyes. But as we are about to discover, the destruction of the bridges will prove an act of appalling futility.

Don Lancer has miraculously survived. Crossing seconds ahead of the demolition to his new vantage point, he is able to describe the tripods wading unperturbed into the river. For a moment there is a glimmer of hope as the massed artillery fires in unison and brings down one of the tripods, but then Lancer reports on a great cloud of black smoke that the remaining tripods have begun to disgorge. Too late he realizes that the Martians are using poison gas. It is destined to be his final report as the advancing gas chokes off his words.

The news is now relentlessly grim. The tripods appear to be doing their best to destroy any means of communication, ripping up railway lines and punching holes in highways, while still others are reported advancing on many fronts. Dunkirk is said to be deserted and the newsroom staff are abandoning their posts and trying to reach their families. WKBW-TV anchor Irv Weinstein is now the "last surviving" reporter in Buffalo and has holed up in the communication center in City Hall. As tripods ring the city, he and Jeff Kaye tally their colleagues' death toll on two-way radios. As they talk, the eerie screeching sound of the Martians intrudes and Kaye comes to realize that as a communications hub, City Hall is a likely target. Kaye implores Weinstein to leave, but it is too late and City Hall is knocked off the air.

Kaye realizes he is now the only surviving newsman on the air, and shows every sign of cracking under the immense strain. Taking a mobile microphone with him, he descends to street level and paints a vivid picture of streets choked with abandoned cars. "It looks like a used car lot," he laughs hysterically, as the power fails and in the distance comes the sound of explosions and the terrible keening drone of the Martians. And then in a significant departure from the 1938 broadcast and the original novel, WKBW abruptly ends its drama on this desperately morbid note, with Kaye facing a lonely death in the street as the lights go out in America, literally and figuratively.

Dan Neaverth then returns to the air, asking listeners to imagine how they might react in a real alien invasion. He also explains that in the original novel the Martians are defeated, but this tacked-on epilogue does nothing to detract from what was an extraordinary 110 minutes. As a loving homage to the original 1938 broadcast, WKBW's version had more than lived up to the high bar set by the Mercury Theatre, and it might even be fair to say that in some ways they surpassed it. Even today and forearmed with the knowledge that one is listening to a drama, this disturbing production has the power to shock and unnerve, though it appears this was nothing compared to the upset visited upon listeners on the actual night of the broadcast.

It was program director Jeff Kaye who wrote the extraordinary script, with able technical assistance from engineer director Dan Kriegler, whose spectacular sound effects did so much to bring events to life. With the 30th anniversary of the Orson Welles broadcast approaching, Kaye had harbored ambitions to simply rebroadcast the original Mercury Theatre production, but he was unable to find a complete copy of the show. His next thought was to reenact the Howard Koch script word for word, but CBS refused him permission, so he made the decision to completely reimagine the story using a cast he drew from the WKBW newsroom.

Unfortunately, rehearsals revealed a serious flaw in this plan; the newsmen did not sound at all convincing when asked to stick to the scripted dialogue. So Kaye rewrote the script again, shifting the action from the sort of small, rural New Jersey community envisaged by Howard Koch to Grand Island, a larger and better-known location for both his news team and listeners. He also threw away much of the scripted dialogue, taking advantage of the one undoubted quality his inexperienced actors could bring to the production: the ability to think fast on their feet.

Now, rather than ask them to read stiffly from a script, he simply gave them a basic idea of what he wanted to happen next in a scene and a cue to start. Free to ad lib, the cast members now brought an unparalleled degree of realism to their work, and to their considerable credit they really do sound as if events are unfolding before their very eyes. The realism even went so far as to have Jim Fagan and other newsmen record their parts from news cruisers parked outside the station, with the added pops, hisses and squelches of the transmission adding immeasurably to the suspenseful quality of the drama.

Dan Kriegler deserves considerable credit for crafting the extraordinary sound texture of the WKBW broadcast, which was a carefully honed mix of live and recorded material. The initial 11 P.M. news summary which kicked off the broadcast was delivered live, as was the contribution of DJ Sandy Beach, whose regular program was scheduled directly after the news, but other portions of the broadcast were pre-recorded, or (in the case of many sound effects) actually incorporated live on air by Kriegler as the script demanded. This approach was quite deliberate, as the sound recording equipment of the time was still relatively primitive by modern standards, and Kriegler wanted to avoid the diminishing sound quality introduced by each successive generation of tape.

Something Kaye and Kriegler also wanted to avoid was another scare, so great care was taken to ensure that no one would be taken by surprise. The *War of the Worlds* broadcast was actually scheduled to be the culmination of a night of spooky Halloween programming, with Jeff Kaye and Dan Neaverth narrating a number of classic tales throughout the evening, including Edgar Allan Poe's "Tell Tale Heart" and Washington Irving's "Legend of Sleepy Hollow." The evening was extremely well publicized, both on WKBW and in the local press. The *Buffalo Evening News* prominently headlined the events in its radio and TV news page of October 31 and letters about *The War of the Worlds* were sent out on three separate occasions to the police, fire services and civil defense members of eight surrounding counties. Speaking in 1998 on Buffalo television reporter Bob Koshinski's WNED-TV documentary about the broadcast, Kaye recalls, perhaps with tongue slightly in cheek, that they even visited streets on Grand Island where the broadcast was to be set and bought the residents pizza.[3] But all the free pizza in the world was to prove futile, and as the broadcast picked up speed and intensity, so the inevitable frightened calls began.

As Kaye began to realize the gravity of the situation, an astoundingly familiar tableau was playing out in the control room. In 1938 John Houseman had physically prevented CBS producer Davidson Taylor from interrupting the broadcast to issue a disclaimer. In 1968 Jeff Kaye confronted Dan Kriegler in much the same way, with Kriegler determined that the show must go on and Kaye equally adamant that there had to be an announcement to try and calm the situation. As Kaye recalls, the two men squared off before the big tape rack where the pre-recorded elements of the broadcast were playing, with Kaye issuing a firm ultimatum to his colleague: "If you don't let me go on the air, I'm going to rip this tape right out of this machine and run like hell onto Main Street with it, and you'll never finish it."[4] Kriegler relented, and at 55 minutes and eight seconds into the broadcast Kaye breaks in, just moments after Don Lancer had succumbed to a cloud of Martian gas. Kaye delivers his plea for calm in slow, measured tones (tinged with an unmistakable hint of desperation) but it seemed to have no discernable effect and the calls kept coming.

So was this 1938 revisited? Not quite, as the reach of WKBW, while impressive, was still limited in comparison to the national network of CBS, but certainly there seems to have been a reaction from listeners that evokes a strong sense of déjà vu. According to one account, a man who was raving about a Martian invasion entered a Buffalo police station. He was thought drunk, until the radio was switched on and a rattled chief of police began breaking out the firearms. It was only the lucky intercession of a station break that prevented an armed and excited posse setting out to battle the Martians.[5] Another story tells of a county civil defense unit that went on alert and started calling up its members. Most extraordinarily of all, both Jeff Kaye and Dan Kriegler recall visits from aggrieved listeners to the station. Kriegler tells of tearful people beating on the door of the control room in their terror, while Kaye claims, "One man came to the back door with a baseball bat and was threatening to bash my brains out"[6] since in his haste to reach

Grand Island and rubberneck at the carnage, he had wrapped his car around a utility pole. Colorful stories indeed, but what about all those telephone calls? Do they reveal anything of the extent of the panic and the state of mind of listeners that night?

Kriegler recollects calls from police chiefs and off-duty officers volunteering their services,[7] and the total number of calls received by Buffalo police, newspaper and telephone company switchboards is put by some sources at over 4000,[8] though this high volume of calls is contradicted by several credible sources. The *New York Times* of November 1 quoted a Buffalo police switchboard operator as saying that calls numbered several a minute. The *Buffalo Evening News* on November 1 reported on the broadcast's aftermath in distinctly low-key terms, relegating the story to its radio and television page. According to this article, some 200 calls were received by the Buffalo police. It is not entirely clear if the newspaper figures are for a single precinct or represent an aggregated tally, but this potential disparity between the reported numbers of calls in secondary accounts with what can actually be found in primary sources does call into question the legendary nature of the WKBW broadcast, and it is not hard to find another major inconsistency.

One of the abiding legends of the broadcast is that Canadian National Guard units responded to the broadcast and began rushing to the Peace Bridge, Rainbow Bridge and Queenston Bridge border crossings with the United States.[9] Regretfully, this appears to be little more than urban legend. For one thing, there is no such thing as a Canadian national guard, and members of the Lincoln and Welland Regiment, who would have most likely responded to such a call to action, flatly deny that any such deployment occurred.[10] Yet just because the impact of the WKBW broadcast might have to be reassessed does not make it any less special or important, and it is still right and proper to acknowledge that many listeners were well and truly spooked.

But were people scared for broadly the same reasons as with previous broadcasts, or can we identify anything new this time? Television, as intimated at the beginning of this chapter, likely shares some blame. The eminent science fiction writer Harlan Ellison famously disparaged it as "the glass teat," and certainly watching television and listening to radio are as different as chalk and cheese. Listening to the radio is a deeply immersive experience, requiring a great deal of attention and participation on the part of the listener. Watching TV requires no such effort from the viewer, so it would be fair to argue that television had robbed Americans of the crucial ability to engage perceptively with demanding dramatic content. But much else had changed since the golden age of radio. Not only had scripted drama largely disappeared from the radio, but the relationship between broadcaster and listener had also changed beyond recognition, with a new generation of celebrity disc jockeys taking to the airwaves and connecting with their listeners on a personal level inconceivable in 1938. With the likes of Sandy Beach and the newsroom team playing themselves, this intimacy would have added an extra frisson of realism to the listener's experience.

One of the factors most obviously missing from the WKBW broadcast is the lack of what could be termed a Charlie McCarthy moment. There was clearly no one point in the WKBW broadcast that received a sudden influx of unsuspecting listeners because they happened to switch from another channel. However, there was certainly a lot more opportunity for random dial-surfers to be swept up in the story. Remember that the 1938 version switched at approximately the midpoint to a conventional drama, while the WKWB broadcast remained "in character" as a news broadcast from very beginning to end. In fact, given that the number of competing stations was so much higher than in 1938 and the audience far more fickle, it seems likely that there were a great many individual Charlie McCarthy moments that night.

This effect would have been further exacerbated by the striking realism of the drama. Speaking in 1971, Jeff Kaye indicated that before the scheduled transmission time, calls were coming in asking when the show was going to start, but that these calls continued after the 11 P.M. start time.[11] It is therefore clear that the seamless integration of the story into the regular programming schedule of the station was extremely effective in beguiling listeners. If people who had actually tuned into the station with the intent of listening to *The War of the Worlds* couldn't tell they were listening to a drama, what chance would a random dial-surfer have of sifting fact from fiction?

The answer is: very little, given how well performed and produced the show was. The sound effects are superb, with the call made by the conquering Martians best described as somewhere between the drone of an angry nest of wasps and fingernails down a blackboard. It's a deeply unpleasant sound: raw, unsophisticated and irritatingly monotonous. In a word, alien. The constant back-and-forth chatter of the newsmen, with all the genuine pauses and blemishes that mar their dialogue, amplifies the fear and uncertainty of the situation, and in this regard, special mention must go to the largely amateur cast assembled by Jeff Kaye. It appears that only Irv Weinstein had any prior acting experience, having started out as a child actor on radio, but all excel in their portrayal of an unimaginably strange situation. It is in all particulars a pitch-perfect performance, but perhaps scariest of all is the disconcerting loss of control we hear in their voices. As radio historian Jason Loviglio of the University of Maryland has observed, no matter how terrible the news, it is usually delivered in calm and authoritative tones. The voice over the radio may be delivering the most distressing news, but that regular trusted figure we hear night after night can always be counted on to explain the situation and even assuage our fears. Loviglio contends that in 1938 Welles caused fear by killing off the newsmen, so no one was left to provide that unemotional perspective.[12] But if that is true, then it must have been far worse in Buffalo. Welles killed off the fictional reporter, Carl Phillips. Jeff Kaye slaughtered the entire WKBW news team. Not only that, but like Carl Phillips before them, the WKBW reporters lost their composure. They appeared fallible and even fearful. If these trusted figures could no longer provide that anchor of calm to their listeners, the cause was surely lost.

Death, destruction and futility are not the only things Kaye accentuated. The script skillfully emphasizes all the most terrifying aspects of the Mercury Theatre broadcast to devastating effect. Though employing the same unreal compaction of time as had Koch, the musical interludes are considerably greater and consequently his story takes much longer to build to its crescendo. The listener has longer to stew and is less inclined to notice the inconsistencies in the pacing. Having achieved his perfect apex of terror, Kaye then holds the high note until the last exquisitely tense moment. In focusing completely on a dizzying blizzard of fragmented news reports he never allows his listeners a moment's respite to take stock, and there is an intimacy to the experience we are sharing with the reporters (whom we know to be real people) that is desperately, unnervingly compelling.

Nor should we forget that this was a very bad time to be toying with the uncertainties of an already jittery nation. Earlier that year, on April 4, the civil rights leader Martin Luther King had been gunned down, and just two months later presidential hopeful Robert F. Kennedy also fell to an assassin's bullet. In the aftermath of King's untimely death, over 100 cities had suffered race riots, while abroad America was embroiled in the hugely divisive Vietnam War. And of course, at the back of everyone's mind was the Cold War and the constant anxiety that a nuclear war might break out with the Soviet Union. The parallels with the situation in 1938 are striking, in that once again events far beyond the control of the general population were driving up levels of anxiety. In 1938, many listeners assumed that the radio had made a mistake and it was German forces that were mounting an attack on America, and while there is no indication that people in 1968 believed they were listening to a Soviet attack, it would not be at all surprising if some jumped to this quite plausible conclusion. Yet there are aspects of the WKBW broadcast that do not quite so easily lend themselves to comparison.

In our discussion of the reasons for the 1938 panic in chapter 8, we examined an intriguing sociological theory which proposed that panics were more likely to occur if a population is presented with a constricting range of options to flee. If all avenues of escape become blocked, the population is less likely to panic, essentially becoming resigned to their fate. However, if an exit still exists but the window of opportunity to seize it is closing the anxiety levels increase, leading to mass panic and flight. When one considers the geography of Grand Island and the way in which the WKBW broadcast emphasized the chaos on the roads and bridges, one might think that the result would be a significant panic, but it appears that the pre-publicity campaign by the station had worked particularly well, and the reports of distressed reactions generally come from much further afield, where the publicity campaign had clearly not reached so well.

As reported in the *Buffalo Evening News* of November 1, calls came from as far afield as Bangor, Maine, and San Francisco, 2,500 miles away. One caller from Albany nervously asked, "Is there anything else happening besides the bombing halt?," in reference to President Johnson's announcement of the cessation of Operation Rolling Thunder. In the same report, students at Alfred University (about two hours southeast of Buffalo) were said to have called to check on relatives living in the area. According to the *New York Times* of November 1, the New York radio station WINS received 18 calls from people enquiring why the all-news station had not yet picked up on the momentous events on Grand Island.

Of course the media should have known from the press releases sent out by WKBW that the broadcast was a drama, though legend has it that despite these sizable precautions, a number of local newspapers dispatched reporters to Grand Island to cover the invasion, sheepishly turning back half way there as the truth of the matter dawned on them. The police, too, should have been prepared, but the *Buffalo Evening News* of November 1 reported that "at least one Buffalo deputy police commissioner hadn't been advised about the broadcast." One can only shudder to think what might have happened if, as in Quito, other news outlets had begun to repeat the story verbatim and the police had mobilized.

Kaye's forethought in publicizing his intentions may well have prevented a panic of considerable scale, since the potent combination of a strikingly realistic drama using real names, places and institutions, coupled with the expropriation of normally scheduled programming and a restricted island location, could easily have caused the situation to spiral out of control.

Indeed, the WKBW broadcast seemed to have all the makings of a perfect storm and if we indulge for a moment in some "what if" historical revisionism, it is intriguing to imagine what might have happened if Welles had been able to use the same degree of realism in his broadcast. The 1938 broadcast was somewhat defanged, with names and places changed to satisfy the censor, but just imagine for a moment what might have happened if Welles had used the likes of Kaltenborn and Murrow as his voices. Had he continued to report the "news" until the very end of the program rather than switch to a more conventional dramatic style for the final act, the terror might well have become unbearable. In 1938 Welles joked that he had "annihilated the CBS," but if passions had become inflamed when his listeners learned of the deception, he might well have found life imitating art to an uncomfortably realistic degree. How might history now view Welles if in the aftermath of his Halloween "boo" the headquarters of a major radio network had been burned to the ground?

Jeff Kaye too was lucky that he had no mob of stone-throwing, torch-wielding rioters to contend with, but when he returned to his office that evening he certainly thought his days as a radio broadcaster were over. Sitting alone at his desk, he sadly typed out his resignation and slipped it under the door of general manager Norm Shrutt. Then the phone rang. Kaye took the call, which to his utter chagrin was from the regional sales manager of one of the country's biggest automobile manufacturers. The hapless Kaye was then subject to a torrent of abuse and the horrifying news that the automobile company was going to pull all its advertising from the station. This seemed to be the final nail in the coffin for Kaye's career, so the next morning he came into work fully prepared to clear out his desk.

But then the impossible happened. Talking to Warren Potash, the WKBW sales manager, Kaye was surprised to learn that his colleague too had received a call from the divisional sales representative of a large automobile company, but he had placed all the company's advertising with WKBW! Kaye couldn't believe his ears. Was this the same man who had turned the air blue with his condemnation of the station? Apparently it was, but as Potash explained, it seems as if the aggrieved salesman had thought it was a rival Buffalo station, WBEN, that had broadcast *The War of the Worlds*. He had got his wires crossed and in the confusion had shifted his entire advertising budget to WKBW.

But Kaye's biggest concern, aside from his belief that he had cost the station vital advertising revenues, was that the Federal Communications Commission would revoke the station's license. Kaye has admitted that he had anticipated some sort of reaction from listeners,[13] which is why he took such great care to publicize the broadcast. He later claimed that the station had put out disclaimers every hour on the hour for 21 days prior to transmission,[14] and in fact it may have been this demonstrated diligence that got WKBW off the hook. If the station really had done everything humanly possible to warn and prepare their listeners, the FCC would find it difficult to allege that any wrongdoing had been contemplated, though Bob Kosinski thinks otherwise. Writing on the website of the Buffalo Broadcasters Foundation, he recalls Dan Kriegler insisting, "They had never intended to scare anyone, just do good radio"—but, as Kosinski dryly adds, "I didn't believe him for a minute."[15]

But the FCC received no complaints, or it simply chose to ignore them. No censure was forthcoming and a much-relieved Kaye kept his job. In fact, so blasé was the management of WKBW that it even repeated the broadcast on several other Halloween nights, each time updating the production with the latest chart songs and changes to personnel. In the 1971 version, Jackson Armstrong replaced Sandy Beach and Dan Kriegler bowed out completely, objecting to Kaye editing out some 12 minutes of the show for lack of time. In another significant departure from the 1968 version, Kaye opened the story with a detailed monologue on the history of *The War of the Worlds* on radio, including his own unfortunate contribution to what was now the most sustained series of radio hoaxes in history. Perhaps it was the longer introduction that served to better prepare people for the story to come, because though the show is still very good the effect was mild in comparison to what happened in 1968, though incredibly there were still a few calls to the station. A final version made in 1975 passed completely without incident, but without the oversight of Kaye (who had by then left the station) it is generally considered the weakest of the three. However, this was not quite the end of the story for the Jeff Kaye script. In 1974 it was passed into the hands of a radio station in the state of Rhode Island, setting the scene for a final assault on American soil, but for now the Martians had other plans, and it was the unfortunate citizens of Brazil who were once again to bear the brunt of their aggression.

14

MARS 2, BRAZIL 0
The Siege of São Luís

In 1954 Brazil had suffered its first attack by the Martians, but less than twenty years later the invaders would return to wreak far greater havoc, selecting as their target this time the city of São Luís, the island capital of the northeastern state of Maranhão. It was a textbook military operation, with the Martians landing their forces next to the only bridge connecting the city to the mainland and effectively isolating the terrified inhabitants. Meanwhile other Martian armadas were said to be launching simultaneous attacks all over the world. In reality, of course, those behind the invasion were perfectly human, and motivated this time by nakedly commercial considerations. The radio station involved was losing money and needed a spectacular event to increase listening figures, but as the dust settled the next day, the staff of Rádio Difusora must have wished they had found a much less contentious way of promoting their station.

Of all the many versions of *The War of the Worlds* broadcast over the years, the drama transmitted by Rádio Difusora on October 30, 1971, was arguably the one most calculated to cause an adverse reaction in its listeners. Orson Welles' true intentions will forever be a matter for conjecture and debate; the catastrophic broadcast in Ecuador in 1949 has been characterized as the malicious intent of a lone individual, while other events such as the previous Brazilian scare in 1954 were purely accidental or a misreading of the potential consequences. But at Rádio Difusora it appears a high-level decision was made to create a landmark event in order to combat encroaching competition and declining listenership.

At the time there were four other competing radio stations in the Maranhão region of Brazil: Rádio Ribamar, Rádio Gurupi, Rádio Timbira and Rádio Educadora. Rádio Difusora was part of a powerful media group owned by the Bacelar family, whose holdings also included the only television station in the region. Surveys had shown that the introduction of television had had a serious effect on listener numbers and that Rádio Educadora in particular was becoming a serious threat, and so something spectacular was needed to grab audience share from their rivals. It was the board of Rádio Difusora that proposed the idea of producing a program that would grip the public attention in a big way, though they may have been thinking of something a little less imperiling to their business than the idea that was eventually settled upon.

At this point in our story the imposing figure of Sérgio Brito enters the frame. Brito is a major name in the history of Brazilian radio who also held a number of political offices (he was in the cabinet of the governor of Maranhão in 1967) and edited several newspapers and magazines during his extremely varied career. He was born in 1939 in the city of Itapecuru-Mirim, and in 1963 began his radio career broadcasting from Rádio Gurupi, moving the same year to Rádio Timbira. The following year he joined Difusora, working for both the radio and television arms of the company before briefly leaving the region to pursue other interests in Rio de Janeiro. Returning in 1970, he was approached by Magno Bacelar to help solve the disastrous slump in ratings, and especially to combat the threat from their major competitor Rádio Educadora.

Brito's first passion had always been radio, and he accepted the challenge with relish, asking only for 24 hours to come up with an idea. It happened that Brito had in his possession a copy of a relatively new magazine in Brazil called *Ele Ela* (He and She) which contained a single-page article on the 1938 broadcast. This would be Brito's inspiration. When he presented the idea, however, he was asked skeptically if he could actually extrapolate a complete program from a single page of information. Brito saw this as a challenge. Securing a copy of the original novel, he set out to write his own radio version of *The War of the Worlds*.

Brito was clearly quite certain of what he was doing. His brief was to create a program that would cause a sensation, and he was well aware that listeners might react in an extreme fashion. Quoted in the *Jornal da Rede Alfredo de Carvalho*, Brito candidly admitted, "I knew that it could generate a panic and that people would want to run away from the city, as it happened in the USA."[1] His solution was certainly original, though not without a certain degree of cold calculation. Brito landed his invasion fleet at the Campo de Perizes, an area directly adjacent to the only point of egress from the island of São Luís. His reasoning was that if people did become alarmed and consider fleeing, they would quickly realize there was no escape over the bridge and so remain in the city. It's an extraordinary idea, though as we've already seen in previous chapters, one that is actually quite sound from a sociological perspective. People do indeed become resigned to their fate if they are shown there is no escape from a dangerous situation, though of course this does not preclude them enduring a great deal of suffering in the process.

Brito has gone on record as saying that he never heard the 1938 broadcast, and since it was in English it would have done him little good in any case,[2] though judging from the surviving material from his version, it seems that he was in some manner able to incorporate dialogue that bears a striking similarity to certain scenes in the Howard Koch script. Perhaps there were sufficient clues in the *Ele Ela* article for him to replicate some key scenes, but however he did this, the fact remains that his script retains the basic framework of a series of news flashes interrupting a regularly scheduled program.

The chosen vehicle for Brito's version of *The War of the Worlds* was the top-rated Saturday morning program *Paradão do Rayol* (Rayol's Choice), hosted by Rayol Filho, though the date chosen of October 30 actually had no connection at all to the original Orson Welles broadcast. Halloween has only in recent years become a recognized event in Brazil (much to the annoyance of many Brazilians who see it as an example of cultural imperialism) and the date was actually chosen for Brito's *War of the Worlds* broadcast because it happened to be the founding date of Rádio Difusora.

It appears that on October 29 there was an announcement on Difusora television that the radio station was planning something special for the following day, but there was no evidence to suggest that any kind of campaign was mounted (as in Buffalo) to promote the program. Difusora did, however, go to great lengths to ensure that listeners were thoroughly caught up in the drama, integrating the script into both its radio and television properties.

The show prior to *Paradão do Rayol* was *Quem manda é você* (You're in Charge), hosted by José Branco. Branco was bringing his program to a close when he announced to listeners a special extra item. The well-known television host Bernardo de Almeida had a scoop for listeners. An astronomer, "Professor Galvão," from the National Observatory was passing through São Luís on his way to investigate the alleged landing of a spacecraft near the city of Cururupu, and because de Almeida's program did not air until 3 P.M. and the astronomer was on a tight schedule, he was going to interview him live on the radio that very morning.

The interview with Professor Galvão (played by Reinaldo Faray) reveals that while investigating the supposed landing site of a UFO (in an area where deposits of a phosphate called monazite had been discovered) a piece of magnesium had been recovered that had an incredibly high degree of purity. Listeners were told that such purity was impossible to duplicate on Earth. With this uncertainty planted in listeners' heads, *Paradão do Rayol* began as usual, with all the advertisements and jingles that listeners were accustomed to. Just after the third song an unexpected news report interrupts proceedings, heralded by a trumpet fanfare very similar to that used by the well-known *Esso Reporter* news program. The story is that at 5 A.M. local time, a Professor Farrell of the Mount Palomar Observatory has reported witnessing regular explosions of gas on the surface of Mars. Tellingly, the use of the name Farrell is a clear indicator that to some degree Brito was working from the Howard Koch script, given that this very same name was used in exactly the same context in the 1938 broadcast.

Professor Mario Cordelini of the National Observatory at Rio de Janeiro provides additional confirmation of the explosions, and adds the news that something has been expelled along with the gas on a trajectory toward Earth. He describes the explosions as like blue sparks from the muzzle of a gun. At this stage the announcer informs the listeners that the station is arranging a live connection with the observatory at Rio de Janeiro. There follows a ten-second silence, another song, and then, at approximately 9:40 A.M. local time, the connection is made with the observatory. Professor Cordelini is interviewed and offers the opinion that the explosions are really nothing to be concerned about, though while he is on the air, more worrying news arrives reporting further activity on the surface of Mars.

Brito's script now deviates significantly from any previous version of *The War of the Worlds*, taking on a distinctly global perspective. The United Nations is reported to have declared a state of emergency as the Martian spacecraft are tracked into the Earth's atmosphere, while the superpowers go on high military alert and communications become erratic as the Martians begin jamming signals. From reporter Jota Alves comes word from Tiririçal airport (located on the outskirts of São Luís) that Martian spacecraft have been seen following aircraft, while from Vatican Radio comes an urgent appeal from the pope for the people of the Earth to pray for salvation.

Then from the tallest building in Rio de Janeiro a reporter (played by Brito) describes the destruction rained down on the city as the Martians fly over the beachfront commu-

nity of Botafogo. This is followed by the alarming news that the Martians are also landing close to the airport in the region of São Luís known as the Campo de Perizes. Ignor-
ing entreaties to take care, Alves and his technician Heracias Medeiros bravely set out to
report on the situation.

This incredibly action-packed drama is now having a serious effect on listeners. The
phones at Rádio Difusora are ringing off the hook with desperate people trying to discover what has happened in Rio de Janeiro, fearing that their friends and relatives may
have perished in the attack. Meanwhile on the radio, the fictional military response gathers pace, with the 24th Hunters Battalion (military police) based in São Luís reported to
be mobilizing. The station even receives one call from a military police captain who offers
to place his troops on the streets, though in reality the battalion too is busy fielding phone
calls from terrified residents.

Alves and his colleague, along with Professor Galvão, have now arrived at the Campo
de Perizes and, in a scene strikingly similar to Carl Phillips' report from Grover's Mill,
describes for viewers a chaotic scene as onlookers throng about the Martian ship, which
appears to be about 30 meters wide and constructed of a strange metal. Alves then interviews Mr. Sebastião, the owner of the Santa Marta ranch, on whose land the Martian
spacecraft has descended. Sebastião explains that he was knocked from his chair by the
impact and compares the strange noise the object made to a piercing sound like São João
fireworks.*

Suddenly Alves screams and the transmission is cut off. Rayol Filho makes frantic
attempts to raise his colleague, but when this fails, he announces that in light of the
tragedy that seems to have befallen them, the station will switch to playing solemn music,
starting with a funeral march. As if this isn't enough to unnerve listeners, several unexpected events now occur. In the skies over Maranhão, a squadron of Brazilian air force
jets on a training mission from Belém do Pará (around 220 miles from São Luís) pick up
the radio transmissions and seek clarification from the control tower at Tirirical airport.
Luckily the tower is able to clarify the situation, but by now the planes have overflown
the city. This unusual activity serves only to spook people even more, and when the
weather over the city turns unexpectedly cloudy, listeners are further convinced that the
reports they are hearing of Martian gas attacks must also be true.

Finally, the broadcast comes to its exhausting conclusion, with Reinaldo Faray repris-
ing his role as Professor Galvão to explain that he is the sole survivor of the entire human
race, but that the Martians have also perished, wiped out by bacteria. It had been an
extraordinary day in São Luís, but for the staff of the station, the drama was far from
over. Brazil in 1971 was under a dictatorship, and torture and murder were commonplace
tools of repression, so Brito had to take extraordinary measures to protect himself and
his staff. He had transmitted a warning the night before, but this had clearly been
insufficient to allay fears or prevent the chaos that engulfed São Luís. The Federal Police
had actually approved the show prior to the broadcast, which provided one mitigating
circumstance in the station's favor, but the police were now demanding a copy of the
broadcast to study, so in an bold move, Brito had the recording doctored, inserting every

*Annual fireworks displays, which take place at beginning of the Brazilian winter and are dedicated to Saint John.

10 minutes a statement to the effect that the broadcast was only science fiction and not to worry.

While Brito and his team worked on the recording, a meeting called by the commander of the 24th Hunters Battalion was convened, attended by federal judges, the minister of justice and a representative of the Federal Police. The decision was made to shut down the station immediately, but when Colonel Coutinho of the Federal Police arrived at the station at 1 P.M. to listen to the recording, he appears to have been mollified enough by the deception to let the station off the hook. This should have been the end of matters, but at 2 P.M., furious at the chaos that had been caused in the city, the commander of the 24th Hunters Battalion orders his men to occupy the station under the pretext that it might come under attack from a civilian mob bent on revenge, though in fact the city was quite calm and the crowd that did gather outside the station was far more interested in observing the comings and goings of the military and Federal Police.

With the station occupied, the MPs then remove many of the personnel to the battalion barracks for interrogation, but this action triggers something of a crisis in the city, as the Federal Police felt that their authority had being slighted by the military. Arriving at the 24th Hunters Battalion barracks, Colonel Coutinho demands the immediate release of the station personnel and that the MPs withdraw from the station. His demands are met, and the crowd gathered around the station jeer at the retreating soldiers.

Difusora had almost been the victim of its own success, but against all the odds it fooled the authorities and even avoided further sanctions, which could have come from the Departamento Nacional de Telecomunicações (National Department of Telecommunications), otherwise known as Dentel. However, São Luís was a city in shock, and while it is difficult to confirm the exact nature and scope of the reactions experienced by its citizens, it was clearly substantial. It has even been said that the family of Difusora's owner was caught up in the chaos. Additionally, a document prepared by the commander of the Security Division of the 3rd Air Zone of the Ministry of Aviation speaks of widespread panic.[3] But it is Sérgio Brito who has the most illuminating tales to tell, some comical, others harrowing. Speaking at a conference specially convened to discuss the broadcast,[4] Brito revealed that to his knowledge, there had been one miscarriage, a suicide pact (thankfully not carried out) and a priest who had gathered his family to read from the Book of Revelation. At the opposite end of the spectrum, Brito also tells of an unfaithful husband who, believing he is about to die, confesses his infidelities to his wife. "That's fine," retorts his wife, "but if this is a time for confessions, you ought to know that you're not the father of our son!"

In the days following the broadcast São Luís slowly returned to normal, though when Difusora finally got back on the air at 10 A.M. the next day, it was ordered to repeat every half hour a statement explaining that *The War of the Worlds* had been a hoax. The Difusora television station was also required to make the same half-hourly admission. But what had caused such an outpouring of emotion in this particular case? If we turn first to the production itself, it is notable that Brito's *The War of the Worlds* is closer in tone to the WKBW version mounted in Buffalo than it is to the original 1938 broadcast. Brito dropped his drama directly into the scheduled mix of programs and used familiar names and voices to relay events. Jota Alves, "incinerated" by the Martians at the Campo de Perizes, was a regular reporter for Difusora, and Bernardo de Almeida was a well-known commentator, and of course Rayol Filho was extremely familiar to listeners. All this would certainly have served to convince listeners that they were hearing a real account of events. The sound engineer José de Ribamar Elvas Ribeiro has been described as "one of the most versatile sound designers in Maranhão,"[5] so with a director as talented as Brito at the helm, the potential seems high for a very convincing drama.

It should also be considered that the communication infrastructure in Brazil was then quite primitive by modern standards, lacking, for instance, direct dial telephones. Calls had to be made through an exchange operator, so bringing such a system to its knees was relatively easy. Of course, this does not explain why people did not simply switch to any of the other four radio stations available, or the television, though the latter would likely not have been in as many homes as radio. Dictatorship certainly seems a likely contributing factor, given that people living under such a system are routinely conditioned not to question the things they hear from the media that they know is controlled by the state; but once again, we should not let a desire to find a sociological or political smoking gun for these events blind us to the simple fact that it takes a special kind of talent to pull this kind of rabbit from the hat. Sérgio Brito thus joins a long line of creative thinkers who deserve full recognition for their dogged determination to stretch the rules to breaking point and beyond. He would not be the last.

15

PERIL IN PROVIDENCE
The Last American Campaign

In 1974 a Providence, Rhode Island, AM radio station called WPRO landed a last Martian task force on American soil, and this time it was not only the radio listening public that saw red. For this final invasion to target America, an island was once again the chosen landing site of the Martian forces, bridges were destroyed, traffic was reported halted and reporters delivered hysterical reports of the destruction visited upon the terrified population. The unfortunate focal point this time was the community of Jamestown on Conanicut Island, a tiny island of less than 10 square miles located in Narragansett Bay. When WPRO program manager Jay Clark wrote the script (which to his recollection took several months) he took great pains to localize his story, shrewdly selecting Jamestown for its close proximity to Newport Naval Station, which he felt occupied an ideal position to protect the mainland from the Martians.[1] With a population at the time of less than 3,000 persons* Conanicut Island was even smaller and more isolated than Grand Island had been during the WKWB broadcast, and it seems that the WPRO version touched a particularly raw nerve with its residents. As Jim Pemantell, the Jamestown police chief at the time, recalls, "No one and I mean no one in Jamestown thought it was funny."[2]

The WPRO take on *The War of the Worlds* bears many striking similarities to the WKBW version, which is hardly surprising, as a large media conglomerate called Capital Cities Communications owned both stations at the time. As such, the stations shared many ideas back and forth. There are even parallels to be found in the history of the two stations, as WPRO had enjoyed a long period as a mainstay of the local music scene before eventually shifting, as would WKBW, to the talk radio format. However, in marked contrast, it should be noted that the 5,000-watt WPRO was not nearly as powerful as WKBW in terms of the reach of its signal, but it did enjoy a very close relationship with its smaller audience, who counted heavily on the station as a source of news and information.

The broadcast began at 11 P.M. on October 30 and went out over the last hour of the regularly scheduled Holland Cooke show. Like the WKBW version before it, the drama makes conspicuous use of local place-names and is punctuated with songs and advertisements, including a campaign advertisement for the post of state treasurer. Going a step farther than WKBW, it also mentions more genuine state and police officials, such as Major General Leonard Holland (head of the National Guard), police chief Walter A. McQueeney and state governor Phillip W. Noel. The script otherwise follows closely the

---

*Census figures for 1970 put the population at 2,911.

sequence of events laid down by Jeff Kaye, beginning with relatively mild reports of fires on Conanicut Island and building momentum with a series of increasingly alarming news reports of a suspected meteor impact. Before the hour is up the Martians have massacred the defenders at the Newport Bridge and a last despairing message from Jay Clark is transmitted as the victorious Martians close in on the station.

Just as had happened at WKBW, Clark drafted the on-air news staff and had them play themselves, but in contrast to the problems encountered by Jeff Kaye in 1968, Clark's actors did not falter when confronted by the script, and though some small degree of spontaneity may have been sacrificed, the performances are still exceptionally convincing. This was doubtless thanks to the boundless energy of the cast, but also because it appears that many of the ad-libbed scenes that had been perfected for the WKBW version worked their way into the scripted version for WPRO. Clark also strived to ensure that the drama was as realistic to local listeners as possible, even calculating the estimated flight time for military jets to reach Jamestown.[3]

On the technical side, Clark lavishes fulsome praise on the work of the late Austin "Jake" F. Paquin, who at the time was the WPRO production engineer. As described by Clark, Paquin threw himself into the project with gusto. In fact Clark had never seen him quite so energized, describing his work as "just plain incredible."[4] Jeff Kaye had had his actors transmit from their mobile news cars to achieve the intermittent quality of two-way radio communication, but for a studio-bound production, Paquin had to manually insert the static squelches between transmissions. He also created a much richer audio mix than had been attempted at WKBW. The zaps of the Martian death rays are audible in his production, and the clarity and quality of the sound effects are generally far crisper and much more polished. This was a considerable achievement, as Paquin was working with a simple two-track tape machine and, as Holland Cooke recalls, "There was a lot of razor blade and grease pencil and tape editing that went into this thing."[5] The dialogue itself was recorded intermittently over a number of days, with various people making their contributions when they were available. Among the WPRO staff to record their parts in this fashion were Mark Haines (later a regular on CNBC-TV), Barbara Hamilton, Dave Fallon, Barry Parker and Gary Berkowitz.

At first it seemed as if the public was reacting calmly to the broadcast, but this was not to last, and as recalled by Clark, the tipping point for listeners came with the "death" of Mark Haines, at which moment, Clark recalls, "All hell broke loose with our phone lines."[6] This came at the 47-minute mark, with Haines succumbing to a Martian gas attack. Shortly afterwards, and doubtless responding to the growing clamor of outrage and terror from callers to the station, an impromptu statement is read out by DJ Salty Brine to assure listeners that they are listening to a drama, but by then the damage had been done. Looking back, Clark expresses amazement that the broadcast had such a dramatic effect on his listeners. He recounts the particularly alarming story that one woman was preparing to kill her child rather than face death at the hands of the Martians.[7]

Such an extreme reaction is clearly atypical, but the totality of evidence does point to a significant outpouring of distress and anger. A Jamestown police spokesman at the time told the *Evening Bulletin* newspaper of October 31 that people were calling up "swearing at us" as the number of calls to their switchboard approached 100, many from residents demanding that the broadcast be halted. Police chief Jim Pemantell recollects that calls were still being received when he came in for work the following morning.[8] In total the *Bulletin* received up to 500 calls in the space of an hour.

Among the calls received by the *Bulletin* was one from Bruce Whitney of East Providence, who complained angrily, "The neighbor's children are crying and throwing up they're so scared. I'm really upset." From accounts like this can be discerned at least one familiar reason for the depth and scale of the scare. Whitney was woken by a telephone call from his partner, while another unnamed person told the *Bulletin* that a friend had called him at work, warning him that his family in Jamestown was in imminent danger. The frightened man left his night job and headed home in a rush before discovering the true nature of the broadcast. Several letters of complaint to the FCC alluded to similar reactions, with one particularly aggrieved correspondent writing, "We are not alarmists or gullible people but in the hour that we listened we were so afraid we called neighbors and our parents to warn them...."[9]

So it seems abundantly clear that once again, telephone calls to people who were not even listening to the broadcast triggered extreme reactions. So, too, did a simple lack of foreknowledge about the drama. Said an enraged caller to the *Bulletin*, "I've never seen anything so irresponsible in a civil defense station. I was scared to death, running around the house with my gun. I can understand replaying Orson Welles' thing. But I listen to WPRO at morning and night, and I never heard them advertise that program."

But the program had been publicized, albeit with nothing like the saturation levels adopted by WKBW for its 1968 version. Hourly advertisements began airing on WPRO at 12:45 P.M. on the day of the broadcast, with the last going out some 45 minutes before the drama began, but even if there had been weeks of pre-publicity, we know all too well that the very nature of radio disinclines people from hanging on every word. The agitated man with the gun may well have had his radio on all evening, but unless he had been paying very close attention, it is unlikely that the warnings would have been heeded.

Jay Clark was certainly acutely aware of the dangers. With the best intentions he had ensured that letters were sent to local authorities and emergency services to warn them of the impending broadcast, but as the Jamestown Police Department records for that night seem to prove, not everyone received these, or if they had, the message had not been disseminated throughout the ranks. Tellingly, there is no indication from the comments recorded on the Jamestown PD log (which contains numerous references to calls received) of any kind of foreknowledge or prepared answers on the part of the answering officers, and the calls themselves are highly revealing. The *Woonsocket Call* newspaper phoned at 11:26 P.M., followed in close succession by Channel 10 Television and WWON radio. Even more astonishingly, the log records (at 11:40 P.M. and 11:55 P.M.) National Guard members phoning in to find out if they were needed, while a Sergeant Wyhn from the North Kingstown Police Department rang at 11:55 P.M. to say his switchboard was jammed. It seems that plenty of people and institutions that should have known better were in the dark.

Not only had Clark done his best to warn the emergency services; he had also argued vociferously with station general manager Richard Rakovan about how far they should go, with Clark cautioning against opening the broadcast with a fake news story. Rako-

```
                          DAY SHEET          10/30/74  (Page #2)

  11:34 P.M.   All belows calls are the same subject etc...PBJ, how many calls..man..
               woman.....
  11:37 P.M.   Warwick PD...call from a man, same mad.....
  11:38 P.M.   Woman in Pawtucket....man in same place..... woman in Jamestown....sam
               upset.....
  11:39 P.M.   Jerry Taylor....woman in prov....
  11:40 P.M.   Tel. op. in FR ref. have Nat. Guard men calling in to find out if need
  11:41 P.M.   Tel. op in Prov..same, switchboard flooded with calls...
  11:42 P.M.   3 calls.....
  11:43 P.M.   Same as above.....
  11:44 P.M.   Mrs. Dutton, CB'ers on all chanells about same, advised.....
  11:45 P.M.   6 calls.....
  11:46 P.M.   Woman, mad,crying.....
  11:47 P.M.   Man from Lincoln, very upset, what we going to do about it?..not too m
               l can do now..... another woman.....
  11:48 P.M.   WKFD...3 other calls.....
  11:49 P.M.   3 Calls.....
  11:50 P.M.   W. Warwick PD..advised same...2 other calls.....
  11:52 P.M.   Call from 2 women, 1 man.....
  11:53 P.M.   Press Froberg..another from man in Woonsocket, mad.....
  11:54 P.M.   Call from a Sgt. DeBrasse, RI Nat. Guard..advised same.....man called
               ref. same.....woman in Npt..same.....
  11:55 P.M.   Call from Sgt. Wyhn, NKPD, all his lines tied up ref. same, hope we car
               do somthing about sit...ok...if we need any help just call..advised
               our car stated traffic picked up for a few minutes but died off again..
  11:57 P.M.   3 calls.....
  11:58 P.M.   Call from Bob Peckham, was just called by npt. ref. same..advised.....
  11:59 P.M.   3 Calls.....
```

Original day sheet from the Jamestown Police Department showing calls received about the WPRO *War of the Worlds* broadcast (courtesy Jamestown Police).

van had chided Clark as a wimp for his caution, but Clark was extremely concerned that the FCC might revoke the station's license if things went wrong.[10] It was a laudable approach and Clark won the fight, but missing on the night was any kind of opening statement warning listeners that the drama was beginning. Holland Cooke remembers feeling some surprise that the broadcast began without any kind of preamble to warn listeners.[11] Instead it dovetails seamlessly with the top 40 show he was hosting that night. The first inkling listeners had that something unusual might be happening was when he delivered the exact same gag that Sandy Beach had made in 1968 about the blue flames on Mars, with only the name of the local gas company substituted.

Since the show was entirely prerecorded, Cooke was able to leave the studio. Never having heard himself on the radio, he excitedly jumped in his car and drove around Providence listening to the drama unfold. He had intended to make his way to the Newport Bridge to see if anyone actually turned up to watch, but in the event never got that far. However, he saw nothing that night to indicate that any sort of panic was spilling onto the streets,[12] though Jay Clark offers an illuminating story. A woman driving to Boston from Jamestown happened to hear the portion of the drama that included the announcement that fire fighting equipment was being diverted to the island. At that very moment she had the misfortune to pass a fire truck heading in the direction of Jamestown. As Clark relates, this only served to confirm her worst fears: "...so what she did is immediately turn the car around and run into the first place that she could see was open, which was a bar, at which point she informed the entire bar that the world was coming to an end because the Martians had landed."[13]

So in this case we can add inopportune coincidence to the list of reasons for WPRO's success in stirring up their listeners, but just how predisposed were people this time to react irrationally? We have seen it repeatedly demonstrated that political and social conditions are likely catalysts for extreme reactions to radio dramas, but this seems a less likely factor for the WPRO broadcast. The nation had recently endured the Nixon resignation and the worst of the oil crisis, the end of the Vietnam War was in sight and, despite severe economic difficulties, America was not nearly so beset by internal divisions as it has been in 1968. Even the Cold War was enjoying a period of cautious détente, so if people were not so precariously primed to take fright, what other factors might explain the panic in 1974? Jay Clark plausibly attributes much of the reaction to what he perceives as his listeners' unquestioning "belief in the radio station and its tradition of being the news power in the market place." WPRO, says Clark, with more than a hint of pride, "...was the station to listen to for news. We closed all the schools when it snowed, so [for] any big news story, people turned to WPRO."[14] Holland Cooke cites the realism of the broadcast, observing with satisfaction, "It sounded like impromptu AM radio, dancing as fast as we could to cover something that took us by surprise and was bigger than we could handle."[15]

In the aftermath of the broadcast it looked like the repercussions for WPRO would also be hard to handle. With demands mounting up that the station be prosecuted or its license taken away, the Jamestown administrator assigned Chief Pemantell the job of investigating the broadcast. He duly interviewed a senior person at the station, most likely general manager Richard Rakovan, who admitted that the drama had been a mistake, but there was little else Permantell could do in the circumstances and no statute under which he could arrest someone. WPRO did issue an apology to Jamestown residents, though the contrition was slightly at odds with a comment attributed to station news director Barry Parker, who let slip to the *Providence Journal-Bulletin* of October 31 that "the purpose of the hoax was, in fact, to 'scare people a little bit.'" Holland Cooke recalls that Parker received a reprimand from station management for that unfortunately worded statement,[16] but despite the public protestations of regret, Cooke also reveals that there were mixed feelings in the station the following day. He observed, "When the damage was done, we were all gathered around the TV set watching three local TV stations [...] describing the havoc, and we were both embarrassed and proud."

Not only proud, confesses Cooke. "As apologetic and horrified as we wanted to seem after the fact, the stunt was a real competitive coup because we were under attack by three other stations ... what we did that night was the opposite of business as usual and we trumped them."[17] This is not to suggest that there was any premeditated plan to trigger a scare in pursuit of ratings, for as Clark makes abundantly clear, "It caused more panic than I would ever want to cause." Nevertheless, what was done was done, and as Cooke wryly acknowledges, "We were already in the doghouse and loving every minute of it."[18]

This was not a sentiment shared by everyone. The outrage in Jamestown and elsewhere generated many letters of complaint and some unwanted high-level attention. Representative William A Babin, Jr., threatened letters to both WPRO and the Rhode Island delegation in Congress, for although he was not a listener himself, he indignantly told the October 31 *Evening Bulletin* that he was awakened that night by his 19-year-old daughter, who was "really scared." Such was the level of anger that an investigation by the FCC was inevitable, and it didn't take long to start, with a call logged in a Rhode Island police station day sheet from the FCC on October 31, asking for information on the number of calls received and if switchboards had been jammed.

It took a while for the wheels of bureaucracy to turn, but on July 18, 1975, the FCC duly issued a formal reprimand to WPRO. As reported by the *Providence Journal* on July 18, it concluded that "the station did not adequately assure its listeners the program was a hoax" and that the station was in violation of an obscure codicil buried in a 1966 public notice warning against "contests and promotions likely to disrupt public life." Contained within was the following rather comical example of the sort of material the FCC would find objectionable:

> The broadcast of "scare" announcements or headlines which either are untrue or are worded in such a way as to mislead and frighten the public: e.g., a sudden announcement delivered in a tone of excitement to the effect that "amoebas" were invading a certain city, implying that amoebas were dangerous creatures.[19]

WPRO did mount a defense, but it seemed distinctly halfhearted. The station noted that it was unaware of any explicit FCC regulation governing the content of a drama like *The War of the Worlds* and argued unsuccessfully that in any case, the 1966 public notice did not apply. The station drew a particularly scathing response when it tried to imply that since there had been no gathering of onlookers in Jamestown, the impact of the broadcast had clearly been inconsequential. An FCC official dryly retorted, "It would be reasonable to assume that the last place that those people misled by the broadcast would want to gather is at the landing site."[20] The FCC went on to observe, "The only way to assure adequately that the public would not be alarmed in this case would be an introductory statement repeated at frequent intervals throughout the program."[21]

The FCC response was not unanimous. Commissioner Abbott Washburn echoed feelings expressed in 1938 that the FCC should not be in the business of censoring radio stations unless there was absolute certainty that the audience found it impossible to recognize the program as a hoax. Washburn felt that in the case of WPRO, the number of complaints was not large, and the precautions taken by the station had been sufficiently diligent that the public had been adequately informed of their intentions.

So in the end the FCC did not go so far as to threaten the station's license, but it is notable that its response to the WPRO scare was the first time the commission had ever set out clearly their position on the matter of fake broadcasts, and that stations contemplating such broadcasts were henceforth required to tread very carefully indeed. Responding to the FCC judgment, Richard Rakovan told the *Providence Journal* of July 18, "Our intention was not in any way to alarm people. The premise of the program was, frankly, to entertain. I'm sure that if anyone had considered the content at all alarming, we probably would have taken greater steps to indicate it was truly a dramatization." A suitably contrite position for sure, but you could also argue that seasoned broadcasters should have known better and that WPRO management surely betrayed some naivete in thinking the drama would pass without serious incident. In fact as seems clear, there were misgivings felt about the potential for trouble and sensible steps taken, but in the final analysis we should not forget that it is all too easy to assume that past follies are symptomatic of a less enlightened era. If *The War of the Worlds* should have taught us anything, it is that no matter how sophisticated an audience may seem, we must never underestimate just how thin is the veneer of civilization. Though America finally claimed victory over the Martians at the battle of Jamestown, that alarming reality was still not appreciated in other parts of the world and, incredibly in the years to come, there were yet more hard lessons to be learned.

16

THE FINAL CAMPAIGNS
Portugal 1988 and 1998

Lightning is said never to strike in the same place twice, but the Martians have demonstrated no such reluctance in their campaigns, assailing the United States in 1938, 1968 and 1974. Yet if we are looking for patterns, there is more to consider than geography. Language, too, has been a significant factor, and it seems that the invaders have exhibited a marked predilection for countries where Portuguese is spoken. Brazil was targeted twice, in 1954 and 1971, and Portugal itself was struck in 1958, but that was just the beginning, for Portugal also has the distinction of being the last place on Earth (for now at least) to have suffered a Martian attack. This occurred in 1998 and centered on the town of Palmela, located some 16 miles south of Lisbon. Against all the odds, ten years previously another Portuguese city had also come under the scrutiny of the Martians. It is to this penultimate invasion we will turn next.

Braga is a picturesque city in the northwest of the country known as the Portuguese Rome for its great concentration of religious architecture. Its population is also considered among the most pious (even fanatical) in the country, which, given the religious dimensions associated with the 1958 *War of the Worlds* broadcast, should have sounded warning bells to the staff of Rádio Braga when the idea was first floated to produce a new version. As with almost all these extraordinary occasions in broadcast history, a single passionate individual is at the heart of the events. José Manuel Coelho was born on May 1, 1956, in Braga, and after some time spent as a teacher took up a post with Rádio Braga in 1986. Even before he began his radio career he had developed a reputation as an artistic innovator, though the idea to reimagine *The War of the Worlds* would not have occurred to him if not for a radio documentary he heard in September 1988, which told the story of the 1938 broadcast. It captured his imagination, and his desire to recreate that magic increased when he realized that the 50th anniversary of the broadcast was fast looming. Could he possibly write and produce a complex dramatization in the time remaining before the anniversary date, which was then only a month away?

Orson Welles and the Mercury Theatre achieved the impossible in just seven days, but Coelho did not have a Koch or a Houseman to help him, nor the backing of a team of actors and technicians well practiced in working together to tight deadlines. Coelho had to put together his own Mercury Theatre for the occasion and so his first thought was to find a well-known radio personality to be the voice of his broadcast, a search that led him to a meeting with the journalist Ferreirinha Antunes. Antunes was the host of the very popular Sunday morning discussion program *Encontro às Dez* (Meeting at Ten), which aired on Rádio Braga between 10 A.M. and 1 P.M. A trusted and respected journalist, Antunes was the perfect person to lend the necessary degree of authenticity to proceedings. Better yet, he was an enthusiastic convert to the idea, and as luck would have it a regular edition of his show would fall on October 30.

With a key member of the cast secured and a date and time agreed for the broadcast, Coelho was able to turn his attention to the script. He appears not to have referred to the original Howard Koch script, preferring to dissect the original novel meticulously and craft his own unique, modernized version of the story for radio. To this end he spent three weeks working from the book, only turning in the first part of the script to his colleagues on October 25. Meanwhile he had begun to assemble his cast and crew, selecting Luis Santos to create the sound effects and asking Maria José, Gloria Fernandes and Francisco Costa to take on various roles within the production. Coelho himself assumed the role of the reporter who first alerts the world to the existence of the Martians and follows their remorseless rampage toward Braga.

With the date of transmission fast approaching, concerns began to surface, with Manuel Moreira, one of the senior managers at the station, expressing misgivings and asking to see a copy of the script. Coelho had already dismissed the idea that the drama might cause a panic like the one in 1938, though one might think he should have been more concerned by the impact of the Portuguese version created by Matos Maia in 1958. Coelho's composure aside, the station insisted on precautions, issuing a press release to local newspapers that on Sunday morning they would be broadcasting a special tribute to Orson Welles in commemoration of the 50th anniversary of the celebrated CBS radio broadcast. But this was only released late on the afternoon of October 29, and since the station was unwilling to pay for any advertising in the newspapers the story did not receive a great deal of exposure. Some advertising was aired, but this also came late in the day on October 29.

Meanwhile the situation in the studio echoed that in 1938, with a tense last-minute rush to complete the program. There was some argument as to whether it should be recorded or go out live, but in the end it was decided that a recording would be best. It was two in the morning on October 30 before the work was complete, and then the exhausted cast adjourned to listen to the result of their labors. Coelho was not convinced that they had achieved their aims, but by 4 A.M. it was too late to do anything more. Forgoing sleep, he waited tensely for the dawn in the company of Maria José and Luis Santos. The dawn arrived with a highly symbolic bang as a loud thunderstorm shook the region.

At 10 A.M., Ferreirinha Antunes took to the air to deliver what sounded like his normal program. In an attempt to boost the normal listening figures, it had been announced earlier that a special interview with an important local person would take place later in the program, and while we are lacking any indication of the actual numbers who tuned in, it seems likely that a good many would have been blissfully unaware of what was about to happen. At first Antunes delivers his program live to air as per usual, and for about a quarter of an hour nothing untoward happens, but at approximately 10:18 A.M. the recording is switched on. Costa Guimarães, a manager at the station, is heard to enter the studio and interrupt Antunes, who protests vainly at this unwarranted intrusion. Surely, whatever story has broken, it can wait until the next scheduled news program at 11? But

Guimarães is adamant that this news is so important they must connect immediately to José Manuel Coelho, who is standing by in the town of Cabanelas.

Cabanelas is a tiny parish of the county of Vila Verde located a little over 10 kilometers west of Braga, just the sort of isolated community perfect for this kind of deception. Coelho is hastily connected with the studio and immediately launches into a detailed description of a thirty-meter-long cylindrical object, which has crashed in the vicinity. It is a dark gray in color, radiates great heat and periodically discharges large volumes of white vapor, making it very difficult to get close. Cleverly, Coelho works in some modern-sounding speculation as to the origin of the object, proposing that it may be a secret military device from a foreign power rather than an extraterrestrial spacecraft. As the minutes tick by Antunes, Guimarães and Coelho continue to speculate at length on the nature of the object, and at first there is much excitement that they are lucky enough to be present at what may be a landmark moment in the history of the world. Coelho interviews several witnesses to the landing of the object and reports that as it has cooled, a rhythmic banging has been heard emanating from within. This he interprets as the sound of occupants.

By now a huge crowd, perhaps 1,000 people, has gathered around the object, with many taking photographs, but then the excitement turns to terror as Coelho interrupts the studio chatter with an impassioned description of a Martian creature that has unexpectedly emerged from the cylinder. Coelho is stricken with fright at the sight of the Martians, which he has reimagined as a curious hybrid of human beings and the classic tentacled creatures of the original novel. It is a not altogether successful idea, as the rather confused description dilutes the essential otherworldly quality of the Martians, which of course made them such successful monsters in the first place, but there is little time for listeners to ponder their appearance as the pace of events is quickening.

Back in the studio, Costa Guimarães has disturbing news of a second landing on the beach of Portinho da Arrábida just to the south of Lisbon, but before listeners can digest this new information, Coelho is urgently returned to the air with an even more frightening report. The Martian heat-ray has savagely struck down a peace delegation, and the crowd surrounding the cylinder has fled in terror. Coelho is able to continue to report from a safe distance, informing listeners that the army is expected on the scene shortly and that the authorities are issuing pleas for calm, though in what feels like a pointed political barb, he reports that local residents are criticizing the response of the authorities, and were these events happening in America, it would surely all be resolved by now. The broadcast has now reached its halfway point, and there is a musical intermission, featuring the tracks *I Can't Believe It's Real* and *Climbing Devil's Tower* from the film *Close Encounters of the Third Kind*.

After a 25-minute interlude the drama resumes with Ferreirinha Antunes and Costa Guimarães summarizing the events of the last hour before receiving an update from Coelho on the escalating situation in and around Cabanelas. Coelho reports that he has found temporary refugee at a small café a few kilometers from the landing site, but this is likely to be evacuated soon. A military column has been wiped out by poison gas and the Martians may soon have Braga in their sights.

In the studio Antunes and Guimarães are finding it difficult to convey the enormity of the situation, and can only advise their listeners to stay tuned for any further developments. At this point Maria José enters the studio with the news that she has received a telephone call from a resident of Merelim São Paio (a few miles from the landing site at Cabanelas) who claims to have witnessed enormous Martian war machines on the march, sowing death and destruction as they go. This terrible report is corroborated by Coelho, who piles on the horror with considerable skill, describing a blackened, charred landscape littered with the bodies of the dead.

Following cautiously in the footsteps of the Martian tripods, he then delivers a final devastating report. The Martians are capturing human prisoners and sucking the blood from their bodies, and should they continue on their present course will reach Braga within a matter of minutes. In the studio, Guimarães informs listeners that the train station is at that moment being obliterated and that he and his colleagues are preparing to flee for their lives. Antunes is the last to speak. He says, "May God be merciful and save us from this catastrophe. We have to leave the city!"[1]

And with this despairing statement, the drama came to its planned abrupt ending, with two classical music pieces played from the soundtrack to the film *2001: A Space Odyssey.* First came Gyorgy Ligeti's haunting *Requiem for Soprano, Mezzo Soprano, Two Mixed Choirs & Orchestra,* then on a lighter note (intended to signify rebirth after a terrible ordeal) came *Blue Danube* by Johann Strauss II. The plan was then to assemble the entire cast for a roundtable discussion of the program, but in the unsettling circumstances that were fast developing this was the last thing possible, for in the space of just over an hour the atmosphere in the studio had changed considerably.

At first it seemed as if the program would pass without serious incident and Coelho and his colleagues were in high spirits, even if the first call received at around 10:30 had been derisive of their efforts. Then a second call arrived, this time from the Guimarães Radio Foundation, to ask what was happening in Braga. The foundation had had several inquiries and wanted to know what to tell people. Another caller asks to speak to Orson Welles, prompting Maria José to reply mischievously that he can't come to the phone as he is in the studio. At first this is all very amusing and exciting, but little by little the volume of calls is increasing, as is the apparent level of apprehension from the listeners. Other local stations such as Rádio Trofa and Rádio Barcelos begin to call in demanding information, and the volunteer fire department from Vila Verde sends out a patrol to investigate.

Outside the weather is going from bad to worse, and to compound matters further the local branch of the Portuguese Red Cross had scheduled a drill that morning to simulate a major accident on the Avenida de la Liberdade, the most important street in the city, located just a few hundred yards from the radio station. It seems not at all implausible to imagine that someone looking out of their window onto the storm-lashed streets of Braga that morning would, between the thunder and the Red Cross vehicles, have had their very worst fears confirmed. The *Correio do Minho* (Minho Post) of October 31 offers the intriguing alternative perspective that some listeners thought the radio broadcast and the Red Cross exercise had been prearranged together, prompting the Red Cross to issue a statement categorically denying any such connection.

By now the two phones in the studio are ringing non-stop and the news filtering through is beginning to seriously alarm everyone. There are reports of entire families fleeing their homes and large queues forming at petrol stations on the roads leading out of Braga. At 11 A.M., with some 45 minutes of the drama yet to go, Coelho and his cast become aware that an agitated crowd of several hundred persons are gathering outside the station. Luckily the police are on hand to defend the station, but even so, some protesters succeed in climbing the stairs to the studio door where a brief fracas develops. Aside from the insults and threats, Francisco Costa is injured in the arm. With security restored but the crowd continuing to lay siege to the entrance, the suggestion is made that the transmission be halted, but Coelho is determined to see things through to the end and insists that with just 10 minutes left to go, they should not give in to intimidation. At approximately 11:44 A.M. the drama reaches its natural conclusion.

Realizing that it is imperative that calm be restored, both Antunes and Guimarães take turns to reassure listeners that they have been listening to a play, but the drama is not yet over for those still effectively trapped in the studio. At midday officers of the Public Security Police arrive and invite the station director, Manuel Moreira, to their headquarters for an interview. The police take with them the reel containing the broadcast and the script. Luckily for Moreira, Portugal was by 1988 a democracy and the dreaded secret police that had threatened Matos Maia were a thing of the past, so any interrogation he faced would have been a lot less intimidating. Indeed, later that afternoon Moreira was able to call the station with instructions to immediately begin transmitting a regular disclaimer making clear to listeners the true nature of the broadcast.

Though the situation finally appears to be calming, there is a further moment of alarm when a call is received from a person purporting to be a sympathetic listener warning that an attack is being planned on the station. The attackers allegedly intend to destroy the station with all those in it. Fearing the worst, station personnel lock the doors and windows and call the police, but as time wears on it soon becomes apparent that the call was, ironically, a hoax. A second call later in the afternoon claiming that a bomb has been planted in the station also turns out to be untrue, but such is the level of anxiety that two private security firms are hired to protect the station overnight. In a further indication of the lingering alarm and anger among the population, it is reported that in the municipalities of Póvoa de Lanhoso and Vieira do Minho, armed police patrol the streets until the early evening.

The following morning, the story was front page news and Coelho was kept busy answering telephone calls from all over the world, including one from the BBC, but as with every previous radio scare examined in this book the same pivotal questions arise: was there really a significantly agitated reaction from the public, and if there was, what exactly did they do and why did they react in such an extreme manner? In truth, the volume of calls to the station was not particularly high, with Paulo Sousa, a reporter at Rádio Braga, putting the number at approximately 100. The *Correio do Minho* of October 30 offers up information indicating that a considerable number of calls were also directed to the authorities all across the district, such as fire and police stations and the armed forces. The *Correio do Minho* additionally reports on large numbers of residents who fled their homes in Braga carrying their valuables, with chaos on the main roads leading out of the city as they attempted to reach the nearby cities of Porto and Barcelos. The suggestion that the

Vila Verde fire department dispatched trucks to the scene is also corroborated, with a member of the department quoted as claiming to have witnessed "a large throng of people fleeing from their homes with their children."

But among the most compelling evidence for a large scale scare in Braga is the account of events recorded by José Manuel Coelho himself in his book *Os Marcianos em Braga* (The Martians in Braga). Coelho's book (now long out of print) offers a detailed account of the making of the broadcast and the events that it triggered and is backed up by dozens of newspaper clippings from around the world. While this impressive volume doesn't vouch for the accuracy of the story, the fact that the 1988 broadcast was keenly reported all across Europe and as far afield as the Dominican Republic and Hong Kong means that the reported scale of events cannot be so easily dismissed or diminished.

It seems quite likely then that Braga was in the throes of a major disturbance on the morning of October 30, 1988, and we must then ask why. A particularly intriguing quote is attributed to Costa Guimarães in the *Correio do Minho*, in which he suggests that a form of autosuggestion was at work, with several calls received at the station from people wholly convinced they were experiencing the events they were hearing. Said Guimarães, "They even called in saying that more than 500 people had already been killed." Something similar happened in 1938, when people reported they could see the flames of battle on the New York skyline, but it seems likely that the highly religious inhabitants of Braga were particularly susceptible to this kind of self-delusion. Indeed Wells' imagery, replete with bloodsucking, fire-breathing monsters is loaded with religious resonance, and Coelho does not shy from graphically describing these things in his script. In 1938 some people thought they were under attack not by Martians but by Nazis. Might it be that in Portugal in 1988, some listeners came to the conclusion that they were being invaded by the denizens of Hell?

Unfortunately the author has been unable to hear the Braga broadcast, but as seems clear from the published script, Coelho was eminently successful in his adaptation and as in so many other events of this nature, the impassioned delivery of well-written dialogue from a seemingly trusted source was enough to bypass the normal critical faculties of his listeners. Factor in a combination of religious preconditioning to apocalyptic imagery with an unfortunate confluence of appalling weather and a training exercise by the emergency services and all the pieces fall into place for another classic Martian radio scare. It cannot have helped either that at no point during the broadcast was there a disclaimer or explanation, though past experience teaches us that when people become caught up in the moment, there is little chance of them heeding a warning, no matter how forcibly it is presented.

Despite the chaos and upset it caused, Rádio Braga suffered no censure for its actions. In the final analysis the broadcast probably did more good than harm to the reputation and ratings of the station. Perhaps this is secretly what had been hoped for, for no matter how hard anyone protests their innocence in such a situation, the suspicion must be that the perpetrators knew exactly what they were doing. The fact remains that even if the reaction of listeners had genuinely caught Coelho completely and utterly by surprise, he clearly knew in a relatively short space of time that his broadcast was causing a major upheaval in Braga, yet resisted calls to stop the transmission and calm the situation. This does not necessarily make Coelho out as a villain. Instead, it is as if the performers in these extraordinary circumstances become as carried away by the momentum of the situation as their listeners, and that once under way these events are then almost impossible to bring to a halt.

It also seems impossible to stop people repeating the error, no matter how many times it has resulted in calamity and mishap. It is therefore not at all surprising that the Martians were able to launch one last invasion in the closing years of the 20th century, though there are perhaps serious grounds for concern that people could still fall so easily for essentially the same hoax 60 years after the original. Orson Welles would no doubt have been delighted, though the inhabitants of the Portuguese town of Palmela were likely a lot less pleased that they should be the latest and last victims of the longest and most sustained series of hoax events in the history of radio broadcasting. We can however take some comfort that this final Martian invasion was the least troublesome of all to the inhabitants of Earth, with not nearly the same scale of alarm as has been recorded for previous assaults.

This last Martian assault was the work of Antena 3, a radio station in Lisbon operated by the Portuguese Public Service Broadcasting Corporation. The hour-long drama, which was intended as a 60th-anniversary celebration of the original 1938 broadcast, aired between 8 A.M. and 9 A.M. on Friday, October 30, 1998, and landed the Martians in the town of Palmela. Speaking to the *Público* newspaper of October 31, a spokesperson from Antena 3 indicated that Palmela was chosen "for no specific reason," though it ticks all the relevant boxes for the kind of place most suited to a Martian invasion. The town is located some 40 kilometers northwest of Lisbon, and is a relatively small community in the shadow of the Arrábida mountain range. It is therefore sufficiently remote that most listeners would not easily be able to investigate the story themselves, but close enough to a major population center that a palpable sense of impending threat could easily be provoked. The reaction as recorded in the *Público* the next morning followed an all too familiar pattern, with a flood of concerned calls to the authorities, some from as far afield as the town of Moimenta da Beira, 400 kilometers north of Lisbon. Among the testimony recorded in *Público* is the story of a schoolteacher who sent her charges home and locked the gates against the Martians, and the boss of a construction firm who arrived at his building site to discover that his workers had abandoned their tools, though it is not recorded if they had run home or to the nearest bar.

It would be interesting to learn if airing the show when many people would have been in their cars on the way to work in any way contributed to listener reaction, for confronting someone with a potential threat to life and limb while behind the wheel of an automobile would certainly seem to be tempting fate. If, as sociologists maintain, people are more inclined to panic if they are presented with a narrowing range of escape options, then telling thousands of people they are in mortal danger during rush hour could be judged a particularly reckless thing to do. Unfortunately (or perhaps thankfully) no evidence has come to light revealing what drivers did that morning, but it could be that Antena 3 had a particularly lucky escape, especially given the exacerbating role religion has played in previous Portuguese broadcasts, for in randomly selecting the town of Palmela as the location of their Martian beachhead the station may have inadvertently tempted fate even more. Palmela is well known in Portugal as a major religious center,* which could certainly imply that its inhabitants would be particularly susceptible to suggestion. Ironically, it may be that another equally powerful kind of religion saved the region from descending into chaos and upheaval, for according to *Público*, the local radio station serving Palmela was running a competition that morning to win tickets to a big soccer match. As fate would finally have it, many potential listeners were completely oblivious to all the excitement. This could be considered an inauspicious end to the Martian designs on Earth, but as we will see in the next chapter, the original 1938 broadcast has had an incredibly lasting effect on American popular culture. In the final analysis, the Martians may have lost all the battles, but they could very plausibly claim to have won the war.

*Palmela is renowned for festivals dedicated to Our Lady of Escudeira.

17

REMEMBERING 1938
An American Myth

There are some things that simply never go away—they become a part of the fabric of society. As with a loose thread, the urge to tug and see what might happen is never far away. Ever since Orson Welles first showed the world how easy it was to unravel our carefully ordered society, there have been plenty of other equally inspired (some might say reckless) people who have followed in his footsteps, but where in other countries the furor has been short-lived and quickly consigned to a footnote in history, in America the original 1938 broadcast has become something to be celebrated and remembered. Its explosive effect has rippled out over the intervening decades, inspiring and shaping some of the best-known motifs in modern science fiction. Many of the biggest and most bombastic Hollywood blockbusters owe a seldom-acknowledged debt to both Orson Welles and H. G. Wells, but the original broadcast itself has also become something of a cult item, with references to it slipping almost unnoticed into the most unexpected of places.

If not for the adamant resistance of Orson Welles, the broadcast might have achieved even greater fame. Fresh from his triumph with the Mercury Theatre and *The War of the Worlds*, Welles accepted in July 1939 what has often been described as the greatest contract ever offered by a movie studio to an artist, though in fact it was not quite so revolutionary as Welles and the studio publicity machine liked to pretend. It is true that in unprecedented fashion, RKO had given a contract to a raw 24-year-old with the only a passing experience of movie making, and it is equally true that he was allowed considerable freedom in his choice of material, but other provisions in the contract effectively gave him just six rolls of the dice. This was the number of ideas Welles was allowed to pitch, none of which RKO was obliged to accept. After that, RKO got six chances to pitch to Welles, but if at the end of this process neither party could agree on the subject of a first movie, then the contract was to be declared null and void. This is not to say that contract was not revolutionary in many ways, especially as regards the freedom Welles was promised on set and in the editing suite, but as with most things in Welles' life, there was an inevitable degree of self-aggrandizement at work. While Welles was milking his good fortune in the press, behind the scenes he was under considerable pressure to turn his talents to an obvious first project, a movie version of *The War of the Worlds*.

It is not entirely clear what form a *War of the Worlds* movie was to take. Would it be a reenactment of the broadcast or an adaptation of the book, or perhaps some hybrid of the two? In truth it had probably not even been considered, but there were those on the RKO board who believed that such a movie would play well given the situation in the world, and especially so with the added publicity to be gained from Welles' involvement. Welles was not actually against the idea of returning to the story, but not for his first movie. RKO head George Schaefer took Welles' side in this conflict, explaining to the board that Welles "does not want to be the horror man."[1] Perhaps this is what Welles had told Schaefer, but it might also be another indication of Welles' nervousness at allowing any scrutiny of the authorship of the broadcast. We have already seen in Chapter 9 how Welles fought furiously to prevent Hadley Cantril crediting *The War of the Worlds* script to Howard Koch, and clearly if any sort of movie relating to the broadcast was made, the role of Koch would have to come to light.

Whatever the true reason for Welles' reluctance to make a *War of the Worlds* movie, it should be lamented as one of the great lost chances in cinema history. Given what Welles achieved with special effects and dramatic techniques in *Citizen Kane*, it is breathtaking to imagine what his version of *The War of the Worlds* might have looked like. Tragically for Welles he never again achieved the same unfettered degree of freedom in Hollywood and the opportunity was lost, but had he gone forth with *The War of the Worlds*, it is tempting to imagine that he might have succeeded in making the genre respectable in the 1940s, ushering in a much earlier age of quality science fiction movies.

In fact it seems very unlikely that RKO could have ever made the movie, since H. G. Wells had sold the movie rights in perpetuity to Paramount in June 1926, with a first treatment produced as early as November of that year by Roy J. Pomeroy, an accomplished special effects man who would go on to win an Oscar in 1928 for his work on the aerial epic *Wings*. Pomeroy's treatment is very much a product of its time, introducing a particularly cumbersome romantic plotline, though it would have been fascinating to see a silent version of *The War of the Worlds*. Several more treatments followed over the years, including most intriguingly a swiftly curtailed attempt to make a movie set during the 1938 broadcast. The originator of this undated idea appears to have been a person named Mel Baker, for whom no biographical information has been found, but also involved was Erwin Gelsey, a jobbing writer who worked at one time or another for most of the major studios between 1932 and the early 1950s.

In a long letter to Gelsey, Baker set out his vision for the movie, which he saw as an opportunity to weave together a multitude of small stories set against the background of the broadcast. He talks of a romantically rejected high school junior, a recently qualified doctor freshly arrived in town, a married couple both of whom are setting out on infidelities, and a newly divorced woman returning alone to her home. Baker reveals himself keen to make full use of the material gathered by Hadley Cantril and the original broadcast audio, but he also allows himself to get carried away with some tall tales, claiming in his enthusiasm that a man rushing to see his priest for final unction was killed when his car left the road and hit a tree. Most interestingly, Baker also apparently saw the movie as something of a public service endeavor, educating the public as to the perils of overreacting to rumors. This altruistic approach may have been motivated by a sense that publicity for the movie could benefit from an association with the authorities, which also helps us to date the project.

In Baker's letter to Gelsey he alludes to A-bomb threats and the likelihood that the formation of a civilian defense organization was imminent. Such an organization was founded in 1950. A further clue to the dating of the project comes in an internal memo sent from Paramount's Bernard Smith to Don Hartman confirming the rejection of the project, as it was not considered a sound commercial idea. The memo goes on to recommend that a movie based on the novel of *The War of the Worlds* would be a better prospect, with an intriguing handwritten addendum added naming directors George Pal and King Vidor. It was of course Pal who would in 1953 finally bring the H. G. Wells novel to the big screen for Paramount.

Paramount would return in spectacular fashion to the story in 2005, producing a big-budget version of *The War of the Worlds* with Steven Spielberg in the director's chair and Tom Cruise in the starring role. Spielberg's movie charts its own unique course in its interpretation of the original novel. Morgan Freeman does a credible job of channeling the spirit of Orson Welles in his introduction. The New Jersey location certainly suggests that Spielberg and his writers were honoring a debt to Welles and Koch. This becomes even more apparent when we consider that several years previously, Spielberg bought at auction one of the last surviving original copies of the 1938 script and has publicly stated that he thought it would make a great movie. It is a great shame that Spielberg chose not to channel his energies into a big-budget retelling of the 1938 broadcast, but plenty of other people have kept the original Howard Koch script alive over the years. It is tempting to say that not a Halloween goes by without the story being reenacted somewhere in the world, either on stage or over the radio, though generally without any deleterious effects.

If there is one place in America that was profoundly affected by the 1938 broadcast, it was, of course, the community of Grover's Mill in New Jersey. It was here that Howard Koch landed his Martian forces and here that the first fatalities of the war were recorded. Grover's Mill was and still is an archetypal model of small-town America. The community takes its name from a mill that has been on the site since at least 1759, when a Daniel Wolsey was recorded as the operator, though it was not until 1868, when Joseph H. Grover bought the mill, that the origin of the name can be pinpointed. The mill has long since ceased to operate, but the building remains in use as a private residence.

After the hubbub caused by the broadcast had subsided, Grover's Mill returned to normality quickly enough, but the residents could not entirely forget (nor were they ever allowed to forget) the events of that night. On another Halloween holiday 31 years later, Howard Koch visited Grover's Mill to discover what, if any, memories still persisted. He found a community plainly exasperated at the attention it continued to receive from reporters every Halloween, but also encountered some residents who were happy to expound at length on their moment of fame. Koch also discovered that the fiction of that night had bled through to the real world, as he was assured in all seriousness that as a young man Orson Welles had in fact stayed in a guest room at a local establishment called Cotswald Cottage.[2] Welles was said to have been writing a book, which could only have been *Everybody's Shakespeare*, which he cowrote with Skipper Hill. Alas, the story cannot be true, for it is well recorded that Welles wrote some of the book while on his extraordinary travels through Africa and Spain in 1933 and the remainder under Hill's strict supervision in Chicago. It also seems utterly implausible that Welles would fail to comment on the spectacular coincidence that Koch had accidentally chosen such a personally familiar location for his Martian beachhead.

The memorial to the 1938 *War of the Worlds* broadcast in Van Nest Park, West Windsor Township, New Jersey (courtesy James Ragucci).

Grover's Mill has long since forgotten its resentment of the indignities heaped upon it, and now regularly celebrates the broadcast with special festivities. In 1988 the community gathered for a 50th-anniversary celebration, which featured among other things a parade, panels (including a special event reuniting people who had experienced the broadcast firsthand), a "panic run" and a dedication ceremony in Van Nest Park for a wonderful monument commemorating the 1938 broadcast. The beautifully sculpted plinth shows Welles at the microphone, a family of frightened listeners at his feet, and looming above them all, a Martian tripod. Howard Koch was on hand to witness the unveiling of the monument, upon which is carved the following dedication:

> On the evening of October 30, 1938, Orson Welles and the Mercury Theatre presented a dramatization of H. G. Wells' *The War of the Worlds* as adapted by Howard Koch. This was to become a landmark in broadcast history, provoking continuing thought about media responsibility, social psychology and civil defense. For a brief time as many as one million people throughout the country believed that Martians had invaded the earth, beginning with Grover's Mill, New Jersey.

For the residents of Grover's Mill the broadcast is now a fun episode to recollect and a welcome boost to the local economy, but the ripples from that night have extended into other areas of society, though some of the connections are more fanciful than others. What seems incontrovertible is the influence the broadcast has had on the entertainment industry, with the use of "news flashes" within dramas becoming commonplace and well-

Logo for the official 50th-anniversary celebration of *The War of the Worlds* at Grover's Mill.

known news anchors being drafted to play themselves to bolster the realism of fictional stories.

Meanwhile, *The War of the Worlds* broadcast of 1938 has made an astoundingly large number of appearances in other media, and while it is often only a throwaway detail in a movie, comic, book or television series, it is extremely significant that entirely fictional stories are referencing another fictional story as if it were real. It is precisely this sort of intertextuality that signals the final, absolute absorption of the broadcast into popular culture. It would be fair to say that few other fictional properties have come close to the same level of reverential devotion, with perhaps only the science fiction television show *The Twilight Zone* enjoying a similar degree of penetration into the popular imagination. *The War of the Worlds* broadcast has also become a common phrase in the lexicon of reporters and commentators, as news stories make oblique references to the broadcast in a multitude of generally apocalyptic contexts, from the war on terror to the see-saw state of the world's financial systems.

The very first reference to the 1938 *War of the Worlds* broadcast came only a few years after its transmission, in, of all things, the pages of the April 1940 issue of the comic book *Batman*. Not just any Batman comic, it should be emphasized, but the very first issue of this historic publication. Original copies now cost tens of thousands of dollars, though it would be pure hubris to suggest that this value is in any way enhanced by the inclusion of a reference to the 1938 broadcast. It is, however, a story that capitalizes on lingering memories of the broadcast, featuring a first devilish turn from Batman's arch-nemesis the Joker, who in the opening panels hijacks a radio program to predict that the millionaire Henry Claridge will be killed at midnight and the Claridge diamond stolen. One listener is less than impressed, laughing it off as a hoax like "that fellow who scared everybody with that story about Mars the last time." Of course, the prediction does come true, and the Joker then proceeds to make a series of similar radio announcements, each time fulfilling his prophecy and leaving behind victims scared by his hideous trademark rictus grin.

Another wonderful nod to our broadcast came in 1946, in the unlikely sounding setting of a Porky Pig cartoon. Robert "Bob" Clampett designed the timeless character of Porky Pig in 1935 and was one of a legendary team of animators including Tex Avery and Chuck Jones who made their home in Warner Brothers' famous "Termite Terrace" studios located on Sunset Boulevard in Los Angeles. From this dilapidated wooden building, so named for its massive infestation of termites, came a series of cartoons and characters that have become synonymous with a golden age at the studio. Among any number of landmark productions, *Kitty Kornered* is widely held to be one of Clampett's finest cartoons from this period. It is a freewheeling and anarchic flow of wacky ideas that pits Porky against a gang of fractious felines who are determined to stay in the warm on a cold winter's night and who counterattack by staging their own fake radio invasion from Mars.

Though there is not the slightest reference in the cartoon to Orson Welles or the 1938 broadcast, the debt is obvious, though it would be intriguing to learn what had prompted Clampett to include his reference to *The War of the Worlds* in *Kitty Kornered*. A possible clue is to be found in an earlier project that he worked on. In 1931 Clampett approached the author of the John Carter of Mars books, Edgar Rice Burroughs, for permission to attempt a groundbreaking series of cartoon shorts based upon his Martian stories. Clampett received an enthusiastic reception and, together with Burroughs' son Jack, worked for a number of years to bring this remarkable idea to fruition. They got close, producing much material including a superb test reel, but alas the project was sunk by a nervous studio. Perhaps *Kitty Kornered* was an oblique nod to that earlier Martian experience.

From the sublime to ridiculous is a phrase that neatly sums up the next reference to the broadcast, as Orson Welles himself takes a starring role in a 1950 issue of the *Superman* comic book, though precisely how it came about is a matter of conjecture. No biography of Welles makes reference to a collaboration with DC Comics, nor is there any indication that the publisher sought permission for the use of Welles' name and likeness, though promotional tie-ins between comic book companies and movie studios were not then unknown. Welles was starring in an Italian-made movie that year called *Black Magic*. Tellingly, the comic book story is called *Black Magic on Mars*, so this may very well have been an early example of creative cross-promotion between the studio and a comic book company. The timing is certainly right, with the movie released in America in late 1949 and the cover of the comic dated January/February 1950. In fact, the timing was probably even more opportune, since it was routine at the time for comics to hit the newsstands cover dated months ahead of their actual date of publication, as this made them appear fresher than their rivals. Equally plausible is that the writer may have read about Welles' role in the movie and decided to incorporate it into his own story, though it is hard to believe that the notoriously litigious Welles would have allowed an unofficial use of his name and likeness to go unchallenged.

The name of the comic book writer appears to be unknown, and even the artist is a matter of conjecture, though Wayne Boring is a good candidate, with Stan Kaye the likely inker. Whoever the writer was, he rustles up a vividly improbable tale that sees Welles whisked off to Mars, having come across an untended spacecraft while filming *Black Magic* in Italy. Curiosity gets the better of Welles, and he finds himself trapped in the rocket as it soars off for Mars. (As any fan of that era's science fiction will know, this was a common occurrence. Absent-minded scientists were always building rocket ships in obscure locations and leaving the door wide open.)

Two hours later (that was some rocket engine!), Welles is stepping out onto the surface of Mars, still attired in his flamboyant movie costume, where he is swiftly assailed by the Martians and brought before their leader, the Great Martler. The Martians speak English and goose step about like Nazis, for Martler is an admirer of Hitler and has modeled his dictatorship after Nazi Germany, though for some reason the Martians speak English. Welles has arrived on the eve of a Martian invasion, and, turning down Martler's offer of a job as propaganda minister on the soon-to-be-conquered Earth, uses his prop sword to seize control of a radio and broadcast a warning. Of course no one believes a word of it back on Earth. But Superman is not about to take any chances, so he speeds off to Mars, arriving just in time to prevent Welles getting disintegrated for his troubles.

Boring, if he is the artist, does a very credible job of capturing Welles' likeness. The references to the 1938 broadcast are interesting, in that it seems memories of the event were still fresh even a decade later. There are also several intriguing links between Orson Welles and Superman that are worth noting. The man of steel was created by Jerome Siegel and Joe Shuster in 1938, which was of course the year that Welles scared America with his *War of the Worlds* radio broadcast. Welles was also the radio voice of the crime fighter the Shadow, and there is some speculation that Shuster and Siegal took inspiration from the Shadow for the names of their key characters. In the print version of the story, the Shadow was the alter ego of Kent Allard (he was Lamont Cranston on radio), hence Superman's disguise as Clark Kent, while the oft-imperiled Lois Lane was perhaps derived from the name of the Shadow's agent, Margot Lane.

EC Comics (Entertaining Comics) was one of the most controversial experiments in the history of comic books, pushing the prevailing boundaries of taste and decency in the 1950s by daring to publish material that was just as likely to be politically provocative as it was violently shocking. The science fiction titles published by EC are among the finest ever produced, featuring stories and art of unsurpassed quality and imagination. It is noteworthy that EC was a regular publisher of stories by the renowned author Ray Bradbury, including many later collected as *The Martian Chronicles*, and so it seems perfectly fitting that a December 1950 issue of *Weird Science* should have also featured a story which drew upon the 1938 broadcast as its inspiration.

Drawn by EC stalwart Al Feldstein, the story featured in issue 15 of *Weird Science* was called "Panic." In keeping with the EC philosophy of amplifying the horror quotient, this reimagined version of the broadcast is packed with violent imagery, including several suicides and a number of gruesome accidental deaths as crowds panic and flee. The EC writers' take on the broadcast is merely a springboard to allow them to introduce their trademark twist in the tale. The instigator of this particular panic is "Carson Walls," a name just a hair's breadth short of a lawsuit from Orson Welles. Walls is horrified when he discovers the chaos he has unleashed, but memories are short, and several years later (though very much against his better judgment) he is persuaded to repeat the broadcast. This time the papers are full of warnings to the public, so when the broadcast begins, the reaction at first is merely one of mild amusement. Unfortunately for the listening public, they are the victims of a grand deception, for under cover of the broadcast a real invasion is imminent. As the radio frantically issues pleas for the military to intercede, the invaders decimate the defenses of the Earth and assert their dominion over the human race.

EC Comics are a rare treat for anyone with a love of this art form. They had a genuinely dangerous edge and reveled in their reputation as a barb to authority. Their lovingly over-the-top tribute to the 1938 broadcast is a fine addition to this great tradition, featuring stunning artwork and a sparkling script. In fact, such is the quality of the story that it would gain a new lease on life in the 1990s, when it was adapted (rather loosely, it must be said) for the HBO television series *Perversions of Science*.

But America did not have to wait until the 1990s for its first televisual reminder of the events of 1938. This came much sooner than one might imagine, with *The Night America Trembled*, a gem of a production made in 1957 for the renowned Emmy-winning television anthology *Studio One*, though like many television shows at the time it had actually started life on radio. Created in April 1947 for CBS by Canadian émigré Fletcher Markle,* the series had quickly transferred to television, where it ran for a phenomenal 466 episodes and regularly featured many up-and-coming stars, including for this episode a stunning roster of emerging talent, including Warren Beatty, James Coburn, Edward Asner, Warren Oates, Vincent Gardenia and John Astin.

---

*In an entirely unrelated coincidence, Markle was a writer (uncredited) on Orson Welles' 1948 movie *The Lady from Shanghai*.

There is, however, something strange about the episode. Though it is an extremely faithful retelling of events within the studio, going so far as to use the original Howard Koch radio script and musical arrangements, Orson Welles is completely absent, as are any other recognizable characters such as Koch and Houseman. In fact, no one is named at all, which may seem like a particularly cruel omission, except that we know Welles attempted to sue CBS over the *Studio One* production. Perhaps to knock the wind out of his sails they simply removed any reference to him, and as an unfortunate by-product of his intransigence the rest of the Mercury Theatre cast got tossed out with the bathwater.

One inspired piece of casting serves to bridge the gap between this episode and the key participants in the events of 1938. Acting as host is none other than Edward R. Murrow, a particularly resonant casting choice, as his radio reporting of the events leading up to the Second World War did so much to inure American minds to the dangers of foreign invasion. Murrow touches on this very point in his introduction, which he delivers wreathed in his habitual cloud of cigarette smoke.

Clearly at least one person on the production was determined to make the episode as realistic as possible, and that was likely scriptwriter Nelson Bond. A prolific writer for radio in the 1940s, Bond wrote an impressive 46 half-hour crime dramas for the ABC series *Hot Copy* during the 1943-44 season and any number of other episodes for shows such as the *Ford Theatre*, *Mystery on the Air* and *Dimension X*. Bond would therefore have known exactly what a radio studio looked and sounded like. Added up together, the creative talent assembled in front of and behind the camera results in an extraordinary production, boasting a cast that in later years would have cost millions to assemble and a superbly observed script by a writer with an intimate knowledge of the period.

After the unparalleled success of *The Night America Trembled*, American television viewers would have to wait almost two decades for another homage quite as reverential in tone, but cartoon makers had no qualms about purloining the story for their own uses, which has resulted in some wonderful and very unexpected pastiches.

It is rather fitting that Alex Anderson, the creator of the legendary cartoon characters Rocky and Bullwinkle, has acknowledged his debt to radio. In fact he has gone so far as to describe the show as "something between television and radio."[3] Certainly the animation (which was produced in Mexico by a studio apparently lacking staff with an adequate knowledge of English) can be described as very crude, but the show is still beloved by children and adults alike for its surreal take on reality and the surprising sophistication of the scripts. That connection to early radio drama is readily apparent in the cliffhangers that characterized each episode, but none more so than in the very first episode, aired in November 1959, which features a character named Dawson Bells and a mass panic caused by the approach of a mysterious spacecraft from the Moon. The appearance of Bells is so brief that you'll miss it in a moment, and it is interesting to wonder how many children in 1959 would have got this shyly inserted reference. The answer is likely precious few, but the writers clearly remembered the broadcast and knew that parents too would appreciate a joke aimed well above the heads of their children.

Fast forward to 1965 and we find one of the most famous families in American television history next in line for an encounter with the Martians. *The Flintstones* is generally held to be one of the finest cartoon series ever produced, and it made history by becoming the first cartoon series to win a prime-time evening slot. In the sixth season, aired in 1965, the episode "The Masquerade Party" took its inspiration from the 1938 broadcast, entangling perpetual bunglers Fred and Barney in a publicity gimmick for a touring British pop band called The Way Outs, which results in a near riot when a local radio station gets in on the act. The episode was loosely based on an episode of *The Honeymooners* (a show *The Flintstones* was itself modeled on) called "The Man from Space," though that show made no reference at all to *The War of the Worlds*.

Other than the WPRO radio broadcast of 1974, the 1938 broadcast seems to have been largely forgotten in the 1970s, but television did produce one very notable exception, called *The Night That Panicked America*. Inexplicably, it has never been released on home video or DVD. This is a substantial loss, as in very similar fashion to *The Night America Trembled* it beautifully dramatizes the backstory of the 1938 broadcast. Made for television by Paramount and first broadcast on the ABC network on Halloween night in 1975, *The Night That Panicked America* was directed in meticulous detail by Joseph Sargent from a screenplay by Nicholas Meyer and Anthony Wilson. Underpinning his affinity for the material, Meyer also went on to pen and direct *Time After Time*, another historical fantasy in which the author H. G. Wells is revealed to have invented a real time machine that falls into the hands of Jack the Ripper.

Paul Stewart was technical adviser on *The Night That Panicked America*, so we can presume a high degree of authenticity was applied to the replication of the studio environment, and certainly the sense that such shows were produced on a wing and a prayer is authentically captured, especially as regards the highly experimental nature of the sound effects. In this regard it is particularly satisfying to see legendary sound engineer Ora Nichols depicted in the cast of characters by Shelley Morrison, though inexplicably the marvelously world-weary Nichols is never identified by name (except in the credits as "Toni"), even though she is clearly intended to be Nichols. This rather baffling slight aside, it is fitting to note that *The Night That Panicked America* would go on to win an Emmy in 1976 for Outstanding Achievement in Movie Sound Editing.

John Houseman, too, is treated rather strangely in this production, receiving only a passing mention, though unlike *The Night America Trembled*, many other key players are present and depicted correctly, including Howard Koch. Most importantly of all, Orson Welles is at the heart of the story, where he very much belongs, with Paul Shenar capturing the great man's personality and mannerisms with considerable aplomb.

If the 1970s were fallow years, the mid–1980s surely marked the beginning of a golden age, with references to the broadcast coming thick and fast. The first rumblings of this veritable avalanche of veneration came in a very unusual movie called *The Adventures of Buckaroo Banzai Across the Eighth Dimension*. Released in 1984 to a lukewarm reception by critics, it has since assumed a well-deserved cult reputation. Peter Weller plays the titular Buckaroo Banzai, a world-renowned scientist, adventurer, brain surgeon and rock star! Caught up in a plot by the Red Lectoid invaders from a parallel dimension, Banzai and his team trace the invaders to Grover's Mill, where in 1938 the alien invaders first intruded into our dimension.

Director W. D. Richter has some impressive credits to his name, including the screenplay to the extremely well regarded 1978 remake of *Invasion of the Body Snatchers* and a cowriting credit on John Carpenter's *Big Trouble in Little China*. He directs *Buckaroo Banzai* with a keen eye for the absurdities of the situation, and while the script by Earl Mac Rauch is wildly uneven, the charming pulp flavor he injects into the movie is gleefully reciprocated by the cast. John Lithgow steals the show with a trademark manic performance as the insane Red Lectoid leader Lord John Whorfin, while by contrast Peter Weller plays Banzai with a remarkably straight face. Ellen Barkin, Jeff Goldblum and Christopher Lloyd add their own considerable talents to a great ensemble cast that borrows its key conceit from the pulp fiction and radio crime fighter *Doc Savage*, for where Savage had his specialist helpers the Fabulous Five, so Banzai can call upon his Hong Kong Cavaliers to assist him in dicey situations.

We have already encountered several comic book flirtations with the 1938 broadcast in the course of this survey, but the Crimson Avenger is by far the best, a hugely enjoyable paean to the 1930s. Rather aptly, the Crimson Avenger was created in the October 1938 issue of *Detective Comics* and joins the ranks of other great masked crime-fighting figures of the time such as the Shadow and the Green Hornet, all of whom were highly derivative of each other, though the Crimson Avenger is a particularly close match to the Green Hornet. Both of them were newspapermen with a secret identity, both had an Asian valet, and their weapon of choice was a nonlethal gas gun. Numerous rather suspicious similarities aside, the Crimson Avenger does have the unique distinction of being the first masked superhero from DC Comics, predating even Batman.

The Crimson Avenger was essentially a forgotten character by the early 1950s, but in 1986 he was briefly resurrected for a single issue of the comic book *Secret Origins*, which undertook in its 50-issue run to retell or reinvent the histories of various DC super-heroes. In issue 5 it was the Crimson Avenger's turn, and given the auspicious date of the character's first appearance, it would have been criminal not to include in some way a reference to *The War of the Worlds*. But in fact as scripted by comic book legend Roy Thomas, the story goes far beyond a mere reference, weaving the broadcast into the very fabric of the story with great deal of panache and confidence.

It is the eve of the broadcast and the 25-year-old publisher of the *Globe Leader* Lee Travis is in ebullient mood. His newspaper is about to scoop the *New York Times* with the news that Japan is to withdraw from agencies of the League of Nations in protest of "slanderous accusations" from China. His good mood is not shared by his Chinese driver, who is rather more concerned at the casualties inflicted on his homeland by the Japanese. Thomas works these authentic details into the story with considerable dexterity, building in a few frames of dialogue (with able assistance from artist Gene Colon) a vivid sense of a world teetering on the brink of disaster.

Stopping off at his office, Travis takes time out for an interview with a beautiful magazine reporter named Claudia Barker, in which we learn that Travis had fought in the Spanish Civil War against the Fascists, and upon returning home injured had inherited the family newspaper business. The encounter with Barker is bruising but invigorating, and Travis is looking forward to the opportunity to meet her again at a charity masquerade ball that evening in aid of Chinese victims of the war. Travis' secretary has arranged a costume for him, which turns out to be a flamboyantly attired "highway rob-ber." Borrowing his driver's gun to complete the illusion, Travis sets out for the party in a rueful mood, wondering if, as Claudia had insinuated in the interview, he has betrayed his ideals by taking over the *Globe Leader*.

At the party, Travis is confronted with a woman who shrieks that the Martians have landed. The partygoers gather around the radio to hear the news, the dialogue for which is a word-for-word transcript from the Howard Koch script, but Travis is skeptical and his instincts are confirmed when Claudia arrives to announce that they are listening to a drama by Orson Welles. That should be the end of matters, but suddenly the party is interrupted by the arrival of a quartet of tommy-gun-toting Martians demanding (somewhat oddly) that the guests hand over their valuables. As Travis quickly realizes, these are no Martians, but rather an astute gang of criminals out to take advantage of the broadcast.

Claudia makes the same deduction, but on confronting the leader of the "Martian" gang she is fatally wounded. The costumed hoodlums flee the scene of the crime with Travis and his driver in hot pursuit, and there is a superbly crafted car chase, liberally interspersed with more dialogue from the broadcast and scenes of the panic gripping New York. Finally Travis and his driver corner and subdue all but the gang leader, who is moments away from gunning down Travis when he himself is suddenly blasted by a shotgun. In a final twist, Travis' unexpected savior is revealed as none other than Bill Dock, the elderly farmer who famously posed for the press with his shotgun at Grover's Mill the day after the broadcast. Driving off into the night still attired in his masquerade costume, Travis realizes that fate may have shown him a way to continue his fight for justice.

Writer Roy Thomas clearly has a great affection for the time and place of the story and succeeds in packing into less than two dozen pages an impressive amount of fine detail, combining an effective origin story for the Crimson Avenger with a convincing snapshot of the tense world situation in 1938. The plotline featuring the fake Martian invaders could easily have derailed the carefully constructed reality of the story, but to Thomas' credit it is not at all out of place, and the authentic dialogue from the Howard Koch script (including Welles' famous closing remarks) and the final dénouement at Grover's Mill brings the story to an extremely satisfying conclusion.

The principal joy of the Crimson Avenger is in its loving reconstruction of the world of 1938, and this quality is equally to the fore in Woody Allen's *Radio Days*, a hugely affectionate love letter to the lost world of radio in the early 1940s. *Radio Days* is a movie without any discernible pretense of a plot, but suffers not a jot for its meandering structure. Narrated in winsome terms by Allen, the movie is simply a collection of loosely connected stories revolving around the life of a typical Jewish family and the way the radio was woven into the fabric of their daily lives. The hero of the movie is Joe (Seth Green), the youngest member of the family and a habitual radio listener whose greatest passion in life is the crime-busting exploits of fictional radio crime-fighter the Masked Adventurer. His devotion to the show is such that to purchase a "Masked Adventurer Secret Compartment Ring" he steals money from a synagogue collection for the foundation of the Jewish state, but though his eventual exposure as a thief puts him off a life of crime, it does nothing to dampen his abiding interest in radio.

The movie is undoubtedly semiautobiographical, though many of the stories just as likely emerged fully formed from Allen's fertile imagination. Allen captures the mood of the times perfectly, and numerous references to real radio programs such as *The Charlie McCarthy Show* and the first wartime broadcasts create a perfect air of realism. Most intriguingly, the movie features a short segment focusing on the events of *The War of the Worlds* broadcast. (Allen himself was born in 1935 and therefore could not possibly remember the events of that night.)

The story in question focuses on Aunt Bea (Dianne Wiest), whose main aim in life is to find herself a husband, though she has been failing miserably in this task for years. In fruitless pursuit of her goal she has endured a succession of increasingly hopeless and desperate dates, but on this particular night she is on cloud nine because she has at last been asked out by the very eligible Mr. Manulis. Little does Aunt Bea suspect, of course, that the date is heading for disaster. As they are driving home through thick fog, the car runs out of gas, and the assignation comes to an abrupt end when the radio announces that a Martian invasion is under way. With Martians landing at Wilson's Glenn (note the name change from Grover's Mill), the formerly self-assured Mr. Manulis flees into the night, abandoning Aunt Bea to walk home alone.

Allen makes no explicit reference to Orson Welles and the spotlight of the story is very tightly focused on the experience of Aunt Bea, so no one should watch this movie in the hope of seeing a detailed historically accurate retelling of events. This is not the purpose of the movie at all. Allen is primarily concerned with evoking nostalgia for a bygone age, and in this he succeeds admirably, helped in large part by his typically careful and intelligent casting. The movie concludes on a melancholy note, lamenting that an era has passed and the radio voices of yesterday grow dimmer with each passing year.

A television series based not on the broadcast but something closer to the original concept of *The War of the Worlds* was bound to happen one day, and indeed in the mid 1970s George Pal had even dabbled with the idea of a sequel to his 1953 movie, but it was not until 1988 that a writer and producer named Greg Strangis was able to put all the pieces in place. The intriguing and much underrated result (also titled *The War of the Worlds*) was actually intended as a quasi-sequel to the 1953 movie, though in one brilliantly realized episode "An Eye for an Eye," the action is shifted to Grover's Mill in a story which postulates in similar fashion to *Buckaroo Banzai* that the Orson Welles broadcast was a front for a real Martian invasion.

That the first season is so good is a testament to the writers and cast, who by and large rose above the rather weak central premise, which postulated that a form of generalized amnesia has wiped out our collective memories of the 1953 attack. Of course, one can sympathize with the decision, as a direct sequel to the movie would have required the expensive engineering of a completely different history for our planet from 1953 to modern days. Far easier from a production point of view is to set everything in a readily recognizable world, which for the sake of economy meant Canada, where the show was filmed.

Strangis had some serious aspirations for the show, seeing it as an opportunity to highlight what he saw as humanity's poor treatment of the planet, and that the aliens might simply be our destined replacements in the natural scheme of things. Production values are not especially high (budgets ran to about $680,000 per episode) but the series is imaginatively designed and the crew succeeded in getting every dollar on the screen, though the rather gory effects brought some criticism.

An entirely novel approach to incorporating the broadcast into a story was employed in the 1990 movie *Spaced Invaders*, which cleverly inverts the plot by having a crew of inept Martians pick up a Halloween repeat of the broadcast. Being the warlike race that they are, they assume that Mars has opened hostilities and, not wanting to miss out on the glory, blast off for Earth. Unfortunately they crash-land in the town of Big Bean, Illinois, and spend the rest of the movie constantly being thwarted in their desire to inflict some harm, partly because they get mistaken for Halloween trick-or-treaters, but largely because they are idiots.

Unfortunately the cleverest thing about *Spaced Invaders* is the central conceit of the Martians responding to a modern repeat of the 1938 broadcast. The rest of the movie is a terrible muddle and the humor seldom rises much above the level of slapstick. There are a couple of engaging performances from Douglas Barr as the town sheriff and Ariana Richards as his daughter, and the production designs are extremely entertaining, but while this is certainly a very strange film, it is no *Buckaroo Banzai*.

We will be discussing in the final chapter if television might one day prove as effective a medium as radio for triggering mass delusions, but we can examine now how one made-for-television movie ventured a very good attempt at reimagining the 1938 broadcast for a modern audience. *Without Warning* was broadcast on Halloween night, October 31, 1994, on CBS. It has only a superficial resemblance to the plot of the original broadcast, but the antecedents are readily apparent, dropping the viewers into what appears to be a typical crime thriller, before switching to the newsroom for a breaking story. What follows is a quite well realized and often moderately chilling tale of alien invasion told through the eyes of the CBS newsroom and many familiar reporters. It was sufficiently realistic that at least one affiliate station reported it had received concerned calls from viewers.

Programs like this have been very rare due to the sensitivity of the subject matter and concerns by the networks that they might trigger another scare. Several CBS affiliates flatly refused to even consider showing *Without Warning* because of this concern. There have been a few other similar productions (notably *Special Bulletin*, 1983) that can reasonably claim to have been influenced by *The War of the Worlds*, but *Without Warning* is the only time a television network has dared break the explicit taboo of using the breaking-news format in conjunction with a story of alien invasion.

But once again cartoons dare to tread where others fear to walk. We have already encountered several cartoon shows that flirted with the broadcast, but there is one cartoon mouse that is synonymous with the subject. *Pinky and the Brain* must be one of the most outlandish cartoons ever made and in one particularly memorable episode dishes up a superbly wacky take on *The War of the Worlds* radio broadcast, but it would be fair to say that the entire series is nothing less than a celebration of the memory of Orson Welles. The voice of the Brain, a super-intelligent mouse with designs on world domination, was provided by Maurice LaMarche, an avowed fan of Welles who has described the Brain's voice as "65% Orson Welles, 35% Vincent Price"[4] and indeed his performance is spookily reminiscent of Welles' trademark diction. Saddled with his half-wit companion Pinky ("quarter-wit" would be more apt), the Brain plots each night to take over the world, devising ever more ingenious ways to overcome the one crucial impediment to his desires: the fact that he and Pinky are six inches tall and mice.

The story of these two genetically engineered lab mice and their nightly plots to take over the world began life as a segment of *Animaniacs*, an anarchic and freewheeling cartoon series that modeled itself on old variety shows, with a large ensemble cast of characters starring each week in short skits. The show was the creation of Steven Spielberg's Amblin Entertainment and aired on the Warner Brothers network from 1993 to 1998. Such was their popularity that in 1995 Pinky and the Brain were awarded their own series, which ran through 1998. The episode that spoofs *The War of the Worlds* aired on October 28, 1995, and is called "Battle for the Planet." In this episode, Brain recounts to Pinky the story of the Orson Welles panic broadcast, and sets out with the aid of cardboard sets to duplicate the scare in a hijacked television news flash.

"Battle for the Planet" was not the only time *Pinky and the Brain* made clear the connection to Orson Welles. An entire episode, "Yes, Always" was based on an infamous incident in which Welles railed at the poor quality of a script he was reading for a frozen peas commercial; LaMarche apparently regularly used lines from this debacle as warm-up material and writer Peter Hastings was inspired to write an entire episode on the theme. In another episode, Brain became "The Fog," a reference to the time Welles voiced *The Shadow*. There was even an episode that spoofed *The Third Man*, with Brain taking on the Harry Lime role made famous by Orson Welles. Cartoons that pack in cultural references for adult viewers are commonplace nowadays, but most are not half as smart as they'd like to believe. *Pinky and the Brain* is that rare animal, a series that was every bit as clever as it thought it was.

The debt to H. G. Wells and Orson Welles owned by any number of science fiction filmmakers would be worthy of a book of its own, but one particularly good example from 1996 might be fairly described as the movie that dare not speak its name. *Independence Day* is an extraordinarily blatant reworking of *The War of the Worlds*, blending elements of the original novel with aspects of the 1938 broadcast, specifically the appropriation in the latter case of breaking news stories to progress the narrative. The ending in which the plucky human heroes infect a massive alien mother ship with a computer virus is an obvious nod to H.G Wells, as writer and directors Dean Devlin and Roland Emmerich have candidly admitted in the DVD commentary for the movie. None of this prevents the movie from being a bombastic assault on the senses, and the scenes of destruction, especially that of the White House, are rightly regarded as groundbreaking in their own right. Imitation is after all the sincerest form of flattery, and *Independence Day* is just the latest in a long line of movies beginning with classics such as *Invaders from Mars* and *Earth vs. the Flying Saucers** that can proudly trace their lineage to Wells and Welles.

It is comforting to think that the original broadcast belongs to a more refined age, so it comes as something of a shock to find it brought explicitly up to date in the HBO

---

*Footage from *Earth vs. the Flying Saucers* was used by Welles in his film *F for Fake*.

series *Perversions of Science*. The series was loosely based on the old EC Comics titles, which as previously mentioned were particularly gory and violent for their time. It was inevitable then that pairing these stories with a cable service like HBO would result in a quite different approach to the material than had previously been contemplated. The episode "Panic," broadcast in July 1997, is not entirely without merit, though the expletives seem gratuitous and the final twist falls flat. Little of the original EC Comics story survives translation, which means even less of the 1938 broadcast gets to screen, but there is some humor to be derived from the idea that a pair of Martian advance scouts are themselves fooled by the broadcast into believing that a long-planned invasion by Mars has begun.

It's hard to imagine that the writers of *Perversions of Science* cared about honoring their source material, but the same cannot be said of an episode of the cartoon series *Hey Arnold!* that aired on Monday, October 27, 1997. "Arnold's Halloween" is a lovingly crafted tale that benefits immeasurably from the presence of Maurice LaMarche, who took a break from *Pinky and the Brain* to step much more obviously into the shoes of Orson Welles. *Hey Arnold!* tells the day-to-day adventures of neighborhood kid Arnold and his friends in the fictional town of Hillwood (which looks very much like New York City). In this episode, Arnold hatches a plot to scare the adults of Hillwood with a hoax invasion from Mars, but the transmission is picked up by UFO investigator Douglas Cain (LaMarche in full Welles mode) who amplifies the panic tenfold by featuring it on his television show. LaMarche is in marvelous form, chewing up the scenery as Welles in all but name, and the script by series creator Craig Bartlett (with cowriters Joseph Purdy and Antoinette Stella) is finely observed, with many knowing nods to the original broadcast.

Hey Arnold! was not the last time Maurice LaMarche would take on his beloved role of Orson Welles, but he must have longed to play the part without the subterfuge of a pair of mouse ears or a pseudonym. He briefly achieved this on the animated series *The Critic*, but his true moment in the spotlight came when the 1938 broadcast achieved that most iconic seal of pop culture approval, an appearance in *The Simpsons*. This cartoon series has established a laudable tradition of spoofing famous (and not-so-famous) science fiction ideas, notably in the annual Halloween fright-fest episode called "The Treehouse of Horror." "The Day the Earth Looked Stupid" (the title spoofs the classic 1950s science fiction film *The Day the Earth Stood Still*) is a marvelously irreverent 15 minutes of tomfoolery that transposes Springfield, the Simpsons' hometown, to a sepia-tinted 1938 and takes a playful swipe at the gullibility of listeners.

That the Simpsons chose to lampoon the broadcast is a final seal of approval on a 70-year love affair with Orson Welles and his extraordinary hoax, but at the opposite extreme of the spectrum the broadcast has entered the murky world of conspiracy theorists. One hypothesis, proposed by alternative-historian Daniel Hopsicker, suggests that the 1938 broadcast was no mere chance event but rather a planned experiment in psychological warfare conducted by none other than the Rockefeller Foundation. If that sounds outlandish, then rather more plausible is the suggestion that the broadcast has actually influenced the American government's approach to UFOs, on the basis that it offered a clear warning that unfounded rumors of alien visitations were potentially dangerous to public order.

Captain Edward J. Ruppelt was the officer in charge of the famous U.S. Air Force investigation into UFOs called Project Blue Book. In 1956 he wrote an account of his experiences, *The Report on Unidentified Flying Objects*, in which he observed, "The UFO files are full of references to the near mass panic of October 30, 1938, when Orson Welles presented his now famous 'The War of the Worlds' broadcast."[5] If the air force genuinely saw the broadcast as an indication of what might happen if UFO sightings were left unchallenged and unexplained, then Welles may well have inadvertently informed government policy on the subject. After all, such anxiety is not entirely unjustified (as shown by the events that allegedly occurred in Brazil in 1954) but did the U.S. government actually act on these concerns?

It is likely we will never know for certain, but there is certainly no doubt that, with regard to UFO sightings, the air force and other government agencies have long gone to great lengths to promote mundane explanations, no matter how extraordinary or compelling the case evidence. That this has only served to fuel conspiracy theories is ironic, and it is fascinating to imagine that one of the great mysteries of the modern age may owe a large part of its mystique, not to a sinister conspiracy to cover up real alien invaders, but to the actions of a government that was itself spooked by the most famous radio hoax in history.

18

ENVIOUS EYES
Could It Happen Again?

Before embarking on this chapter it would be useful to begin by summarizing how something as mundane as a radio broadcast could convince supposedly rational people that they were under attack by Martian invaders. Flying in the face of all reason, there have been no less than 10 distinctly identifiable events since 1938, though as Auric Goldfinger once remarked to James Bond, "Once is happenstance. Twice is coincidence. The third time it's enemy action." But who or what is the real enemy? In 1938 people heard "Martians" but many assumed "Nazis." A wave of UFO sightings preconditioned the population in 1950s Brazil, and in Portugal, church and state conspired to stifle independent thought by encouraging belief in apocalyptic prophesies. On other occasions dark rumors have swirled that panics have been planned by the broadcasters, while suppression of personal liberties has very likely played its part in countries under dictators, though even in democracies the voice of authority issued from a radio has sometimes proven all too beguiling. These are just some of the many reasons identified in previous chapters, though we should not forget that looming above everything hangs the baleful presence of the planet Mars. Which begs the question; in this modern age, do the Martians still wield any significant power over the people of Earth?

If we are to believe one particularly vocal group of armchair investigators, the answer might well be yes. These tenacious seekers after hidden history contend that NASA is covering up evidence of life on Mars, and to prove their contention, they are scrutinizing every new image that arrives from Mars with a forensic zeal and determination that has vexed the mainstream scientific community for years. The controversy began in 1976, when the *Viking Orbiter 1* was photographing the Cydonia region of Mars on the lookout for suitable landing sites for its sister ship *Viking 2*. One of the images returned to Earth caused a great deal of interest in the media because it appeared to show a huge carving of a face. NASA was quick to dismiss the "face" as an illusion of light and shadow, but for many in the alternative science community, the strange feature became a cause célèbre, proof that Mars had once hosted an advanced civilization.

You might be asking why this is important to the question posed by this chapter, but it is significant, since it shows that for many people, Mars is once again a place of mystery and perhaps even menace, if indeed it ever really ceased to be. If the conspiracy theorists are to be believed, the surface of Mars is liberally littered with the detritus of an ancient civilization. Now, with the ability to easily disseminate these incredible claims on the Internet, the Mars theorists are posing challenges that NASA and other scientific bodies are finding increasingly difficult to ignore. This is no better illustrated by the deci-

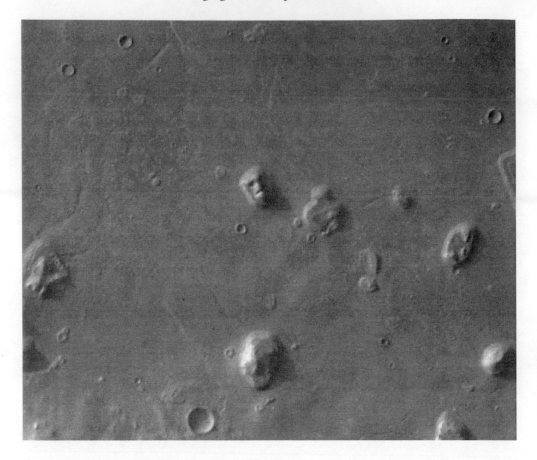

The original image of the so-called Face on Mars in the Cydonia region of Mars, captured July 25, 1976, by the *Viking Orbiter* 1 (NASA).

sion taken by NASA to re-image the Cydonia region in April of 1998 with a much superior camera on their *Mars Global Surveyor* spacecraft. The idea was to finally disprove the theory that the face was artificial, but it didn't entirely work. While the new images appeared to offer compelling evidence that the face was indeed the result of erosion, shadow and a fortuitous camera angle, the most ardent believers were not to be deterred and with the recent arrival on Mars of the *Spirit, Opportunity* and *Phoenix* missions, the "proof" NASA is accumulating has gone from a trickle to a flood. A recent picture snapped by the *Spirit* rover purporting to show a running alien figure on the Martian surface even went global, appearing on news services as diverse as CNN, the BBC and *China Daily*. Once again, there was a perfectly prosaic explanation; wind had sandblasted a rock into the striking shape and a well-known psychological phenomenon known as pareidolia did the rest. This is the process in which the human mind finds familiar shapes and patterns in unexpected places, such as the bark of trees or clouds in the sky. The face on Mars is one of the best-known examples of this phenomenon, but it is also just one facet of a growing movement that seeks to reject conventional scientific wisdom in favor of an alternative world viewed through a very dark lens.

In the television series *The X-Files*,* a poster of a flying saucer in FBI agent Fox Mulder's office proclaimed "I want to believe," and it seems so does a very large segment of the population. A 1997 Gallup poll revealed that 71 percent of Americans believed their government knew more about UFOs than it would admit, and an Associated Press poll in 2007 found that 1 in 4 Americans expected to experience the Rapture that year[1] (one can only assume they were very disappointed to see in 2008). The number of conspiracy theories continues to grow at a dizzying pace, many of

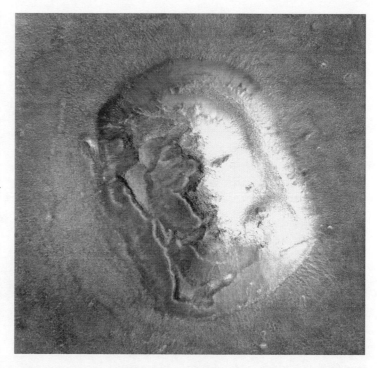

NASA's *Mars Global Surveyor* took this high-resolution image of the so-called Face on Mars in an attempt to refute theories that the feature was an artificial construction. The image seemed to offer conclusive proof that it was a natural geological feature (NASA/JPL/Malin Space Science Systems).

them related to UFOs and nefarious religious cover-ups. Add all these together and one begins to get a sense of the devils' brew of beliefs bubbling on the caldron. Religion and UFOs have both been a factor in previous radio scares, but the volume and reach of these stories has now reached endemic proportions, promulgated on the Internet without the benefit of peer review and entering the mainstream via motion pictures and television. There are even those who believe that a conspiracy of world leaders is plotting a fake alien invasion in order to impose a new world order upon the nations of the Earth. This readiness to believe the impossible should send clear warning signals that, if anything, the propensity for suggestibility is far worse than it has ever been before, and we should not therefore be surprised if history repeats itself.

So if the worst does happen, where can we expect the Martians to strike next? The sociological factors described previously suggest that America is still particularly vulnerable, though in fact it may now be a less likely target, not because people are any less prone to misunderstanding (the very opposite seems likely), but because the FCC has finally clarified its position on broadcasts like *The War of the Worlds*. The first tentative steps toward a clearer understanding of the situation came in 1985, when the FCC with-

---

**The X-Files episode "War of the Coprophages" is set in the town of Miller's Grove in homage to Grover's Mill.

Snapped by the *Spirit* rover in the closing months of 2007, this picture caused enormous interest around the world when a blogger spotted what appeared to be a figure (white arrow) in the Martian landscape (NASA/JPL–Caltech/Cornell University).

drew its 1966 public notice on contests and promotions, voicing the preference that any future infractions be handled at local law enforcement levels, though, significantly, the commission reemphasized that a broadcast in the style of *The War of the Worlds* without disclaimers would breach their guidelines. However, it was still a recommendation without teeth. All this would begin to change in the early 1990s, when a number of ill-judged broadcasts occurred.

On the morning of January 29, 1991, a DJ named John Ulett of KSHE-FM in Crestwood, Missouri, took it upon himself, without the knowledge or consent of station management, to transmit news of a fake nuclear attack against the United States. Ulett broadcast a 10-second tone before his announcement that could have easily been mistaken for that used by the Emergency Broadcast System, used terminology such as "official civil defense warning" and played the sound of an air raid siren. The broadcast was certainly inopportunely timed as the first Gulf War had begun only weeks previously, and though Ulett claimed he was trying to make a serious statement against nuclear war, the FCC could hardly ignore such a serious misappropriation of the airwaves. They slapped a $25,000 fine on the station, and in their judgment again drew parallels to *The War of the Worlds*.

It truth, it seems likely that no one outside the FCC took the KSHE-FM nuclear attack particularly seriously, but the 1990s were awash with similar broadcasts, including a Hartford, Connecticut, station called WCCM-FM that in 1990 informed listeners that a volcano had exploded in their vicinity, and the unfortunate "Confess your crime" hoax of KROQ-FM in Los Angeles, also in 1990, which involved a pair of DJs who arranged for a friend to call in to their program and anonymously "confess" to murdering his girlfriend. There had been no murder, but the police believed there was a genuine crime to be solved, so they spent several fruitless months and many thousands of dollars investigating the case before it was all revealed to be a hoax. Providence, Rhode Island, also found itself back in the news for a fake radio broadcast when WALE-FM news director Thomas Moriarty announced on air that a colleague had been shot dead on the steps of the station. It all added up to one hoax too many, and in November 1991 the FCC set about drafting a new rule covering such broadcasts.

The FCC was still wary of producing legislation that impinged on free speech and quality programming. Commissioner James H. Quello summed this up succinctly when he cautioned the FCC against assuming the role of censor. He made specific reference to the merits of *The War of the Worlds*, calling it a "classic of American radio." The FCC regulation that was eventually issued in 1992 (Section 73.1217 of Title 47 of the Code of Federal Regulations) is therefore a carefully worded text that cautions against faking disasters or crimes but provides significant latitude for broadcasters to continue to make programs like *The War of the Worlds*, as long as sufficient warnings are provided or the broadcast is made in circumstances under which it should be patently obvious to the listener that it is a hoax, for instance on April Fools' Day.* Hopefully the fact there has been no *War of the Worlds* scare in America in over 20 years is not an indication that the regulation has stifled creativity.

So if America now seems a relatively unappealing target for the Martians, where else might we expect them to appear? The obvious answer is those countries either lacking adequate regulations to ensure due care toward listeners, or countries that have simply never experienced anything like *The War of the Worlds* or, in a worst-case scenario, both. An obvious candidate is China, which exhibits many of the necessary prerequisites: a repressive government, a media which is generally seen as a mouthpiece of the state, large rural populations without easy access to alternative news sources, and a lack of experi-

---

*On April Fools' Day 1993, KGB-FM radio in San Diego told listeners that the space shuttle had been diverted due to an emergency and would be landing at a small airport in the heart of a commercial and residential district. The shuttle was not even in space that day, but this did not prevent at least 1,000 people turning up at the airport in the hope of watching it land. The FCC took no action, but the police reported that they would be billing the station for the cost of policing the crowd.

ence of large media hoaxes. One could easily imagine a Chinese *War of the Worlds* broadcast equaling if not exceeding the level of fright experienced in 1938, though of course it would take considerable courage on the part of the broadcasters to attempt such a thing. The Chinese government, while recently relaxing its censorship to a degree, would not look kindly upon such an event, and in a very small way, there has already been at least one recorded example of their likely reaction. In 1993, the *China Youth Daily* (an extremely popular official newspaper) printed a front-page report that the government was to waive its usual one-child policy in the case of Ph.D. holders. The explanation offered was that Ph.D. holders would produce smarter babies and so reduce the nation's need for foreign experts. The story even had a disclaimer on the same page, but it was still picked up as fact by several other newspapers. Predictably, the Chinese government condemned the article and proclaimed April Fools' Day a dangerous Western tradition.

While this book is primarily concerned with the effect radio versions of *The War of the Worlds* have had on listeners, it is only right that this chapter be allowed to stray into discussions of other forms of media that might be used to transmit something similar, the most obvious of these being television. There have been television programs that have attempted to recapture the magic of the 1938 broadcast, most notably the 1994 CBS movie *Without Warning*. Though CBS had no intention of scaring anyone with this alien invasion movie, a Fort Smith, Arkansas, affiliate took dozens of worried calls, and viewers of other stations in the area asked why they were failing to cover such a momentous event. But *Without Warning* is not the only program to have put a chill down viewers' backs. On October 31, 1992, a British mock documentary called *Ghost Watch*, purporting to be coming live from a haunted house, caused outrage among BBC viewers and the press after a sizable number of people fell for the hoax. Though there seems to be no suggestion that the creators of this program had any intention of duplicating the scare caused by the *War of the Worlds* broadcast, the show's impact was widely felt and there was considerable concern that a large number of children had seen the broadcast, as one of the presenters was a well-known figure in children's television.

The most ubiquitous communication device on the planet is now the cell phone. It has spread to every corner of the globe and has become the locus of a new kind of panic. In 2007 in Karachi, Pakistan, cell phone users received a text message warning them that if they received a call from a number containing the digits 0099 they should not answer, as the phone would then transmit a deadly virus-like signal that would cause the recipient to die. Many believed the message, and the cell phone company had to work hard to convince its subscribers that they were not going to die if they answered the phone. Similar events have occurred all over the world, especially in Africa, which seems to be a particularly fertile ground for this sort of mass delusion. For instance, in September 2003 a spate of text messages caused great alarm among Sudanese men with the warning that their penises were in grave danger of melting away as a result of a Zionist plot to wipe out the nation. Of course, it seems unlikely that news of a Martian invasion transmitted by cell phone in Africa would be very effective, as the idea of Mars as an abode of life or source of alien invasion is predominantly a concept associated with the developed world. The phantom penis melter may have much more resonance in certain African cultures, but let us not forget that the Martians have adapted their tactics to suit local conditions more than once. Put the two together and who knows — perhaps they might yet gain a new territory to conquer.

If there is one modern technology that has done more to spread misinformation than any other it is the Internet. As we have already seen, the ready availability of images transmitted from Mars has created a thriving community centered on conspiracy theories, but the Internet is also famous for hoax e-mails, and Mars has figured prominently in this modern phenomenon. Almost every year since 2003, an e-mail has landed in in-boxes purporting to announce that Mars will be at its closest approach for centuries and the planet will appear in the night sky as large as a full moon. It is complete fantasy, of course, but the e-mail keeps resurfacing and despite astronomers' regular attempts to debunk it, people are fooled time and time again. Mars was indeed on a very close approach to Earth in 2003, coming within 35 million miles, and this seems to be the origin of the e-mail, but it could never appear as large as our Moon, though once again we have positive proof of just how susceptible we are to the mythic qualities of Mars.

Nor had the media been oblivious to the marketing potential of ideas shared across the Internet, and there is a growing pool of talented people and advertising agencies that have become adept at seeding the Net with ideas that can be spread purely by word of mouth. The most famous example and the one that brought the concept into the public consciousness was a low-budget horror movie called *The Blair Witch Project*. Made in 1999 by Daniel Myrick and Eduardo Sánchez, it told the story of the disappearance of three students who travel into the Black Hills of Burkittsville, Maryland, to make a documentary film about a local legend, the eponymous Blair Witch. All three vanish without trace, but their cameras and the footage they shot are eventually discovered. This is the basis of *The Blair Witch Project*, but in a very clever move, the producers set out to create an Internet site which gave the impression that the footage discovered and the disappearance of the student filmmakers was in fact entirely real. So successful was this site that many did believe that *The Blair Witch Project* was a true story, but what is particularly striking is that Daniel Myrick has gone on record to acknowledge his debt to Orson Welles and *The War of the Worlds*. He heard a recording of the broadcast as a child; it impressed him so much that he never forgot it, and when his chance came to make a film he made a conscious effort to try and recapture the same lightning in a bottle. Using the Internet Myrick and Sánchez were able to reinvent the concept in a way that would have surely caused Welles a great deal of wry amusement.

But while *The Blair Witch Project* can be dismissed as harmless fun, the potential of the Internet to spur more dangerous behavior is perfectly illustrated by a far more recent case, the inadvertent release of a six-year-old news story concerning the financial plight of United Airlines. Originally published on December 10, 2002, the story reported that the company had filed for Chapter 11 bankruptcy. A news service in Florida then mistakenly reissued the story on September 8, 2008, triggering a massive (though brief) collapse in the company's stock valuation when traders on Wall Street acted on the apparently devastating news that United Airlines had again filed for bankruptcy protection.

Discussion of the role of the Internet in modern hoaxes brings us to an important distinction that has arisen in recent years, between hoaxes perpetrated by organizations and those created by individuals or groups unaffiliated to any media outlet and thus not beholden to any rules of behavior or legislation. Modern consumer computer technology now allows even an individual to create material that just a few years ago would have required a large team of dedicated experts and enormously expensive resources. A recent example has been spectacular footage of a fleet of UFOs flying over Haiti which was posted on numerous websites (including the hugely popular YouTube) and stirred up a great deal of controversy, splitting opinion between those who thought it was genuine footage and others who maintained it was a hoax. Disappointingly it turned out to be the latter, but in a bizarre twist, the creator of the video (who was tracked down by a *Los Angeles Times* reporter) admitted that the footage had actually been produced as a concept test for a movie he was developing. The movie tells the story of two people who fake a UFO video, which then gets taken for the real thing and assumes a life of its own.[2]

Cynics will say that this story has all the hallmarks of a very clever viral marketing campaign, though the movie in question seems not to have surfaced. But while this case amounts to a relatively harmless prank, there have been other much more worrying abuses of technology that may hint at the shape of things to come. On November 26, 1977, television viewers in the United Kingdom were amazed to find the early evening news interrupted by a message "from outer space." At 5:10 P.M. the audio signal from the Hannington transmitter serving the south of England was overridden, and for just over five minutes an alien named "Vrillon" of the "Ashtar Galactic Command" delivered a rather rambling harangue on the dangers faced by the human race. The perpetrators were never caught, but it was a very early example of what can be achieved with a little determination and the right equipment. The truth of this statement would become even more apparent on June 17, 2007, when an award-winning Czech guerrilla art collective known as Ztohoven hacked into a television weather forecast and superimposed a nuclear mushroom cloud on an idyllic panoramic scene of the Krkonoše Mountains. The footage is chillingly realistic, and while it seems the incident went largely unnoticed by the vast majority of viewers (it was aired in the early morning before most people were up and caused more in the way of amusement than upset), the art collective faced a trial on charges of scare mongering (carrying a possible three-year sentence), though the case was thrown out in March 2008 by the presiding judge.

Perhaps the most obvious successors to the Martians are terrorists, and here lies perhaps the most dangerous opportunity for the invaders to reinvigorate their campaign. With the heightened sense of alarm permeating society in the wake of the 9/11 attacks, it takes very little to trigger mass delusions. After anthrax spores were mailed to various targets in the United States in 2001, school pupils in numerous states were afflicted with mysterious rashes that investigators characterized as mass hysteria, with larges numbers of children falling victim in a matter of minutes. No one was hurt or suffered any lasting effects, but reactions like this illustrate how the power of suggestion is heightened in times of national crisis. This was further graphically illustrated on January 31, 2007, when a guerrilla marketing campaign to promote the late-night adult animation series *Aqua Teen Hunger Force* spiraled out of control. Small electronic billboards were positioned at strategic positions in a number of U.S. cities, and went largely unnoticed until people in Boston began reporting suspicious devices to the police. Bomb squads were dispatched across Boston, bringing traffic to a halt and causing a day of major disruption to the city.[3] In hindsight, except for some wires and batteries the displays looked nothing like bombs, yet people ignored the obvious humorous nature of the displays and assumed the worst.

But could we really be so easily fooled again into thinking the Martians are invading? Perhaps the most convincing argument against a recurrence of a *War of the Worlds* scare is that we have seen it all before. It is now so commonplace to see television and film adopt the breaking-news format to convey drama that we are much less likely to be perturbed by it. Equally, special effects have now become so flawlessly integrated into our daily lives that we know instinctively that anything is possible and should be far less willing to take spectacular images at face value. A fifty-year-old grainy film of an indistinct blob of light is paradoxically a far more convincing UFO than the gleaming metallic objects that are now appearing on YouTube. Indeed, nothing is quite what it seems anymore, with manipulation occurring on a daily basis in a thousand different ways. Anyone attempting a fake broadcast now would be hard put to stand out from the crowd.

However, before we dismiss the possibility out of hand, we should not forget that the last known occurrence of a *War of the Worlds* scare occurred not so very long ago in Portugal in 1998, and the complacent assumption on the part of broadcasters that their listeners are wise enough to separate fact from fiction has backfired spectacularly on many previous occasions. We expect that in this world of saturation media coverage, 24-hour news channels and the Internet, that people would think to switch channels and check for corroboration when confronted with a hoax, yet we have seen that this simply does not happen. Given a strong enough motivation, people are swept up by the power of the moment and do little that we would consider sensible, and it continues to happen with surprising frequency. On Wednesday, December 13, 2006, the Belgian public television station RTBF interrupted regular evening programming with a report purporting to claim that the Dutch-speaking half of the country had unilaterally declared independence. It was a hoax, of course, based on concerns that a separatist movement was gaining ground in public opinion, but thousands called the station in a panic, clearly proving that if one taps into public concerns, one can short-circuit people's ability to react rationally and check the facts. "It's very bad Orson Welles, in very poor taste,"[4] said a spokesman for Prime Minister Guy Verhofstadt.

Perhaps most worryingly of all for the possibility of a large-scale repeat of a *War of the Worlds* scare, we now live in a world that offers rational and reasoned explanations for the things we see about us, and we have an unprecedented degree of access to all the information necessary to immunize us against the more extreme notions that exist, yet we continue to believe in the supernatural and in larger and larger numbers are turning our backs on conventional science. This rush to embrace the fringes of belief and a growing distrust in figures of authority, be they governments or scientists, is potentially fertile ground for a future panic.

So in these circumstances, what might a modern *War of the Worlds* hoax be like? This is a flight of pure imagination, but let us imagine that an art collective like Ztohoven decides to create a modern alien invasion. Using technology that already exists in abundance, they clandestinely hijack thousands of home computers, secretly installing software that awaits a specific time and date to trigger. Months before the attack is due to happen and capitalizing on the growing belief in conspiracy theories and alien visitations, other members of the group begin planting fake videos and news stories on social networking sites, setting up an elaborate viral campaign that is allowed to grow, multiply and form new connections organically. Still more experts in the collective work on setting up the equipment to hijack television broadcasts with random static blackouts and disturbing, barely glimpsed images and snatches of dialogue on top of the normal signal. At the appointed date and time, the operation swings into action. Tens of thousands, perhaps millions of compromised computers across the world begin denial-of-service (DOS) attacks* on the main news sites across the Web, bombarding them with so many demands for pages that their servers slow to a crawl. Meanwhile in-boxes across the world are deluged with e-mails purporting to report that Martian spacecraft are descending on major cities across the world. As people attempt to check this news online, their infected computers redirect them invisibly to fake versions of the BBC and CNN websites, which provide horrifying confirmation of events. Terrified, people call friends or forward e-mails, generating a firestorm of online activity that further cripples the infrastructure of the Internet. When people turn to the television, they see that the media services themselves seem to be under attack. In many parts of the world, other news services begin to report on the invasion. Unable to check because communication networks are failing, they can only parrot the news they are able to obtain from the fake websites. Finally, as a last finishing flourish, the hackers crash the computers at a number of power stations, bringing blackouts across large swaths of the developed world. Planet Earth has fallen.

Naturally such a plan would require staggering effort, coordination and luck, so much so that it will very likely remain in the realms of fantasy forever, though worryingly, all the individual elements have been tried successfully in one form or another. Computer viruses can and are programmed to trigger on specific dates; viral campaigns have been run that have convinced thousands of their veracity, and fake news websites have been built and television news services hijacked. Yet perhaps all this speculation is just too clever and too sophisticated for its own good. Could it be that in reality, radio is still the most likely conduit for a new mass delusion involving the Martians? Deprive a media-saturated population of everything but the sounds, and perhaps those atrophied mental muscles we call the imagination might twitch once more into fitful life. After all, we are still burdened with fears. Where once we were scared of Nazis, now we fear losing our house and job in a collapsed economy, or that the environment is teetering on the brink of collapse or we will be caught up in a terrorist attack. Many of the fears may be new or reimagined for the 21st century, but the underlying paranoia that fuels them is something that we have learned to accept as an everyday part of our lives. In a strange way, perhaps the Martians have provided a cathartic release for the pent-up anxieties that our society imposes upon us.

Just days after Orson Welles thoroughly spooked America with his version of *The War of the Worlds*, the influential commentator Dorothy Thompson mounted a strongly worded defense of Welles in her *New York Tribune* column. She made an extraordinary

---

*A denial of service (DOS) attack generally uses many hijacked computers to bombard a target computer with such a large volume of requests for information (generally web pages) that the target computer can no longer function.

statement that sounds as relevant now as it was then: "The technique of modern mass politics calling itself democracy is to create a fear — a fear of economic royalists, or of reds, or of Jews, or of starvation, or of an outside enemy — and exploit that fear into obtaining subservience in return for protection." To Thompson's list we can now add terrorists, and as for the Martians, they are surely the ultimate outside enemy: implacable, unknowable and completely adaptable to the prevailing Zeitgeist of the time. In these circumstances, it is surely only a matter of time before they once more cross the darkness to play on our fears. The question should not be, could it happen again? but, when and where will it happen again?

APPENDIX:
THE WAR OF THE WORLDS
Original Script by Howard Koch
Reprinted by the kind permission of Anne Koch

The script of *The War of the Worlds* by Howard Koch has been officially reprinted a number of times since its first broadcast in 1938, though small inconsistencies have been introduced in each published version. The following script therefore utilizes the text published by Howard Koch in his own account of the broadcast. Where minor discrepancies have been noted between versions, a copy of the original script has been referred to, with the aim of matching as closely as possible the original intentions of the author. Formatting and layout of the text is closely derived from the original copy of the script.

COLUMBIA BROADCASTING SYSTEM
ORSON WELLES AND MERCURY THEATRE ON THE AIR
SUNDAY OCTOBER 30, 1938
8:00 to 9:00 P.M.

    CUE: (COLUMBIA BROADCASTING SYSTEM)
                   (.........30 Seconds.........)

ANNC'R: The Columbia Broadcasting System and its affiliated stations present Orson Welles and the Mercury Theatre on the Air in "The War of the Worlds" by H. G. Wells.

THEME

ANNC'R: Ladies and gentlemen: the director of the Mercury Theatre and star of these broadcasts, Orson Welles....

(WELLES SPEAKS)

ORSON WELLES

We know now that in the early years of the twentieth century this world was being watched closely by intelligences greater than man's and yet as mortal as his own. We know now that as human beings busied themselves about their various concerns they were scrutinized and studied, perhaps almost as narrowly as a man with a microscope might scrutinize the transient creatures that swarm and multiply in a drop of water. With infinite complacence people went to and fro over the earth about their little affairs, serene in the assurance of their dominion over this small spinning fragment of solar driftwood which by chance or design man has inherited out of the dark mystery of Time and Space. Yet across an immense ethereal gulf, minds that are to our minds as ours are to the beasts in the jungle, intellects vast, cool and unsympathetic regarded this earth with envious eyes and slowly and surely drew their plans against us. In the thirty-ninth year of the twentieth century came the great disillusionment.

It was near the end of October. Business was better. The war scare was over. More men were back at work. Sales were picking up. On this particular evening, October 30th, the Crosley service estimated that thirty-two million people were listening in on radios.

ANNOUNCER ONE

.....for the next twenty-four hours not much change in temperature. A slight atmospheric disturbance of undetermined origin is reported over Nova Scotia, causing a low pressure area to move down rather rapidly over the northeastern states, bringing a forecast of rain, accompanied by winds of light gale force. Maximum temperature 66; minimum 48. This weather report comes to you from the Government Weather Bureau.

We now take you to the Meridian Room in the Hotel Park Plaza in downtown New York, where you'll be entertained by the music of Ramon Raquello and his orchestra.

(SPANISH THEME SONG ... FADES)

ANNOUNCER THREE

Good evening, ladies and gentlemen. From the Meridian Room in the Park Plaza in New York City, we bring you the music of Ramon Raquello and his orchestra. With a touch of the Spanish, Ramon Raquello leads off with "La Cumparsita."

(PIECE STARTS PLAYING)

ANNOUNCER TWO

Ladies and gentlemen, we interrupt our program of dance music to bring you a special bulletin from the Intercontinental Radio News. At twenty minutes before eight, Central Time, Professor Farrell of the Mount Jennings Observatory, Chicago, Illinois, reports observing several explosions of incandescent gas, occurring at regular intervals on the planet Mars.

ANNOUNCER TWO (CONT'D)

The spectroscope indicates the gas to be hydrogen and moving towards the earth with enormous velocity. Professor Pierson of the Observatory at Princeton confirms Farrell's observation, and describes the phenomenon as (quote) like a jet of blue flame shot from a gun (unquote). We now return you to the music of Ramon Raquello, playing for you in the Meridian Room of the Park Plaza Hotel, situated in downtown New York.

(MUSIC PLAYS FOR A FEW MOMENTS UNTIL PIECE ENDS ... SOUND OF APPLAUSE)—CUT TO

ANNOUNCER TWO

Now a tune that never loses favor, the ever-popular "Stardust." Ramon Raquello and his orchestra...

(MUSIC)

ANNOUNCER TWO

Ladies and gentlemen, following on the news given in our bulletin a moment ago, the Government Meteorological Bureau has requested the large observatories of the country to keep an astronomical watch on any further disturbances occurring on the planet Mars. Due to the unusual nature of this occurrence, we have arranged an interview with the noted astronomer, Professor Pierson, who will give us his views on this event. In a few moments we will take you to the Princeton Observatory at Princeton, New Jersey. We return you until then to the music of Ramon Raquello and his orchestra.

(MUSIC)

ANNOUNCER TWO

We are ready now to take you to the Princeton Observatory at Princeton where Carl Phillips, our commentator, will interview Professor Richard Pierson, famous astronomer. We take you now to Princeton, New Jersey.

(ECHO CHAMBER)

PHILLIPS

Good evening, ladies and gentlemen. This is Carl Phillips, speaking to you from the observatory at Princeton. I am standing in a large semi-circular room, pitch black except for an oblong split in the ceiling. Through this opening I can see a sprinkling of stars that cast a kind of frosty glow over the intricate mechanism of the huge telescope. The ticking sound you hear is the vibration of the clockwork. Professor Pierson stands directly above me on a small platform, peering through the giant lens. I ask you to be patient, ladies and gentlemen, during any delay that may arise during our interview. Besides his ceaseless watch of the heavens, Professor Pierson may be interrupted by telephone or other communications. During this period he is in constant touch with the astronomical centers of the world ... Professor, may I begin our questions?

PIERSON

At any time, Mr. Phillips.

PHILLIPS

Professor, would you please tell our radio audience exactly what you see as you observe the planet Mars through your telescope?

PIERSON

Nothing unusual at the moment, Mr. Phillips. A red disk swimming in a blue sea. Transverse stripes across the disk. Quite distinct now because Mars happens to be the point nearest the earth ... in opposition, as we call it.

PHILLIPS

In your opinion, what do these transverse stripes signify, Professor Pierson?

PIERSON

Not canals, I can assure you, Mr. Phillips although that's the popular conjecture of those who imagine Mars to be inhabited. From a scientific viewpoint the stripes are merely the result of atmospheric conditions peculiar to the planet.

PHILLIPS

Then you're quite convinced as a scientist that living intelligence as we know it does not exist on Mars?

PIERSON

I should say the chances against it are a thousand to one.

PHILLIPS

And yet how do you account for these gas eruptions occurring on the surface of the planet at regular intervals?

PIERSON

Mr. Phillips, I cannot account for it.

PHILLIPS

By the way, Professor, for the benefit of our listeners, how far is Mars from the earth?

PIERSON

Approximately forty million miles.

PHILLIPS

Well, that seems a safe enough distance.

PHILLIPS

Just a moment, ladies and gentlemen, someone has just handed Professor Pierson a message. While he reads it, let me remind you that we are speaking to you from the observatory in Princeton, New Jersey, where we are interviewing the world-famous astronomer, Professor Pierson ... One moment, please. Professor Pierson has passed me a message which he has just received ... Professor, may I read the message to the listening audience?

PIERSON

Certainly, Mr. Phillips.

PHILLIPS

Ladies and gentlemen, I shall read you a wire addressed to Professor Pierson from Dr. Gray of the National History Museum, New York. "9:15 P.M. eastern standard time. Seismograph registered shock of almost earthquake intensity occurring within a radius of twenty miles of Princeton. Please investigate. Signed, Lloyd Gray, Chief of Astronomical Division." ... Professor Pierson, could this occurrence possibly have something to do with the disturbances observed on the planet Mars?

PIERSON

Hardly, Mr. Phillips. This is probably a meteorite of unusual size and its arrival at this particular time is merely a coincidence. However, we shall conduct a search, as soon as daylight permits.

PHILLIPS

Thank you, Professor. Ladies and gentlemen, for the past ten minutes we've been speaking to you from the observatory at Princeton, bringing you a special interview with Professor Pierson, noted astronomer. This is Carl Phillips speaking. We now return you to our New York studio.

(FADE IN PIANO PLAYING)

ANNOUNCER TWO

Ladies and gentlemen, here is the latest bulletin from the Intercontinental Radio News. Toronto, Canada: Professor Morse of McMillan University reports observing a total of three explosions on the planet Mars, between the hours of 7:45 P.M. and 9:20 P.M., eastern standard time. This confirms earlier reports received from American observatories. Now, nearer home, comes a special announcement from Trenton, New Jersey. It is reported that at 8:50 P.M. a huge, flaming object, believed to be a meteorite, fell on a farm in the neighborhood of Grovers Mill, New Jersey, twenty-two miles from Trenton. The flash in the sky was visible within a radius of several hundred miles and the noise of the impact was heard as far north as Elizabeth.

We have dispatched a special mobile unit to the scene, and will have our commentator, Mr. Phillips, give you a word description of the scene as soon as he can reach there from Princeton. In the meantime, we take you to the Hotel Martinet in Brooklyn, where Bobby Millette and his orchestra are offering a program of dance music.

(SWING BAND FOR 20 SECONDS ... THEN CUT)

ANNOUNCER TWO

We take you now to Grovers Mill, New Jersey.

(CROWD NOISES ... POLICE SIRENS)

PHILLIPS

Ladies and gentlemen, this is Carl Phillips again, at the Wilmuth farm, Grovers Mill, New Jersey. Professor Pierson and myself made the eleven miles from Princeton in ten minutes. Well, I ... I hardly know where to begin, to paint for you a word picture of the strange scene before my eyes, like something out of a modern Arabian Nights. Well, I just got here. I haven't had a chance to look around yet. I guess that's <u>it</u>. Yes, I guess that's the ... <u>thing</u>, directly in front of me, half buried in a vast pit. Must have struck with terrific force. The ground is covered with splinters of a tree it must have struck on its way down. What I can see of the ... object itself doesn't look very much like a meteor, at least not the meteors I've seen. It looks more like a huge cylinder. It has a diameter of ... what would you say, Professor Pierson?

PIERSON (OFF)

About thirty yards.

PHILLIPS

About thirty yards ... The metal on the sheath is ... well, I've never seen anything like it. The color is sort of yellowish-white. Curious spectators now are pressing close to the object in spite of the efforts of the police to keep them back. They're getting in front of my line of vision. Would you mind standing to one side, please?

POLICEMAN

One side, there, one side.

PHILLIPS

While the policemen are pushing the crowd back, here's Mr. Wilmuth, owner of the farm here. He may have some interesting facts to add ... Mr. Wilmuth, would you please tell the radio audience as much as you remember of this rather unusual visitor that dropped in your backyard? Step closer, please. Ladies and gentlemen, this is Mr. Wilmuth.

WILMUTH

I was listenin' to the radio.

PHILLIPS

Closer and louder please.

WILMUTH

Pardon me!

PHILLIPS

Louder, please, and closer.

WILMUTH

Yes, sir — I was listening to the radio and kinda drowsin', that Professor fellow was talkin' about Mars, so I was half dozin' and half...

PHILLIPS

Yes, Mr. Wilmuth. Then what happened?

WILMUTH

As I was sayin', I was listenin' to the radio kinda halfways...

PHILLIPS

Yes, Mr. Wilmuth, and then you saw something?

WILMUTH

Not first off. I heard something.

PHILLIPS

And what did you hear?

WILMUTH

A hissing sound. Like this: sssssssssss ... kinda like a fourth of July rocket.

PHILLIPS

Then what?

WILMUTH

Turned my head out the window and would have swore I was to sleep and dreamin'.

PHILLIPS

Yes?

WILMUTH

I seen that kinda greenish streak and then zingo! Somethin' smacked the ground. Knocked me clear out of my chair!

PHILLIPS

Well, were you frightened, Mr. Wilmuth?

WILMUTH

Well, I--I ain't quite sure. I reckon I---I was kinda riled.

PHILLIPS

Thank you, Mr. Wilmuth. Thank you.

WILMUTH

Want me to tell you some more?

PHILLIPS

No ... That's quite all right, that's plenty.

PHILLIPS

Ladies and gentlemen, you've just heard Mr. Wilmuth, owner of the farm where this thing has fallen. I wish I could convey the atmosphere ... the background of this ... fantastic scene. Hundreds of cars are parked in a field in back of us. Police are trying to rope off the roadway leading into the farm. But it's no use. They're breaking right through. Their headlights throw an enormous spot on the pit where the object's half buried. Some of the more daring souls are venturing near the edge. Their silhouettes stand out against the metal sheen.

(FAINT HUMMING SOUND)

One man wants to touch the thing ... he's having an argument with a policeman. The policeman wins ... Now, ladies and gentlemen, there's something I haven't mentioned in all this excitement, but now it's becoming more distinct. Perhaps you've caught it already on your radio. Listen: (LONG PAUSE) ... Do you hear it? It's a curious humming sound that seems to come from inside the object. I'll move the microphone nearer. Here. (PAUSE) Now we're not more than twenty-five feet away. Can you hear it now? Oh, Professor Pierson!

PIERSON

Yes, Mr. Phillips?

PHILLIPS

Can you tell us the meaning of that scraping noise inside the thing?

PIERSON

Possibly the unequal cooling of its surface.

PHILLIPS

Do you still think it's a meteor, Professor?

PIERSON

I don't know what to think. The metal casing is definitely extra-terrestrial ... not found on this earth. Friction with the earth's atmosphere usually tears holes in a meteorite. This thing is smooth and, as you can see, of cylindrical shape.

PHILLIPS

Just a minute! Something's happening! Ladies and gentlemen, this is terrific! This end of the thing is beginning to flake off! The top is beginning to rotate like a screw. The thing must be hollow!

VOICES

She's a movin'!
Look, the darn thing's unscrewing!
Keep back, there! Keep back, I tell you!
Maybe there's men in it trying to escape!
It's red hot, they'll burn to a cinder!
Keep back there. Keep those idiots back!

(SUDDENLY THE CLANKING SOUND OF A HUGE PIECE OF FALLING METAL)

VOICES

She's off! The top's loose!
Look out there! Stand back!

PHILLIPS

Ladies and gentlemen, this is the most terrifying thing I have ever witnessed ... Wait a minute! Someone's *crawling out of the hollow top*. Some one or ... something. I can see peering out of that black hole two luminous disks ... are they eyes? It might be a face. It might be...

(SHOUT OF AWE FROM THE CROWD)

Good heavens, something's wriggling out of the shadow like a grey snake. Now it's another one, and another. They look like tentacles to me. There, I can see the thing's body. It's large as a bear and it glistens like wet leather. But that face. It ... it's indescrib-able. I can hardly force myself to keep looking at it. The eyes are black and gleam like a serpent. The mouth is V-shaped with saliva dripping from its rimless lips that seem to quiver and pulsate. The monster or whatever it is can hardly move. It seems weighed down by ... possibly gravity or something. The thing's raising up. The crowd falls back. They've seen enough. This is the most extraordinary experience. I can't find words ... I'm pulling this microphone with me as I talk. I'll have to stop the description until I've taken a new position. Hold on, will you please, I'll be back in a minute.

(FADE INTO PIANO)

ANNOUNCER TWO

We are bringing you an eyewitness account of what's happening on the Wilmuth farm, Grovers Mill, New Jersey.

(MORE PIANO)

We now return you to Carl Phillips at Grovers Mill.

PHILLIPS

Ladies and gentlemen. (Am I on?) Ladies and gentlemen, here I am, back of a stone wall that adjoins Mr. Wilmuth's garden. From here I get a sweep of the whole scene. I'll give you every detail as long as I can talk. As long as I can see. More state police have arrived. They're drawing up a cordon in front of the pit, about thirty of them. No need to push the crowd back now. They're willing to keep their distance. The captain is con-ferring with someone. We can't quite see who. Oh yes, I believe it's Professor Pierson. Yes, it is. Now they've parted. The Professor moves around one side, studying the object, while the captain and two policemen advance with something in their hands. I can see it now. It's a white handkerchief tied to a pole ... a flag of truce. If those creatures know what that means ... what anything means! ... Wait! Something's happening!

(HISSING SOUND FOLLOWED BY A HUMMING THAT INCREASES IN INTENSITY)

A humped shape is rising out of the pit. I can make out a small beam of light against a mirror. What's that? There's a jet of flame springing from that mirror, and it leaps right at the advancing men. It strikes them head on! Good Lord, they're turning into flame!

(SCREAMS AND UNEARTHLY SHRIEKS)

Now the whole field's caught fire. (EXPLOSION) The woods ... the barns ... the gas tanks of automobiles ... it's spreading everywhere. It's coming this way. About twenty yards to my right...

(CRASH OF MICROPHONE ... THEN DEAD SILENCE...)

ANNOUNCER TWO

Ladies and gentlemen, due to circumstances beyond our control, we are unable to continue the broadcast from Grovers Mill. Evidently there's some difficulty with our field transmission. However, we will return to that point at the earliest opportunity. In the meantime, we have a late bulletin from San Diego, California. Professor Indellkoffer, speaking at a dinner of the California Astronomical Society, expressed the opinion that the explosions on Mars are undoubtedly nothing more than severe volcanic disturbances on the surface of the planet. We continue now with our piano interlude.

(PIANO ... THEN CUT)

Ladies and gentlemen, I have just been handed a message that came in from Grovers Mill by telephone. Just a moment. At least forty people, including six state troopers, lie dead in a field east of the village of Grovers Mill, their bodies burned and distorted beyond all possible recognition. The next voice you hear will be that of Brigadier General Montgomery Smith, commander of the State Militia at Trenton, New Jersey.

SMITH

I have been requested by the governor of New Jersey to place the counties of Mercer and Middlesex as far west as Princeton, and east to Jamesburg, under martial law. No one will be permitted to enter this area except by special pass issued by state or military authorities. Four companies of State Militia are proceeding from Trenton to Grovers Mill, and will aid in the evacuation of homes within the range of military operations. Thank you.

ANNOUNCER

You have just been listening to General Montgomery Smith commanding the State Militia at Trenton. In the meantime, further details of the catastrophe at Grovers Mill are coming in. The strange creatures after unleashing their deadly assault, crawled back in their pit and made no attempt to prevent the efforts of the firemen to recover the bodies and extinguish the fire. Combined fire departments of Mercer County are fighting the flames which menace the entire countryside.

We have been unable to establish any contact with our mobile unit at Grovers Mill, but we hope to be able to return you there at the earliest possible moment. In the meantime we take you to-----uh, just one moment please.

(LONG PAUSE)

(WHISPER) Ladies and gentlemen, I have just been informed that we have finally established communication with an eyewitness of the tragedy. Professor Pierson has been located at a farmhouse near Grovers Mill where he has established an emergency observation post. As a scientist, he will give you his explanation of the calamity. The next voice you hear will be that of Professor Pierson, brought to you by direct wire. Professor Pierson.

PIERSON

Of the creatures in the rocket cylinder at Grovers Mill, I can give you no authoritative information — either as to their nature, their origin, or their purposes here on earth. Of their destructive instrument I might venture some conjectural explanation. For want of a better term, I shall refer to the mysterious weapon as a heat-ray. It's all too evident that these creatures have scientific knowledge far in advance of our own. It is my guess that in some way they are able to generate an intense heat in a chamber of practically absolute nonconductivity. This intense heat they project in a parallel beam against any object they choose, by means of a polished parabolic mirror of unknown composition, much as the mirror of a lighthouse projects a beam of light. That is my conjecture of the origin of the heat-ray...

ANNOUNCER TWO

Thank you, Professor Pierson. Ladies and gentlemen, here is a bulletin from Trenton. It is a brief statement informing us that the charred body of Carl Phillips has been identified in a Trenton hospital. Now here's another bulletin from Washington, D.C.

Office of the director of the National Red Cross reports ten units of Red Cross emergency workers have been assigned to the headquarters of the State Militia stationed outside of Grovers Mill, New Jersey. Here's a bulletin from State Police, Princeton Junction: The fires at Grovers Mill and vicinity now under control. Scouts report all quiet in the pit, and no sign of life appearing from the mouth of the cylinder ... And now, ladies and gentlemen, we have a special statement from Mr. Harry McDonald, vice-president in charge of operations.

MCDONALD

We have received a request from the militia at Trenton to place at their disposal our entire broadcasting facilities. In view of the gravity of the situation, and believing that radio has a responsibility to serve in the public interest at all times, we are turning over our facilities to the State Militia at Trenton.

ANNOUNCER

We take you now to the field headquarters of the State Militia near Grovers Mill, New Jersey.

CAPTAIN

This is Captain Lansing of the Signal Corps, attached to the State Militia now engaged in military operations in the vicinity of Grovers Mill. Situation arising from the reported presence of certain individuals of unidentified nature, is now under complete control.

The cylindrical object which lies in a pit directly below our position is surrounded on all sides by eight battalions of infantry, without heavy field pieces, but adequately armed with rifles and machine guns. All cause for alarm, if such cause ever existed, is now entirely unjustified. The things, whatever they are, do not even venture to poke their heads above the pit. I can see their hiding place plainly in the glare of the searchlights here. With all their reported resources, these creatures can scarcely stand up against heavy machine-gun fire. Anyway, it's an interesting outing for the troops. I can make out their khaki uniforms, crossing back and forth in front of the lights. It looks almost like a real war. There appears to be some slight smoke in the woods bordering the Millstone River. Probably fire started by campers. Well, we ought to see some action soon. One of the companies is deploying on the left flank. A quick thrust and it will all be over. Now wait a minute! I see something on top of the cylinder. No, it's nothing but a shadow. Now the troops are on the edge of the Wilmuth farm. Seven thousand armed men closing in on an old metal tube. Wait, that wasn't a shadow! It's something moving ... solid metal ... kind of a shieldlike affair rising up out of the cylinder ... It's going higher and higher. Why, it's standing on legs ... actually rearing up on a sort of metal framework. Now it's reaching above the trees and the searchlights are on it. Hold on!

ANNOUNCER TWO

Ladies and gentlemen, I have a grave announcement to make. Incredible as it may seem, both the observations of science and the evidence of our eyes lead to the inescapable assumption that those strange beings who landed in the Jersey farmlands tonight are the vanguard of an invading army from the planet Mars. The battle which took place tonight at Grovers Mill has ended in one of the most startling defeats ever suffered by an army in modern times; seven thousand men armed with rifles and machine guns pitted against a single fighting machine of the invaders from Mars. One hundred and twenty known survivors. The rest strewn over the battle area from Grovers Mill to Plainsboro, crushed and trampled to death under the metal feet of the monster, or burned to cinders by its heat-ray. The monster is now in control of the middle section of New Jersey and has effectively cut the state through its center. Communication lines are down from Pennsylvania to the Atlantic Ocean. Railroad tracks are torn and service from New York to Philadelphia discontinued except routing some of the trains through Allentown and Phoenixville. Highways to the north, south, and west are clogged with frantic human traffic. Police and army reserves are unable to control the mad flight. By morning the fugitives will have swelled Philadelphia, Camden, and Trenton, it is estimated, to twice their normal population. At this time martial law prevails throughout New Jersey and eastern Pennsylvania. We take you to Washington for a special broadcast on the National Emergency ... the Secretary of the Interior...

SECRETARY

Citizens of the nation: I shall not try to conceal the gravity of the situation that confronts the country, nor the concern of your government in protecting the lives and property of its people. However, I wish to impress upon you — private citizens and public officials, all of you — the urgent need of calm and resourceful action. Fortunately, this formidable enemy is still confined to a comparatively small area, and we may place our faith in the military forces to keep them there. In the meantime placing our faith in God we must continue the performance of our duties each and everyone of us, so that we may confront this destructive adversary with a nation united, courageous, and consecrated to the preservation of human supremacy on this earth. I thank you.

ANNOUNCER

You have just heard the Secretary of the Interior speaking from Washington. Bulletins too numerous to read are piling up in the studio here. We are informed that the central portion of New Jersey is blacked out from radio communication due to the effect of the heat-ray upon power lines and electrical equipment. Here is a special bulletin from New York. Cables received from English, French, German scientific bodies offering assistance. Astronomers report continued gas outbursts at regular intervals on planet Mars. Majority voice opinion that the enemy will be reinforced by additional rocket machines. Attempts made to locate Professor Pierson of Princeton, who has observed Martians at close range. It is feared he was lost in recent battle. LANGHAM FIELD, VIRGINIA: Scouting planes report three Martian machines visible above treetops, moving north towards Somerville with population fleeing ahead of them. Heat-ray is not in use; although advancing at express-train speed, invaders pick their way carefully. They seem to be making conscious effort to avoid destruction of cities and countryside. However, they stop to uproot power lines, bridges, and railroad tracks. Their apparent objective is to crush resistance, paralyze communication, and disorganize human society.

Here is a bulletin from Basking Ridge, New Jersey: Coon hunters have stumbled on a second cylinder similar to the first embedded in the great swamp twenty miles south of Morristown. U.S. Army fieldpieces are proceeding from Newark to blow up second invading unit before cylinder can be opened and the fighting machine rigged. They are taking up a position in the foothills of Watchung Mountains. Another bulletin from Langham Field, Virginia — Scouting planes report enemy machines, now three in number, increasing speed northward kicking over houses and trees in their evident haste to form a conjunction with their allies south of Morristown. Machines also sighted by telephone operator east of Middlesex within ten miles of Plainfield. Here's a bulletin from Winston Field, Long Island: Fleet of army bombers carrying heavy explosives flying north in pursuit of enemy. Scouting planes act as guides. They keep speeding enemy in sight. Just a moment please. Ladies and gentlemen, we've run special wires to the artillery line in adjacent villages to give you direct reports in the zone of the advancing enemy. First we take you to the battery of the 22nd Field Artillery, located in the Watchung Mountains.

OFFICER

Range, 32 meters.

GUNNER

32 meters.

OFFICER

Projection, 39 degrees.

GUNNER

39 degrees.

OFFICER

Fire! (BOOM OF HEAVY GUN ... PAUSE)

OBSERVER

140 yards to the right, sir.

OFFICER

Shift range ... 31 meters.

GUNNER

31 meters

OFFICER

Projection ... 37 degrees.

GUNNER

37 degrees.

OFFICER

Fire! (BOOM OF HEAVY GUN ... PAUSE)

OBSERVER

A hit, sir! We got the tripod of one of them. They've stopped. The others are trying to repair it.

OFFICER

Quick, get the range! Shift 50 30 meters.

GUNNER

30 meters.

OFFICER

Projection ... 27 degrees.

GUNNER

27 degrees.

OFFICER

Fire! (BOOM OF HEAVY GUN ... PAUSE)

OBSERVER

Can't see the shell land, sir. They're letting off a smoke.

OFFICER

What is it?

OBSERVER

A black smoke, sir. Moving this way. Lying close to the ground. It's moving fast.

OFFICER

Put on gas masks. (PAUSE) Get ready to fire. Shift to 24 meters.

GUNNER

24 meters.

OFFICER

Projection, 24 degrees.

GUNNER

24 degrees.

OFFICER

Fire! (BOOM)

OBSERVER

Still can't see, sir. The smoke's coming nearer.

OFFICER

Get the range. (COUGHS)

OBSERVER

23 meters. (COUGHS)

OFFICER

23 meters. (COUGHS)

GUNNER

23 meters (COUGHS)

OBSERVER

Projection, 22 degrees. (COUGHING)

OFFICER

22 degrees. (FADE IN COUGHING)
(FADING IN ... SOUND OF AIRPLANE MOTOR)

COMMANDER

Army bombing plane, V-8-43, off Bayonne, New Jersey, Lieutenant Voght, commanding eight bombers. Reporting to Commander Fairfax, Langham Field ... This is Voght, reporting to Commander Fairfax, Langham Field ... Enemy tripod machines now in sight. Reinforced by three machines from the Morristown cylinder. Six altogether. One machine partially crippled. Believed hit by shell from army gun in Watchung Mountains. Guns now appear silent. A heavy black fog hanging close to the earth ... of extreme density, nature unknown. No sign of heat-ray. Enemy now turns east, crossing Passaic River into the Jersey marshes. Another straddles the Pulaski sky-way. Evident objective is New York City. They're pushing down a high tension power station. The machines are close together now, and we're ready to attack. Planes circling, ready to strike. A thousand yards and we'll be over the first ... 800 yards ... 600 ... 400 ... 200 ... There they go! The giant arm raised ... Green flash! They're spraying us with flame! Two thousand feet. Engines are giving out. No chance to release bombs. Only one thing left ... drop on them, plane and all. We're diving on the first one. Now the engine's gone! Eight....

OPERATOR ONE

This is Bayonne, New Jersey, calling Langham Field...
This is Bayonne, New Jersey, calling Langham Field...
Come in, please ... Come in, please...

OPERATOR TWO

This is Langham Field ... Go ahead...

OPERATOR ONE

Eight army bombers in engagement with enemy tripod machines over Jersey flats. Engines incapacitated by heat-ray. All crashed. One enemy machine destroyed. Enemy now discharging heavy black smoke in direction of—

OPERATOR THREE

This is Newark, New Jersey...
This is Newark, New Jersey...
Warning! Poisonous black smoke pouring in from Jersey marshes.
Reaches South Street. Gas masks useless. Urge population to move into open spaces ... automobiles use Routes 7, 23, 24 ... Avoid congested areas. Smoke now spreading over Raymond Boulevard —

OPERATOR FOUR

2 X 2 L ... calling C Q
2 X 2 L ... calling C Q
2 X 2 L ... calling 8 X 3 R
Come in, please...

OPERATOR FIVE

This is 8 X 3 R ... coming back at 2 X 2 L.

OPERATOR FOUR

How's reception? How's reception? K, please. Where are you, 8 X 3 R?
What's the matter? Where are you?

(BELLS RINGING OVER CITY GRADUALLY DIMINISHING)

ANNOUNCER

I'm speaking from the roof of Broadcasting Building, New York City. The bells you hear are ringing to warn the people to evacuate the city as the Martians approach. Estimated in last two hours three million people have moved out along the roads to the north. Hutchison River Parkway still kept open for motor traffic. Avoid bridges to Long Island ... hopelessly jammed. All communication with Jersey shore closed ten minutes ago. No more defenses. Our army wiped out ... artillery, air force, everything wiped out. This may be the last broadcast. We'll stay here to the end ... People are holding service here below us ... in the cathedral.

(VOICES SINGING HYMN)

Now I look down the harbor. All manner of boats, overloaded with fleeing population, pulling out from docks.

(SOUND OF BOAT WHISTLES)

Streets are all jammed. Noise in crowds like New Year's Eve in city. Wait a minute ... Enemy is now in sight above the Palisades. Five great machines. First one is crossing river. I can see it from here, wading the Hudson like a man wading through a brook ... A bulletin's handed me ... Martian cylinders are falling all over the country. One outside Buffalo, one in Chicago, St. Louis ... seem to be timed and spaced ... Now the first machine reaches the shore. He stands watching, looking over the city. His steel, cowlish head is even with the skyscrapers. He waits for the others. They rise like a line of new towers on the city's west side ... Now they're lifting their metal hands. This is the end now. Smoke comes out ... black smoke, drifting over the city. People in the streets see it now. They're running towards the East River ... thousands of them, dropping in like rats. Now the smoke's spreading faster. It's reached Times Square. People are trying to run away from it, but it's no use. They're falling like flies. Now the smoke's crossing Sixth Avenue ... Fifth Avenue ... 100 yards away ... it's 50 feet...

OPERATOR FOUR

2 X 2 L calling C Q
2 X 2 L calling C Q
2 X 2 L calling C Q ... New York.
Isn't there anyone on the air?
Isn't there anyone...
2 X 2 L—

(MIDDLE BREAK)

ANNOUNCER

You are listening to a CBS presentation of Orson Welles and the Mercury Theatre on the Air in an original dramatization of "The War of the Worlds" by H. G. Wells. The performance will continue after a brief intermission.

This is the COLUMBIA.....BROADCASTING SYSTEM.

(FADE THEME 10 SECONDS)

WABC NEW YORK

(ENTIRE BREAK 20 SECONDS)

ANNOUNCER

"The War of the Worlds" by H. G. Wells, staring Orson Welles and the Mercury Theatre on the Air...

(MUSIC)

PIERSON

As I set down these notes on paper, I'm obsessed by the thought that I may be the last living man on Earth. I have been hiding in this empty house near Grovers Mill — a small island of daylight cut off by the black smoke from the rest of the world. All that happened before the arrival of these monstrous creatures in the world now seems part of another life ... a life that has no continuity with the present, furtive existence of the lonely derelict who pencils these words on the back of some astronomical notes bearing the signature of Richard Pierson. I look down at my blackened hands, my torn shoes, my tattered clothes, and I try to connect them with a professor who lives at Princeton, and who on the night of October 20th, glimpsed through his telescope an orange splash of light on a distant planet. My wife, my colleagues, my students, my books, my observatory, my ... my world ... where are they? Did they ever exist? Am I Richard Pierson? What day is it? Do days exist without calendars? Does time pass when there are no human hands left to wind the clocks? .... In writing down my daily life I tell myself I shall preserve human history between the dark covers of this little book that was meant to record the movements of the stars ... but to write I must live, and to live, I must eat ... I find mouldy bread in the kitchen, and an orange not too spoiled to swallow. I keep watch at the window. From time to time I catch sight of a Martian above the black smoke.

The smoke still holds the house in its black coil ... but at length there is a hissing sound and suddenly I see a Martian mounted on his machine, spraying the air with a jet of steam, as if to dissipate the smoke. I watch in a corner as his huge metal legs nearly brush against the house. Exhausted by terror, I fall asleep ... It's morning. Sun streams in the window. The black cloud of gas has lifted, and the scorched meadows to the north look as though a black snow storm has passed over them. I venture from the house. I make my way to a road. No traffic. Here and there a wrecked car, baggage overturned, a blackened skeleton. I push on north. For some reason I feel safer trailing these monsters than running away from them. And I keep a careful watch. I have seen the Martians feed. Should one of their machines appear over the top of trees, I am ready to fling myself flat on the earth. I come to a chestnut tree. October, chestnuts are ripe. I fill my pockets. I must keep alive. Two days I wander in a vague northerly direction through a desolate world. Finally I notice a living creature ... a small red squirrel in a beech tree. I stare at him, and wonder. He stares back at me. I believe at that moment the animal and I shared the same emotion ... the joy of finding another living being .... I push on north. I find dead cows in a brackish field. Beyond, the charred ruins of a dairy. The silo remains standing guard over the waste land like a lighthouse deserted by the sea. Astride the silo perches a weather cock. The arrow points north.

Next day I come to a city vaguely familiar in its contours, yet its buildings strangely dwarfed and leveled off, as if a giant had sliced off its highest towers with a capricious sweep of his hand. I reached the outskirts. I found Newark, undemolished, but humbled by some whim of the advancing Martians. Presently, with an odd feeling of being watched, I caught sight of something crouching in a doorway. I made a step towards it ... and it rose up and became a man---a man, armed with a large knife.

STRANGER

Stop ... Where did you come from?

PIERSON

I come from ... many places. A long time ago from Princeton.

STRANGER

Princeton, huh? That's near Grovers Mill!

PIERSON

Yes.

STRANGER

Grovers Mill ... (LAUGHS AS AT A GREAT JOKE) ... There's no food here. This is my country ... all this end of town down to the river. There's only food for one ... Which way are you going?

PIERSON

I don't know. I guess I'm looking for----for people.

STRANGER

(NERVOUSLY) What was that? Did you hear something just then?

PIERSON

Only a bird ... (MARVELS) ... A live bird!

STRANGER

You get to know that birds have shadows these days ... Say, we're in the open here. Let's crawl into this doorway and talk.

PIERSON

Have you seen any Martians?

STRANGER

They've gone over to New York. At night the sky is alive with their lights. Just as if people were still living in it. By daylight you can't see them. Five days ago a couple of them carried something big across the flats from the airport. I believe they're learning how to fly.

PIERSON

Fly?

STRANGER

Yeah, fly.

PIERSON

Then it's all over with humanity. Stranger, there's still you and I. Two of us left.

STRANGER

They got themselves in solid; they wrecked the greatest country in the world. Those green stars, they're probably falling somewhere every night. They've only lost one machine. There isn't anything to do. We're done. We're licked.

PIERSON

Where were <u>you</u>? You're in a uniform.

STRANGER

What's left of it. I was in the militia — national guard ... That's good! Wasn't any war any more than there's war between men and ants.

PIERSON

And we're eatable ants! I found that out ... What will they do to us?

STRANGER

I've thought it all out. Right now we're caught as we're wanted. The Martian only has to go a few miles to get a crowd on the run. But they won't keep on doing that. They'll begin catching us systematic like---keeping the best and storing us in cages and things. They haven't begun on us yet!

PIERSON

Not begun!

STRANGER

Not begun. All that's happened so far is because we don't have sense enough to keep quiet ... bothering them with guns and such stuff and losing our heads and rushing off in crowds. Now instead of our rushing around blind we've got to fix ourselves up according to the way things are now. Cities, nations, civilization, progress---

PIERSON

But if that's so, what is there to live for?

STRANGER

There won't be any more concerts for a million years or so, and no nice little dinners at restaurants. If it's amusement you're after, I guess the game's up.

PIERSON

And what is there left?

STRANGER

Life ... that's what! I want to live. And so do you! We're not going to be exterminated. And I don't mean to be caught, either and tamed, and fattened, and bred like an ox!

PIERSON

What are you going to do?

STRANGER

I'm going on ... right under their feet. I gotta plan. We men as men are finished. We don't know enough. We gotta learn plenty before we've got a chance. And we've got to live and keep free while we learn. I've thought it all out, see.

PIERSON

Tell me the rest.

STRANGER

Well, it isn't all of us that are made for wild beasts, and that's what it's got to be. That's why I watched you. All these little office workers that used to live in these houses--they'd be no good. They haven't any stuff to 'em. They just used to run off to work. I've seen hundreds of 'em, running wild to catch their commuters' train in the morning for fear they'd get canned if they didn't; running back at night afraid they won't be in time for dinner. Lives insured and a little invested in case of accidents. And on Sundays, worried about the hereafter. The Martians will be a godsend for those guys. Nice roomy cages, good food, careful breeding, no worries. After a week or so chasing about the fields on empty stomachs they'll come and be glad to be caught.

PIERSON

You've thought it all out, haven't you?

STRANGER

You bet I have! And that isn't all. These Martians will make pets of some of them, train 'em to do tricks. Who knows? Get sentimental over the pet boy who grew up and had to be killed. And some, maybe, they'll train to hunt us!

PIERSON

No, that's impossible. No human being---

STRANGER

Yes they will. There's men who'll do it gladly. If one of them ever comes after <u>me</u>----

PIERSON

In the meantime, you and I and others like us ... where are we to live when the Martians own the earth?

STRANGER

I've got it all figured out. We'll live underground. I've been thinking about the sewers. Under New York are miles and miles of 'em. The main ones are big enough for anybody.

Then there's cellars, vaults, underground storerooms, railway tunnels, subways. You begin to see, eh? And we'll get a bunch of strong men together. No weak ones, that rubbish, out.

PIERSON

As you meant me to go?

STRANGER

Well, I gave you a chance, didn't I?

PIERSON

We won't quarrel about that. Go on.

STRANGER

And we've got to make safe places for us to stay in, see, and get all the books we can---science books. That's where men like you come in, see? We'll raid the museums, we'll even spy on the Martians. It may not be so much we have to learn before--just imagine this: four or five of their own fighting machines suddenly start off--heat-rays right and left and not a Martian in 'em. Not a Martian in 'em. But *men*--men who have learned the way how. It may even be in our time. Gee! Imagine having one of them lovely things with its heat-ray wide and free! We'd turn it on Martians, we'd turn it on men. We'd bring everybody down to their knees!

PIERSON

That's your plan?

STRANGER

You and me and a few more of us we'd own the world!

PIERSON

I see.

STRANGER

Say, what's the matter? Where are you going?

PIERSON

Not to your world.... Good-bye, stranger...

PIERSON

After parting with the artilleryman, I came at last to the Holland Tunnel. I entered that silent tube anxious to know the fate of the great city on the other side of the Hudson. Cautiously I came out of the tunnel and made my way up Canal Street.

I reached Fourteenth Street, and there again were black powder and several bodies, and an evil ominous smell from the gratings of the cellars of some of the houses. I wandered up through the Thirties and Forties; I stood alone on Times Square. I caught sight of a lean dog running down Seventh Avenue with a piece of dark brown meat in his jaws, and a pack of starving mongrels at his heels. He made a wide circle around me, as though he feared I might prove a fresh competitor. I walked up Broadway in the direction of that strange powder — past silent shop windows, displaying their mute wares to empty sidewalks — past the Capitol Theatre, silent, dark — past a shooting gallery, where a row of empty guns faced an arrested line of wooden ducks.

Near Columbus Circle I noticed models of 1939 motorcars in the showrooms facing empty streets. From over the top of the General Motors Building, I watched a flock of black birds circling in the sky. I hurried on. Suddenly I caught sight of the hood of a Martian machine, standing somewhere in Central Park, gleaming in the late afternoon sun. An insane idea! I rushed recklessly across Columbus Circle and into the Park. I climbed a small hill above the pond at Sixtieth Street and from there I could see, standing in a silent row along the mall, nineteen of those great metal Titans, their cowls empty, their steel arms hanging listlessly by their sides. I looked in vain for the monsters that inhabit those machines.

Suddenly, my eyes were attracted to the immense flock of black birds that hovered directly below me. They circled to the ground, and there before my eyes, stark and silent, lay the Martians, with the hungry birds pecking and tearing brown shreds of flesh from their dead bodies. Later when their bodies were examined in laboratories, it was found that they were killed by the putrefactive and disease bacteria against which their systems were unprepared ... slain, after all man's defenses had failed, by the humblest thing that God in His wisdom put upon this earth.

Before the cylinder fell there was a general persuasion that through all the deep of space no life existed beyond the petty surface of our minute sphere. Now we see further. Dim and wonderful is the vision I have conjured up in my mind of life spreading slowly from this little seed-bed of the solar system throughout the inanimate vastnesses of sidereal space. But that is a remote dream. It may be, that the destruction of the Martians is only a reprieve. To them, and not to us, is the future ordained perhaps.

Strange it now seems to sit in my peaceful study at Princeton writing down this last chapter of the record begun at a deserted farm in Grovers Mill. Strange to see from my window the university spires dim and blue through the April haze. Strange to watch children playing in the streets. Strange to see young people strolling on the green, where the new spring grass heals the last black scars of a bruised earth. Strange to watch the sightseers enter the museum where the dissembled parts of a Martian machine are kept on public view. Strange when I recall the time when I first saw it, bright and clean-cut, hard, and silent, under the dawn of that last great day.

(MUSIC)

ORSON WELLES

This is Orson Welles, ladies and gentlemen, out of character to assure you that THE WAR OF THE WORLDS has no further significance than as the holiday offering it was intended to be. The Mercury Theatre's own radio version of dressing up in a sheet and jumping out of a bush and saying Boo! Starting now, we couldn't soap all your windows and steal all your garden gates, by tomorrow night ... so we did the next best thing. We annihilated the world before your very ears, and utterly destroyed the C. B. S. You will be relieved, I hope, to learn that we didn't mean it, and that both institutions are still open for business. So good-bye everybody, and remember, please, for the next day or so, the terrible lesson you learned tonight. That grinning, glowing, globular invader of your living room is an inhabitant of the pumpkin patch, and if your doorbell rings and nobody's there, that was no Martian ... it's Halloween.

(MUSIC)

CHAPTER NOTES

Chapter 1

1. William Sheehan, *The Planet Mars: A History of Observation and Discovery* (Tucson: University of Arizona Press, 1996). http://www.uapress.arizona.edu/onlinebks/mars/chap02.htm.
2. http://www.uapress.arizona.edu/onlinebks/mars/chap07.htm
3. Percival Lowell, *Mars* (New York: Elibron Classics, 2004), 150.

Chapter 2

1. David C. Smith, *H. G. Wells: Desperately Mortal* (New Haven: Yale University Press, 1986), 6.
2. "Report of a Debate." *Science Schools Journal* (November 1888): 58.
3. Anthony West, *H. G. Wells: Aspects of a Life* (New York: Penguin, 1985), 221.
4. H. G. Wells, *The Time Machine* (New York: Berkley, 1963), 43.
5. Bernard Bergonzi, *The Early H. G. Wells: A Study of Scientific Romances* (Manchester: Manchester University Press, 1961), 124.
6. Ibid.
7. Ibid., 125.
8. H. G. Wells, *Experiment in Autobiography, Volume 1* (London: Victor Gollancz, 1934), 275.
9. Unsigned review. *The Spectator.* In *H. G. Wells: The Critical Heritage*, ed. Patrick Parrinder (London: Routledge, 1997), 66.
10. Unsigned review. *Academy.* In *H. G. Wells: The Critical Heritage*, ed. Patrick Parrinder (London: Routledge, 1997), 70.

Chapter 3

1. Barbara Leaming, *Orson Welles* (London: Phoenix, 1993), 5.
2. Frank Brady, *Citizen Welles* (London: Coronet, 1991), 2.
3. Simon Callow, *Orson Welles: The Road to Xanadu* (London: Jonathan Cape, 1995), 9.
4. Barbara Leaming, *Orson Welles* (London: Phoenix, 1993), 8.
5. Ibid., 10.
6. Simon Callow, *Orson Welles: The Road to Xanadu* (London: Jonathan Cape, 1995), 44.
7. Frank Brady, *Citizen Welles* (London: Coronet, 1991), 13.

8. Orson Welles and Peter Bogdanovich, *This Is Orson Welles* (London: HarperCollins, 1993), 45.
9. Micheal MacLiammoir, "All for Hecuba." In *Citizen Welles*, Frank Brady (London: Coronet, 1991), 27.
10. Orson Welles, Interview by Leslie Megahey, "The Orson Welles Story," *Arena*, BBC, 1982.
11. Catherine Cornell, "I Wanted to Be an Actress." In *Citizen Welles*, Frank Brady (London: Coronet, 1991), 52.
12. John Houseman, *Unfinished Business* (London: Columbus Books, 1988), 71.
13. Geraldine Fitzgerald, Interview by Leonard Maltin, *Theatre of the Imagination: The Mercury Company Remembers*, 1988.
14. Orson Welles and Peter Bogdanovich, *This Is Orson Welles* (London: HarperCollins, 1993), 10.
15. Barbara Leaming, *Orson Welles* (London: Phoenix, 1993), 153.
16. John Houseman, *Unfinished Business* (London: Columbus Books, 1988), 177.
17. Ibid., 175.

Chapter 4

1. John Houseman, "The Men from Mars." *Harper's*, December 1948, 75.
2. Michele Hilmes, *Radio Voices* (Minneapolis: University of Minnesota Press, 1997), 123.
3. Simon Callow, *Orson Welles: The Road to Xanadu* (London: Jonathan Cape, 1995), 370.
4. John Houseman, *Unfinished Business* (London: Columbus Books, 1988), 176.
5. John Houseman, interview by Leonard Maltin, *Theatre of the Imagination: The Mercury Company Remembers*, 1988.
6. John Houseman, "The Men from Mars." *Harper's*, December 1948, 76.
7. Howard Koch, *As Time Goes By* (New York: Harcourt Brace Jovanovich, 1979), 4.
8. Jill Wilson, "*War of the Worlds* Original Script Offered on eBay." *Metropolitan Washington Old Time Radio Club.* http://www.mwotrc.com/rr2003_06/warworlds.htm.
9. Howard Koch, *The Panic Broadcast* (New York: Avon Books, 1971), 15.
10. Howard Koch, *As Time Goes By* (New York: Harcourt Brace Jovanovich, 1979), 4.
11. John Houseman, *Unfinished Business* (London: Columbus Books, 1988), 184.
12. John Houseman, "The Men from Mars." *Harper's*, December 1948, 76.

13. Ibid.

14. Steven C. Smith, *A Heart at Fire's Center: The Life and Music of Bernard Herrmann* (Berkeley: University of California Press, 2002), 66.

15. William Alland, interview by Leonard Maltin, *Theatre of the Imagination: The Mercury Company Remembers*, 1988.

16. John Houseman, *Unfinished Business* (London: Columbus Books, 1988), 180.

17. Ibid.

18. Richard Wilson, interview by Leonard Maltin, *Theatre of the Imagination: The Mercury Company Remembers*, 1988.

19. Frank Brady, *Citizen Welles* (London: Coronet, 1991), 166.

20. Quoted in Simon Callow, *Orson Welles: The Road to Xanadu* (London: Jonathan Cape, 1995), 400.

21. John Houseman, *Unfinished Business* (London: Columbus Books, 1988), 191.

22. Ibid., 197.

Chapter 5

1. John Houseman, "The Men from Mars." *Harper's*, December 1948, 79.

2. Hal Davies, *Wideworld*, The Open University for Channel 5, 1997.

3. John Houseman, "The Men from Mars." *Harper's*, December 1948, 82.

4. Charles Jackson, "The Night the Martians Came." In *The Aspirin Age, 1919–1941*, ed. Isabel Leighton (New York: Simon and Schuster, 1949), 437.

Chapter 6

1. Howard Koch, *The Panic Broadcast* (New York: Avon Books, 1971), 24.

2. Ibid., 29.

3. Hadley Cantril, *The Invasion from Mars* New York: Harper Torchbooks, 1966, 48.

4. Ibid., 52.

5. Ibid., 50.

6. Ibid., 53.

7. Hal Davies, *Wideworld*, The Open University for Channel 5, 1997.

8. Norman Corwin, interview by author. Tape recording, October 30, 2007.

9. Howard Koch, *The Panic Broadcast* (New York: Avon Books, 1971), 89.

10. Ibid., 96.

11. Simon Callow, *Orson Welles: The Road to Xanadu* (London: Jonathan Cape, 1995), 403.

Chapter 7

1. Gwenyth L. Jackaway, *Media at War: Radio's Challenge to the Newspapers, 1924–1939* (Westport, Conn.: Greenwood Publishing Group, 1995), 20.

2. Ibid., 22.

3. Ibid., 24.

4. Ibid., 26.

5. Frank Brady, *Citizen Welles* (London: Coronet, 1991), 176.

6. Sheldon Judson, to the author, October 1998.

7. Erving Press is quoted in an unattributed article, "Run! Men from Mars." *Princeton Recollector* V, no. 1 (October 1979): 1.

8. Ibid.

9. Howard Koch, *The Panic Broadcast* (New York: Avon Books, 1971), 120.

10. From the records of the New Jersey State Police Museum and Learning Center in Trenton.

11. Hadley Cantril, *The Invasion from Mars* (New York: Harper Torchbooks, 1966), xiii.

12. John Houseman, *Unfinished Business* (London: Columbus Books, 1988), 199.

13. Norman Corwin, interview by author. Tape recording, October 30, 2007.

14. Howard Koch, *The Panic Broadcast* (New York: Avon Books, 1971), 94.

Chapter 8

1. Hadley Cantril, *The Invasion from Mars* (New York: Harper Torchbooks, 1966), 82.

2. Peter Heyer, *The Medium and the Magician: Orson Welles, the Radio Years, 1934–1952* (Lanham, Md.: Rowman & Littlefield Publishers, 2005) 82.

3. Hadley Cantril, *The Invasion from Mars* (New York: Harper Torchbooks, 1966), 82.

4. Ibid., 83.

5. Ibid., 60.

6. Erich Goode, *Collective Behavior* (Fort Worth, Tex.: Saunders College Publishing, 1992), 314.

7. Hadley Cantril, *The Invasion from Mars* (New York: Harper Torchbooks, 1966), 140.

8. Jerry W. Knudson, *In the News: American Journalists View Their Craft* (Lanham, Md.: Rowman & Littlefield, 2000), 177.

9. Ronda Grogan, "We Must Declare Martial Law." American Studies, The University of Virginia. http://xroads.virginia.edu/~1930s/RADIO/WOTW/frames.html.

10. Hans Kaltenborn, *Fifty Fabulous Years, 1900–1950* (New York: Putnam, 1950), 208.

11. Hadley Cantril, *The Invasion from Mars* (New York: Harper Torchbooks, 1966), 53.

12. Ibid., 100.

13. Ibid., 160.

14. David L. Miller, *Introduction to Collective Behavior* (Belmont, Calif.: Wadsworth Publishing Company, 1985), 104.

15. Hadley Cantril, *The Invasion from Mars* (New York: Harper Torchbooks, 1966), 106–107.

16. *Theatre of the Imagination*. Radio program. 1988.

17. Hadley Cantril, *The Invasion from Mars* (New York: Harper Torchbooks, 1966), 69.

18. Ibid., 70.

19. Neil J. Smelser, *Theory of Collective Behavior* (New York: The Free Press, 1962), 131.

20. David L. Miller, *Introduction to Collective Behavior* (Belmont, Calif.: Wadsworth Publishing Company, 1985), 98.

21. Erich Goode, *Collective Behavior* (Fort Worth, Tex.: Saunders College Publishing, 1992), 335.

22. William Sims Bainbridge, "Collective Behavior and Social Movements." In *Sociology, Second Edition*, ed. Rodney Stark (Belmont, Calif.: Wadsworth Publishing Company, 1987), 554.

23. Hadley Cantril, *The Invasion from Mars* (New York: Harper Torchbooks, 1966), 142.

24. Ibid., 123.

25. Ibid., 47.

26. Ibid., ix.

27. Neil J. Smelser, *Theory of Collective Behavior* (New York: The Free Press, 1962), 136.

28. David L. Miller, *Introduction to Collective Behavior* (Belmont, Calif.: Wadsworth Publishing Company, 1985), 106.

29. Frank Brady, *Citizen Welles* (London: Coronet, 1991), 173.

30. Ibid., 174.

31. Barbara Leaming, *Orson Welles* (London: Phoenix, 1993), 163.

32. Orson Welles and Peter Bogdanovich, *This Is Orson Welles* (London: HarperCollins, 1993), 19.

33. Simon Callow, *Orson Welles: The Road to Xanadu* (London: Jonathan Cape, 1995), 407.

34. Frank Brady, *Citizen Welles* (London: Coronet, 1991), 175.

35. Alex Lubertozzi and Brian Holmsten, eds. *The Complete War of the Worlds* (Naperville, Ill.: Sourcebooks, 2001), 16.

36. Ibid.

37. Howard Koch, "The Radio Years: Orson Welles on the Air." The Museum of Broadcasting, 1988, p. 30.

38. *All Things Considered*. Radio program. National Public Radio, 1988.

39. Peter Heyer, *The Medium and the Magician: Orson Welles, the Radio Years, 1934–1952* (Lanham, Md.: Rowman & Littlefield, 2005), 98.

Chapter 9

1. John Houseman, *Unfinished Business* (London: Columbus Books, 1988), 200.

2. Frank Brady, *Citizen Welles* (London: Coronet, 1991), 176.

3. John Houseman, *Unfinished Business* (London: Columbus Books, 1988), 200.

4. *All Things Considered*. Radio program. National Public Radio, 1988.

5. John L. Flynn, War of the Worlds *from Wells to Spielberg* (Owings Mills, Md.: Galactic Books, 2005), 42.

6. Justin Levin, "A History and Analysis of the Federal Communications Commission's Response to Radio Broadcast Hoaxes." *Federal Communications Law Journal* 52, no. 2 (March 2000): 285.

7. Ibid.

8. Ibid., 286.

9. Ibid., 280.

10. Frank Brady, *Citizen Welles* (London: Coronet, 1991), 175.

11. Simon Callow, *Orson Welles: The Road to Xanadu* (London: Jonathan Cape, 1995), 490.

12. Frank Brady, *Citizen Welles* (London: Coronet, 1991), 177.

13. Simon Callow, *Orson Welles: The Road to Xanadu* (London: Jonathan Cape, 1995), 490.

14. Ibid.

15. Ibid.

16. Ibid.

17. Martin Grams, Jr., "*The War of the Worlds* Revisited: Another Perspective." Old Time Radio Logs and Reviews. http://www.old-time.com/otrlogs2/wow_mg.html.

18. John Houseman, *Unfinished Business* (London: Columbus Books, 1988), 228.

19. Barbara Leaming, *Orson Welles* (London: Phoenix, 1993), 163.

20. Peter Heyer, *The Medium and the Magician: Orson Welles, the Radio Years, 1934–1952* (Lanham, Md.: Rowman & Littlefield, 2005), 149.

21. *The Orson Welles Sketchbook*, BBC Television, May 21, 1955.

22. Orson Welles and Peter Bogdanovich, *This Is Orson Welles* (London: HarperCollins, 1993), 20.

23. Barbara Leaming, *Orson Welles* (London: Phoenix, 1993), 288.

24. Martin Grams, Jr., "*The War of the Worlds* Revisited: Another Perspective." Old Time Radio Logs and Reviews. http://www.old-time.com/otrlogs2/wow_mg.html.

Chapter 10

1. Unknown author, "Those Men from Mars." *Newsweek*, November 27, 1944, 89.

2. Tom Weaver, *Double Feature Creature Attack: A Monster Merger of Two More Volumes of Classic Interviews* (Jefferson, N.C.: McFarland, 2003), 42.

3. Julio Hurtado, "Los Marcianos Llegaron Ya ... (The Martians Have Arrived)." *El Mercurio de Valparaiso*. http://www.mercuriovalpo.cl/prontus4_noticias/site/artic/20050829/pags/20050829143256.html.

4. Diego Zuñiga, "War of the Worlds." *Pensar*, October/December 2005, 9.

5. Ibid.

6. Julio Hurtado, "Los Marcianos Llegaron Ya ... (The Martians Have Arrived)." *El Mercurio de Valparaiso*. http://www.mercuriovalpo.cl/prontus4_noticias/site/artic/20050829/pags/20050829143256.html.

7. Ibid.

8. Ibid.

9. Diego Zuñiga, "War of the Worlds." *Pensar*, October/December 2005, 9.

10. Luís Roberto, "Eduardo Alcaraz (1915–1987)." Soap Opera Biographies. http://www.network54.com/Forum/223031/message/1049053904/Biograf%EDa+de+Eduardo+Alcaraz.

11. Rodolfo Pérez, "Biography of Blanca Salazar Bautista." Biographical Dictionary of Ecuador. http://www.diccionariobiograficoecuador.com/tomos/tomo15/sl.htm.

12. José Villamarín Carrascal, "La Noche que los Marcianos Invadieron Cotocollao (The Night the Martians Invaded Cotocollao)." *La Hora*. http://www.dlh.lahora.com.ec/paginas/temas/caleidoscopio28.htm.

13. Ibid.

14. Ibid.

15. Kingman, Nicolás. "La Invasión de los Marcianos (The Invasion of the Martians)." The Complete Works of Nicolás Kingman. *La Hora*. http://www.dlh.lahora.com.ec/paginas/kingman/tomo66.htm.

16. César Larrea Velásquez, *70 Años de la Vida Nacional 1906–1975. (70 Years of National Life 1906–1975)* (Quito: Diario El Comercio, 1976), 49.

17. Unknown author. "La Noche Que Incendiaron Radio Quito (The Night Radio Quito Burned)." El Universo, June 15, 2003. Article reproduced on http://gonzalobenitez.spaces.live.com/blog/cns!86C9C39EE39C3070!192.entry.

18. José Villamarín Carrascal, "La Noche que los Marcianos Invadieron Cotocollao (The Night the Martians Invaded Cotocollao)." La Hora. http://www.dlh.lahora.com.ec/paginas/temas/caleidoscopio28.htm.

19. Rodolfo Pérez, "Biography of Blanca Salazar Bautista." Biographical Dictionary of Ecuador. http://www.diccionariobiograficoecuador.com/tomos/tomo15/s1.htm.

20. Ibid.

21. Maria Beltrán Testagrossa, interview by Jad Abumrad, War of the Worlds, Radio Lab, WNYC, March 7, 2008.

22. Unknown author. "La Noche Que Incendiaron Radio Quito (The Night Radio Quito Burned)." El Universo, June 15, 2003. Article reproduced on http://gonzalobenitez.spaces.live.com/blog/cns!86C9C39EE39C3070!192.entry.

23. José Villamarín Carrascal, "La Noche que los Marcianos Invadieron Cotocollao (The Night the Martians Invaded Cotocollao)." La Hora. http://www.dlh.lahora.com.ec/paginas/temas/caleidoscopio28.htm.

24. Unknown author. "Windows 2006." Diario Hoy, January 14, 2006. http://www.hoy.com.ec/NoticiaNue.asp?row_id=223845.

25. Joseph Bulgatz, Ponzi Schemes, Invaders from Mars and More Extraordinary Popular Delusions and the Madness of Crowds (New York: Harmony Books, 1992), 139.

26. Unknown author. "Windows 2006." Diario Hoy, January 14, 2006. http://www.hoy.com.ec/NoticiaNue.asp?row_id=223845.

27. Nicolás Kingman, "La Invasión de los Marcianos (The Invasion of the Martians)." The Complete Works of Nicolás Kingman. La Hora. http://www.dlh.lahora.com.ec/paginas/kingman/tomo66.htm.

28. Unknown author. "Windows 2006." Diario Hoy, January 14, 2006. http://www.hoy.com.ec/NoticiaNue.asp?row_id=223845.

29. César Larrea Velásquez, 70 Años de la Vida Nacional 1906–1975 (70 Years of National Life 1906–1975) (Quito: Diario El Comercio, 1976), 51.

30. Ibid.

31. Moore, Don. "The Day the Martians Landed." Patepluma Radio. http://www.pateplumaradio.com/south/ecuador/martians.html.

32. José Villamarín Carrascal, "La Noche Que los Marcianos Invadieron Cotocollao (The Night the Martians Invaded Cotocollao)." La Hora. http://www.dlh.lahora.com.ec/paginas/temas/caleidoscopio28.htm.

Chapter 11

1. Alexandre Busko Valim, "Os Marcianos Estão Chegando! (The Martians Are Coming!)." *Revista de História da Biblioteca Nacional (Journal of History of the National Library),* October 1, 2005, http://www.revistadehistoria.com.br/v2/home/?go=detalhe&id=336&pagina=1.

2. Ibid.

3. Colin M. MacLachlan, *A History of Modern Brazil* (Wilmington, Del.: Scholarly Resources, 2003), 122.

4. Luke Ford, "24 Oct 1954 — Gravatai AFB, Brazil." *UFO DNA.* http://www.ufodna.com/uf02/uf3/023431.htm.

5. Unknown author. "In Their Own Revealing Words (Quotes on UFOs)." *UFO Evidence.* http://www.ufoevidence.org/documents/doc1220.htm.

6. Olavo T. Fontes, "Report from Brazil." PROJECT1947. http://www.project1947.com/articles/fontes1.htm.

7. Olavo T. Fontes, "The UAO sightings at the island of Trinidade." *NICAP.* http://www.nicap.org/fontesarticle.htm.

Chapter 12

1. Matos Maia, "Como Nasceu 'A Invasão dos Marcianos'" (How "The Martian Invasion" was born). Clássicos da Rádio. http://www.classicosdaradio.com/InvasaoMarcianos.htm.

2. Matos Maia, *A Invasão Dos Marcianos: + 3 Fantasias Radiofonicas* (Alfragide, Portugal: Dom Quixote, 1996), 39.

3. Matos Maia, "Como Nasceu 'A Invasão dos Marcianos'" (How "The Martian Invasion" was born). Clássicos da Rádio. http://www.classicosdaradio.com/InvasaoMarcianos.htm.

4. David Birmingham, *A Concise History of Portugal, Second Edition* (Cambridge: Cambridge University Press, 2007), 165.

Chapter 13

1. Unknown author. "Number of TV Households in America." Television History: The First 75 Years. http://www.tvhistory.tv/Annual_TV_Households_50-78.JPG.

2. Michael C. Keith, *Talking Radio: An Oral History of American Radio in the Television Age* (New York: M.E. Sharpe, 2000), 25.

3. *The Making of WKBW's* War of the Worlds, WNED-TV, Buffalo, 1998.

4. Ibid.

5. Alex Lubertozzi and Brian Holmsten, eds. *The Complete* War of the Worlds (Naperville, Ill.: Sourcebooks, 2001), 77.

6. Robert E. Bartholomew and Hilary Evans, *Panic Attacks* (Stroud, U.K.: Sutton Publishing, 2004), 64.

7. *The Making of WKBW's* War of the Worlds, WNED-TV, Buffalo, 1998.

8. Alex Lubertozzi and Brian Holmsten, eds. *The Complete* War of the Worlds. (Naperville, Ill.: Sourcebooks, 2001), 77.

9. Ibid.

10. John Gosling, "Did You Help Repel a Martian Invasion in 1968?" Army.ca Forums. http://forums.army.ca/forums/index.php?topic=69862.0;all.

11. Jeff Kaye, Introduction. *The War of the Worlds*, WKBW, 1971.

12. Jason Loviglio, interview by Jad Abumrad, *War of the Worlds*, Radio Lab, WNYC, March 07, 2008.

13. Robert E. Bartholomew and Hilary Evans, *Panic Attacks* (Stroud, U.K.: Sutton Publishing, 2004), 64.

14. Jeff Kaye, Introduction. *The War of the Worlds*, WKBW, 1971.

15. Bob Kosinski, "WKBW and *The War of the Worlds*." Buffalo Broadcasters. http://www.buffalobro adcasters.com/hist_kbwow.asp.

Chapter 14

1. Jaqueline Moucherek, "A Versão Maranhense da Guerra dos Mundos (The Maranhese Version of *War of the Worlds*)," *Jornal da Rede Alfredo de Carvalho* 4, no. 48 (2004). http://www.redealcar.jornalismo.ufsc.br/boletins/jornal48.htm.

2. Ed Wilson Ferreira Araújo, "A Guerra dos Mundos em São Luís do Maranhão (*The War of the Worlds* in São Luís do Maranhão)," *Jornal da Rede Alfredo de Carvalho* 4, no. 48 (2004). http://www.redealcar.jornal ismo.ufsc.br/boletins/jornal48.htm.

3. Alexandre Busko Valim, "Os Marcianos Estão Chegando! (The Martians Are Coming!)." *Revista de História da Biblioteca Nacional (Journal of History of the National Library)*, October 1, 2005. http://www.revis tadehistoria.com.br/v2/home/?go=detalhe&id=336&pa gina=1.

4. Jaqueline Moucherek, "A Versão Maranhense da Guerra dos Mundos (The Maranhese version of *War of the Worlds*)," Jornal *da Rede Alfredo de Carvalho* 4, no. 48 (2004). http://www.redealcar.jornalismo.ufsc.br/boletins/jornal48.htm.

5. Ed Wilson Ferreira Araújo, "A Guerra dos Mundos em São Luís do Maranhão (*The War of the Worlds* in São Luís do Maranhão)," *Jornal da Rede Alfredo de Carvalho* 4, no. 48 (2004). http://www.redealcar.jornal ismo.ufsc.br/boletins/jornal48.htm.

Chapter 15

1. Jay Clark, interview by the author. May 2, 2008.

2. Pemantell, Jim. E-mail correspondence with the author. April 24, 2008.

3. Jay Clark, Interview by the author. May 2, 2008.

4. Ibid.

5. Cooke, Holland. Interview by the author. May 16, 2008.

6. Ibid.

7. Ibid.

8. Pemantell, Jim. E-mail correspondence with the author. 24 April 2008.

9. Justin Levin, "A History and Analysis of the Federal Communications Commission's Response to Radio Broadcast Hoaxes." *Federal Communications Law Journal* 52, no. 2 (March 2000): 288.

10. Jay Clark, interview by the author. May 2, 2008.

11. Holland Cooke, interview by the author. May 16, 2008.

12. Ibid.

13. Jay Clark, Interview by the author. May 2, 2008.

14. Ibid.

15. Holland Cooke, Interview by the author. May 16, 2008.

16. Ibid.

17. Ibid.

18. Ibid.

19. Justin Levin, "A History and Analysis of the Federal Communications Commission's Response to Radio Broadcast Hoaxes." *Federal Communications Law Journal* 52, no. 2 (March 2000): 289.

20. Ibid., 288.

21. Ibid., 289.

Chapter 16

1. José Manuel Coelho, *Os Marcianos em Braga (The Martians in Braga)* (Porto: Ediçõesdo Litoral, 1989), 121.

Chapter 17

1. Simon Callow, *Orson Welles: The Road to Xanadu* (London: Jonathan Cape, 1995), 451.

2. Howard Koch, *The Panic Broadcast* (New York: Avon Books, 1971), 127.

3. John Province, "Interview with Alex Anderson." Hogan's Alley, the Online Magazine of the Cartoon Arts. http://cagle.msnbc.com/hogan/interviews/anderson/ho me.asp.

4. Adam Arseneau, "Pinky and the Brain: Volume 1." DVD Verdict. http://www.dvdverdict.com/reviews/pinkyandbrainvol1.php.

5. Edward Ruppelt, *The Report on Unidentified Flying Objects* (New York: Doubleday & Company, 1956), 58.

Chapter 18

1. "Poll: 1 in 4 Expects 2007 to Bring Second Coming of Christ; More Expect Terrorist Attack." *USA Today*. http://www.usatoday.com/news/nation/2006-12-31-new-year-predictions_x.htm.

2. David Sarno, "It Came from Outer Space." *Los Angeles Times*. http://www.latimes.com/entertainment/news/newmedia/la-et-ufo22aug22,0,2266445.story?page=1.

3. Dan Lothian and Deborah Feyerick, "Two Held after Ad Campaign Triggers Boston Bomb Scare." CNN. http://edition.cnn.com/2007/US/01/31/boston.bomb scare/index.html.

4. "Viewers Fooled by 'Belgium Split.'" BBC News. http://news.bbc.co.uk/1/hi/world/europe/6178671. stm.

ANNOTATED BIBLIOGRAPHY AND FILMOGRAPHY (INCLUDING RADIO, AUDIO AND TELEVISION)

The original *War of the Worlds* script by Howard Koch has been performed on radio and stage dozens of times since 1938. A comprehensive list of references to these performances is beyond the scope of this book. The following books, comics and productions are listed because they have all made oblique or overt reference to the original 1938 *War of the Worlds* broadcast. This is distinct from the Recommended Research Sources that can be found in the following section.

Books

Sideslip. Written by: Ted White and Dave Van Arnam. Pyramid Books, 1968. A distinctly odd (and not entirely successful) mix of hard-boiled detective story and science fiction, which sees a tough gumshoe transported to an alternative Earth where an alien invasion (not Martians) occurred on the same night Orson Welles was scheduled to make his *War of the Worlds* broadcast. Regretfully, the connection is never expanded on, and for the purposes of the story the date of the invasion appears to be purely coincidental.

The War of the Worlds Murder. Written by: Max Allan Collins. Berkley Prime Crime, 2005. Walter Gibson, the writer of *The Shadow*, becomes embroiled in a murder mystery on the eve of the 1938 broadcast. Invited by Orson Welles to meet with him to discuss a possible movie of *The Shadow*, Gibson is privy to the last-minute preparations for the transmission, but just before the Mercury Theatre is due to go on the air the body of a missing CBS receptionist is discovered, her throat cut by a knife that belongs to Welles. While Welles goes on the air, it is up to Gibson to turn real-life detective and find the murderer. Full of wonderfully authentic detail, this is a superb murder mystery that effortlessly transports the reader back to 1938.

Movies

Kitty Kornered. Director: Bob Clampett. Cast: Mel Blanc (voice). June 8, 1946. Running time: 7 minutes. *Kitty Kornered* is a delightful example of the work of legendary cartoonist Robert "Bob" Clampett. Pitted against Porky Pig (one of Clampett's greatest and most enduring creations) is a querulous gang of delinquent cats who will stop at nothing to invade his warm home, even if that means broadcasting a faked Martian invasion over Porky's radio. Colorful, anarchic and gleefully contravening the laws of reality in every single frame, *Kitty Kornered* is rightfully regarded as a cartoon classic. *Available on DVD. Looney Tunes Golden Collection, Volume Two. Warner Home Entertainment.*

The Adventures of Buckaroo Banzai across the 8th Dimension. Director: W. D. Richter. Script: Earl Mac Rauch. Cast: Peter Weller, John Lithgow, Ellen Barkin, Jeff Goldblum, Christopher Lloyd. 1984. Running time: 103 minutes. A truly baffling science fiction comedy boasting a charming retro feel that harks back to the golden age of the pulp crime fighters like Doc Savage. Alien invaders from a parallel dimension have taken up residence in Grover's Mill and it is up to Banzai (Peter Weller) and his talented team of misfit helpers to save the day. There is certainly much to criticize in this thoroughly muddled movie, but like a diamond with a deep flaw, Buckaroo Banzai has gained a deserved cult reputation. *Available on DVD. MGM.*

Radio Days. Director: Woody Allen. Script: Woody Allen. Cast: Mia Farrow, Seth Green, Julie Kavner, Dianne Wiest. 1987. Running time: 88 minutes. A joyful romp seen through rose-tinted spectacles, drawing partly on recollections from Woody Allen's childhood, and with particular emphasis on the importance of radio to himself and his family. Among the many touching and funny tales on offer is an account of an aunt's traumatic experience during the 1938 *War of the Worlds* broadcast. The facts of what happened that night are clearly of much less importance to Allen than are the opportunities presented to delve into the lives and motivations of his characters, but the broadcast is clearly recognizable and this heartfelt movie comes highly recommended. *Available on DVD. 20th Century–Fox Home Entertainment.*

Spaced Invaders. Director: Patrick Read Johnson. Script: Patrick Read Johnson and Scott Lawrence Alexander. Cast: Douglas Barr, Royal Dano, Ariana Richards, J. J. Anderson, Gregg Berger. 1990. Running time: 100 minutes. A neat inversion of the core concept of the 1938 broadcast is squandered in this slapstick tale of a cadre of inept Martian soldiers who mistake an anniversary transmission of *The War of the Worlds* as a call to arms. They descend onto Earth, but their efforts to conquer the planet are thwarted largely by their own stupidity, but also because the Earthlings repeatedly mistake the Martians as Halloween trick-or-treaters. There are some genuinely funny moments and the production designs are superb, but the movie does not stand up to repeat viewing. *Available on DVD. Walt Disney Video.*

Independence Day. Director: Roland Emmerich. Script: Dean Devlin and Roland Emmerich. Cast: Will Smith, Bill Pullman, Jeff Goldblum, Mary McDonnell. 1996. Running time: 145 minutes (special edition: 153 minutes.) *The War of the Worlds* in all but name, this blockbuster owes at least as much to H. G. Wells as it does to Orson Welles. While there is no specific reference to the 1938 broadcast, there are clear antecedents in the way *Independence Day* utilizes modern television scrolling news feeds to tell the story of a massively destructive alien invasion. *Available on DVD. 20th Century–Fox Home Entertainment.*

Comics

Batman. Written by: Bill Finger. Illustrated by: Bob Kane. DC Comics. Issue 1, April 1940. The first comic book appearance of the chillingly depraved Joker sees Batman's arch-nemesis hijack radio programs to announce his crimes in advance. Reference is made to the 1938 broadcast in this masterfully written and drawn comic.

Superman: Black Magic on Mars. Written by: Unknown. Illustrated by: attributed to Wayne Boring. DC Comics. Issue 62, January/February 1950. Wonderfully quirky adventure which lands a very recognizable Orson Welles on a Mars ruled by a despotic leader with evil designs on Earth. Welles manages to transmit a warning to Earth, but naturally no one believes a word he says. Only Superman gives him the benefit of the doubt, and he arrives on Mars just in time to avert a full-scale invasion of the Earth.

Weird Science: Panic. Written and illustrated by Al Feldstein. EC Comics. Issue 15, December 1950. Delightfully macabre illustrations of panic and carnage leap off the page as the story of the 1938 broadcast is given an extreme makeover by the masters of horror at EC Comics. Radio producer Carson Walls has never forgiven himself for the carnage his fake invasion from Mars caused, so is understandably reluctant to repeat the same mistake twice. Against his better judgment he is convinced it can be done safely if sufficient warnings are made to the public. Unfortunately the publicity is so effective that when a real Martian invasion is launched under cover of the broadcast no one in the military responds to the frantic calls for help.

UFO Flying Saucers. Written by: Unknown. Illustrated by: Unknown. Gold Key. Issue 5, February 1975. *UFO Flying Saucers* promoted itself as a publication concerned with telling real-life stories of encounters with flying saucers and their alien occupants, though apparently the writers were not averse to making them up when the occasion demanded it. Most striking about Gold Key comics were the superbly detailed paintings that graced many of their covers, lending them a sophistication that set them apart from their rivals. *UFO Flying Saucers* boasted some particularly fine covers, but unfortunately this rather stultifying account of the 1938 broadcast was deemed unworthy of this particular honor, which is rather a shame, as it might have elevated this dull effort from relative mediocrity.

Secret Origins: The Crimson Avenger. Written by: Roy Thomas. Illustrated by: Gene Colon. DC Comics. Issue 5, August 1986. Superbly crafted tale that poignantly captures the mood of the American nation in October 1938. Weaving in actual dialogue from the Howard Koch script, this single-issue story retells the origin of the masked crime fighter the Crimson Avenger, whose first comic book appearance, coincidentally, was also in October 1938. The story pits him against a gang of opportunist thieves who invade a Halloween party disguised as green-skinned Martians, though in a considerable feat of writing Thomas works in a great deal of the politics of the time, including the Spanish Civil War and the military conflict between China and Japan.

The Shadow Strikes: To Cloud Men's Minds. Written by: Gerard Jones. Illustrated by: Rick Magyar. DC Comics. Issue 7, March 1990. Though no overt reference is made to the 1938 broadcast, this issue focuses heavily on a radio and theater star named Grover Mills who is transparently modeled on Orson Welles. Audaciously combining elements of Welles' real life and career with the fictional adventures of the Shadow (a character played by Welles on radio), the story convincingly suggests that there would have been an almighty clash of personalities had fact and fiction ever come face to face, but after sharing a perilous adventure together the two become reconciled to each other's existence and Mills has the glimmer of an idea for a radio show about Martian invaders.

Superman: War of the Worlds. Written by: Roy Thomas. Illustrated by: Michael Lark. DC Comics. October 1998. After his success reinventing the Crimson Avenger, Roy Thomas triumphantly returns to 1930s America, pitting Superman against an invading army of Martians in a story oozing with period charm. Proclaiming its debt to the 1938 broadcast and the original novel with pride in every beautifully drawn panel, the story brings the Martians to Earth in the small American town of Woking, an obvious nod to H. G. Wells, though clearly it is Grover's Mill in all but name. On his first assignment as a reporter at Woking, Clark Kent must go into battle for the first time as the Man of Steel, a test that pits him against the equally powerful tripods of the invaders. Published under the umbrella of the Elseworlds series, *Superman: War of the Worlds* should not be considered as part of Superman's "official" history, but rather stands alone as an alternative version of what might have been had Superman and the Martians existed in the same frame of reference.

Radio and Audio Productions

Adventures in Odyssey: Terror from the Skies. Director: Paul McCusker. Script: Paul McCusker. Cast: Earl Boen, David Griffin, Gabriel Encarnacion. Broadcast: October 30, 1993. Running time: 23 minutes. This long-running Christian radio series (over 20 years and 600 episodes to date) tackles the subject of the 1938 invasion. The town of Odyssey is in an uproar as the local radio station dramatizes an attack by aliens, and a series of coincidences such as a power outage only serves to compound matters. *Terror from the Skies* is an adeptly produced program with strong production values and a well-written script and, perhaps surprisingly, it is not at all overburdened by an overtly religious message.

Doctor Who: Invaders from Mars. Director: Mark Gatiss. Script: Mark Gatiss. Cast: Paul McGann, India Fisher, Ian Hallard, Jonathan Rigby, David Benson. CD Release Date: January 2002. Running Time: 92 minutes. The time-traveling Doctor Who has been a mainstay of British science fiction for decades, and in this audio adventure he fetches up in the New York of 1938, right in the middle of preparations for *The War of the Worlds* broadcast. But there are real aliens in New York, as well as Russian and German spies, and all have their own nefarious plans. It is nice to hear Orson Welles and John Houseman portrayed in this production, but it suffers from what can only be described as acute overproduction, with sound effects and dialogue merging into a headache-inducing cacophony. *Available on CD. Big Finish Productions Ltd.*

Television Shows

The Night America Trembled. Director: Tom Donovan. Script: Nelson Bond. Cast: Edward R. Murrow, Robert Blackburn, Alexander Scourby, Warren Beatty, James Coburn, Edward Asner, Warren Oates, Vincent Gardenia and John Astin. Broadcast: September 9, 1957. Running time: 50 minutes. Made for the landmark television series *Studio One*, this is a tautly mounted retelling of the story of the 1938 broadcast, though Welles' name is conspicuously absent, possibly due to legal action he took against the production. Released for home video (as a double feature with the Lights Out episode "The Martian Eyes") under the title *Mars Invades the Earth*. *Available on DVD. Alpha Video.*

Rocky and His Friends: Jet Fuel Formula. Director: Gerard Baldwin. Script: Bill Scott. Cast: Edward Everett Horton, June Foray, Paul Frees, William Conrad, Bill Scott. Broadcast: November 19, 1959. Running time: 15 minutes. The landmark cartoon series that enthralled generations of children (but famously slipped in innumerable cultural references, some quite obscure) featured a brief but charming tip of the hat to the 1938 broadcast in its very first episode. Rocky and Bullwinkle are returning from a trip to the Moon but are mistaken in their rocket for alien invaders, prompting an alarming warning from a familiar-sounding television commentator by the name of Dawson Bells. Released for home video as part of *The Rocky & Bullwinkle Show — Complete Season 1. Available on DVD. Genius Productions, Inc.*

The Flintstones: The Masquerade Party. Directors: Joseph Barbera, William Hanna. Script: Warren Foster. Cast: Alan Reed, Jean Vander Pyl, Mel

Blanc, Bea Benaderet. Broadcast: November 26, 1965. Running time: 30 minutes. Choosing a bad night to dress up as a spaceman for a costume ball, Fred inadvertently becomes embroiled in a radio publicity gimmick for a visiting British rock band, who might, the radio station claims, actually be aliens. Released for home video as part of *The Flintstones: The Complete Season 6. Available on DVD. Turner Home Entertainment.*

The Night That Panicked America. Director: Joseph Sargent. Script: Nicholas Meyer, Anthony Wilson. Technical adviser: Paul Stewart. Cast: Joshua Bryant, Walter McGinn, John Ritter, Meredith Baxter, Tom Bosley, Paul Shenar. Broadcast: October 31, 1975. Running time: 92 minutes. This television movie earns high marks for its beautifully observed depiction of the making of the 1938 broadcast and the ensuing panic. The show won an Emmy in 1976 for Outstanding Achievement in Film Sound Editing. Often rebroadcast around Halloween. *Not currently available on DVD.*

Pinky and the Brain: Battle for the Planet. Director: Alfred Gimeno. Script: Peter Hastings. Cast: Maurice LaMarche, Rob Paulsen. Broadcast: October 28, 1985. Running time: 8 minutes. It was all but inevitable that an irreverent cartoon series starring a mouse that sounds suspiciously like Orson Welles would produce an episode spoofing the 1938 broadcast, and "Battle for the Planet" does not disappoint. Maurice LaMarche excels as the Brain, a super-intelligent lab mouse who is generally thwarted in his aim of taking over the world by the ineptitude of his partner Pinky. This episode proves no exception to the rule, as Brain's plan to reenact the 1938 broadcast on television proves anything but horrifying to an audience tickled pink by the bad acting and cardboard sets. Released for home video under the title *Animaniacs Volume 1. Available on DVD. Warner Home Video.*

Dennis the Menace: The Martians Are Coming. Director: Michael Maliani. Script: Unknown. Broadcast: December 17, 1986. Running time: 7 minutes. The hugely successful comic strip *Dennis the Menace* has transferred a number of times to television, and this 1987 cartoon series offered a not particularly inventive take on the 1938 *War of the Worlds* broadcast. Dennis accidentally transmits a school play over the air to the surrounding town. Real Martians then arrive, but they become alarmed by the panic and retreat back to Mars. *Not currently available on DVD.*

War of the Worlds: An Eye for an Eye. Director: Mark Sobel. Script: Tom Lazarus. Cast: Jared Martin, Lynda Mason Green, Richard Chaves, Philip Akin. Broadcast: October 31, 1988. Running

Time: 50 minutes. A much underrated television series sequel to the George Pal *War of the Worlds* movie (1953) that produced several outstanding episodes, not least *An Eye for an Eye*, which brought the revived aliens back to Grover's Mill in search of a long buried and forgotten War Machine. It was criticized for its high gore quotient and hampered by poor ratings, and a much retooled second season was far less interesting, but the first-season episode set in Grover's Mill is an absolute triumph. Released for home video under the title *War of the Worlds: Complete First Season. Available on DVD. Paramount.*

Talespin: War of the Weirds. Director: Script: Cast: Ed Gilbert, Sally Struthers, R.J. Williams, Alan Roberts, Pat Fraley. Broadcast: November 13th 1990. Running time: 23 minutes. Disney plundered its back catalog of characters to create this new vehicle for Baloo the Bear, first seen in much more dignified circumstances in *The Jungle Book.* Here Baloo is reimagined as the pilot for a ramshackle air freight company. In the episode "War of the Weirds," Baloo attempts to purloin a free two-week holiday by pretending he has flown to Mars, but the deception gets out of hand when an overzealous military intelligence officer overhears and believes his radio broadcasts from "Mars." Released for home video under the title *Talespin—Volume 2. Available on DVD. Walt Disney Video.*

TazMania: The Man from M.A.R.S. Director: Douglas McCarthy. Script: Bill Kopp, Art Vitello. Cast: Jim Cummings. Broadcast: October 9, 1993. Running time: 9 minutes. Taz the Tasmanian Devil, perennial foe of Bugs Bunny, is transplanted back to Tasmania in this cartoon series. Spooked by a radio show about invading Martians, Taz heads for the hills but has the misfortune to run into Marvin the Martian. It's wonderful to see this classic Martian character finally paired up with the 1938 broadcast, though the episode in question is hardly on a par with the golden age cartoons that made him such a star. *Not currently available on DVD.*

Without Warning. Director: Robert Iscove. Story: Jeremy Thorn, Walon Green, Peter Lance. Teleplay: Peter Lance. Cast: Sander Vanocur, Bree Walker, Jane Kaczmarek, Brian McNamara. Broadcast: October 30, 1994. Running Time: 100 minutes. Shown in celebration of the 1938 broadcast, this excellent TV movie draws heavily on the Howard Koch script for inspiration, with an implacable and unseen alien foe raining destruction upon the Earth (Grover's Mill is the first target) in the full glare of the American media. Despite the best efforts of CBS to warn viewers, a small number believed the movie was real breaking news. *DVD released in 2003 but no longer generally available. Madacy Records.*

The New Adventures of Madeline: Madeline's Halloween. Director: Judy Reilly. Script: Betty G. Birney. Cast: Andrea Libman, Tracey-Lee Smythe, Louise Vallance, Vanessa King. Broadcast: September 3, 1995. Running time: 30 minutes. The first Madeline book was written only a year after *The War of the Worlds* broadcast, and the stories have continued to enthrall children ever since. In this episode of the cartoon series, Madeline visits a radio studio and accidentally transmits a story about giant ants invading New York. *Released on VHS but no longer generally available. Madeline's Halloween Spooktacular. Trimark Home Video.*

The X-Files: War of the Coprophages. Director: Kim Manners. Script: Darin Morgan. Cast: David Duchovny, Gillian Anderson, Bobbie Phillips. Broadcast: January 5, 1996. Running time: 45 mins. FBI investigator Fox Mulder takes an impromptu weekend vacation in the town of Miller's Grove, but is drawn into a mystery concerning a series of attacks by cockroaches. Aside from the obvious reference to the 1938 broadcast, there is little else to connect this episode to *The War of the Worlds*, other than a growing sense of public panic at the bizarre activities of the bugs. Released for home video under the title *The X-Files: The Complete First Season. Available on DVD. 20th Century–Fox.*

Touched by an Angel: The Sky Is Falling. Director: Victor Lobl. Script: Glenn Berenbeim. Cast: Roma Downey, Della Reese, John Dye, Brian Keith. Broadcast: November 3, 1996. Running Time: 45 minutes. The long-running series about a group of angels lending a guiding hand to the needy on Earth makes a credible attempt at working the 1938 broadcast into this story, which tells of an embittered writer whose father, a state trooper, died in a car accident on the way to Grover's Mill. The way the original recording of the broadcast is used as a device to cut back and forth between the past and present is extremely effective, but the overall impact of the story is severely lessened by the heavy moralizing tone. Released for home video under the title *Touched by an Angel: The Complete Third Season. Available on DVD. Paramount Home Entertainment.*

Perversions of Science: Panic. Director: Tobe Hooper. Script: Andrew Kevin Walker. Cast: Maureen Teefy, Jamie Kennedy, Harvey Korman, Jason Lee, Edie McClurg. Broadcast: July 2, 1997. Running Time: 25 minutes. A disappointing adaptation of the 1950 *Weird Science* comic book, which was itself inspired by the 1938 broadcast. Little that is recognizable survives the translation from broadcast to comic to TV, and the profanity for which HBO is famous seems to have been inserted entirely for shock value rather than any kind of legitimate artistic expression. A curiosity for its strange and convoluted lineage, but largely lacking in any redeeming characteristics. *Not currently available on DVD.*

Hey Arnold!: Arnold's Halloween. Director: Jamie Mitchell. Script: Craig Bartlett, Joseph Purdy, Antoinette Stella. Cast: Phillip Van Dyke, Jamil Walker Smith, Francesca Smith, Dan Castellaneta, Maurice LaMarche. Broadcast: October 27, 1997. Running Time: 23 minutes. The cartoon series *Hey Arnold!* is a wry observational comedy about a bunch of street-smart kids living in a New York–like inner-city neighborhood. In this episode the great Maurice LaMarche is once again on hand to channel the spirit of Orson Welles, this time playing a paranormal investigator who is caught up in Arnold's Halloween plot to convince the adults in their neighborhood that a Martian invasion is under way. The superb episode maintains a pleasant referential tone throughout, with plenty of authentic moments and some nicely understated humor. Released for home video under the title *Nicktoons Halloween: 6 Tales of Fright. Available on DVD. Paramount.*

Arthur: D.W. Aims High. Director: Unknown. Script: Rose Compagine. Cast: Jason Szwimer, Cameron Ansell. Broadcast: May 19, 2006. Running time: 11 minutes. A sweet-natured cartoon series with an above-average respect for the intelligence of its young target audience. In this episode Arthur's younger sister explores the history of Mars and learns about the 1938 broadcast. It's a fleeting reference, but the episode (and the series as a whole) is to be praised for its commendable educational ethos. Released for home video under the title *Arthur: Season 10. Available on DVD. WGBH Boston Video.*

The Simpsons: Treehouse of Horror XVII, The Day the Earth Looked Stupid. Directors: David Silverman and Matthew Faughnan. Script: Peter Gaffney. Cast: Dan Castellaneta, Hank Azaria, Harry Shearer, Julie Kavner, Nancy Cartwright, Yeardley Smith, Maurice LaMarche. Broadcast: November 5, 2006. Running Time: 7 minutes. The 1938 broadcast is awarded the ultimate pop culture accolade with a superb pastiche that transports "America's favorite family" to a sepia-tinted version of their hometown of Springfield. Maurice LaMarche shines yet again in the role he was born to play (though actually spoofing dialogue originally spoken by Frank Readick) and the script gleefully pokes fun at Welles and his penchant for perfect sound effects. *Not currently available on DVD.*

Cold Case: World's End. Director: Roxann Dawson. Script: Gavin Harris. Cast: Kathryn Morris, Danny Pino, John Finn, Jeremy Ratchford, Thom Barry, Tracie Thoms. Broadcast: November 4, 2007. Running Time: 44 minutes. Celebrating the 100th episode of this forensic crime series, the detectives of the Philadelphia homicide squad investigate the murder of a woman who was last seen alive on the night of October 30, 1938. *The War of the Worlds* broadcast is woven into the story with a great deal of loving care, and while the panic is undoubtedly portrayed with a degree of artistic license, the period detail is superb and the murder mystery itself extremely satisfying, with a very poignant denouement. *Not currently available on DVD.*

Ben 10: Alien Force: Everybody Talks About the Weather. Director: Dan Riba. Script: Dwayne McDuffie. Broadcast: April 26, 2008. Running time: 23 minutes. A cartoon series about a young boy who acquires superpowers from an alien device he stumbles upon while on a camping trip. The episode in question is set in a community called Grover's Mill, though this is the only reference to the 1938 broadcast and the episode is otherwise unconnected to *The War of the Worlds* broadcast. Released for home video under the title *Ben 10: Alien Force: Season One, Vol. 1. Available on DVD. Warner Home Video.*

RECOMMENDED RESEARCH SOURCES

Books

Bainbridge, William Sims. "Collective Behavior and Social Movements." In *Sociology* (2nd edition, ed. Rodney Stark), 554. Belmont, Calif.: Wadsworth Publishing Company, 1987.

Bartholomew, Robert E., and Evans, Hilary. *Panic Attacks*. Stroud, U.K.: Sutton Publishing, 2004.

Bergonzi, Bernard. *The Early H. G. Wells: A Study of Scientific Romances*. Manchester, U.K.: Manchester University Press, 1961.

Birmingham, David. *A Concise History of Portugal*, 2nd edition. Cambridge, U.K.: Cambridge University Press, 2007.

Brady, Frank. *Citizen Welles*. London: Coronet, 1991.

Bulgatz, Joseph. *Ponzi Schemes, Invaders from Mars and More Extraordinary Popular Delusions and the Madness of Crowds*. New York: Harmony Books, 1992.

Callow, Simon. *Orson Welles: The Road to Xanadu* (London: Jonathan Cape, 1995).

Cantril, Hadley. *The Invasion from Mars*. New York: Harper Torchbooks, 1966.

Coelho, José Manuel. *Os Marcianos em Braga (The Martians in Braga)*. Porto: Edições do Litoral, 1989.

Flynn, John L. *War of the Worlds from Wells to Spielberg*. Owings Mills, Md.: Galactic Books, 2005.

Goode, Erich. *Collective Behavior*. Fort Worth, Tx.: Saunders College Publishing, 1992.

Heyer, Peter. *The Medium and the Magician: Orson Welles, the Radio Years, 1934–1952*. Lanham, Md.: Rowman & Littlefield, 2005.

Hilmes, Michele. *Radio Voices*. Minneapolis: University of Minnesota Press, 1997.

Houseman, John. "The Men from Mars." *Harper's*, December 1948, 75.

_____. *Unfinished Business*. London: Columbus Books, 1988.

Jackaway, Gwenyth L. *Media at War: Radio's Challenge to the Newspapers, 1924–1939*. Westport, Conn.: Greenwood Publishing Group, 1995.

Jackson, Charles. "The Night the Martians Came." In *The Aspirin Age, 1919–1941* (ed. Isabel Leighton), 437. New York: Simon and Schuster, 1949.

Kaltenborn, Hans. *Fifty Fabulous Years, 1900–1950*. New York: Putnam, 1950.

Keith, Michael C. *Talking Radio: An Oral History of American Radio in the Television Age*. New York: M.E. Sharpe, 2000.

Koch, Howard. *As Time Goes By*. New York: Harcourt Brace Jovanovich, 1979.

_____. *The Panic Broadcast*. New York: Avon Books, 1971.

Leaming, Barbara. *Orson Welles*. London: Phoenix, 1993.

Levin, Justin. "A History and Analysis of the Federal Communications Commission's Response to Radio Broadcast Hoaxes." *Federal Communications Law Journal* 52, no. 2 (March 2000): 285.

Lowell, Percival. *Mars*. New York: Elibron Classics, 2004.

Lubertozzi, Alex, and Holmsten, Brian, ed. *The Complete War of the Worlds*. Naperville, Ill.: Sourcebooks, 2001.

Maia, Matos. *A Invasão Dos Marcianos: + 3 Fantasias Radiofonicas*. Alfragide, Portugal: Dom Quixote, 1996.

Miller, David L. *Introduction to Collective Behaviour*. Belmont, Calif.: Wadsworth Publishing Company, 1985.

Ruppelt, Edward. *The Report on Unidentified Flying Objects*. Norfolk, Va.: The Project Blue Book Archive, 2008.

Sheehan, William. *The Planet Mars: A History of Observation and Discovery*. Tucson: University of Arizona Press, 1996.

Smelser, Neil J. *Theory of Collective Behavior*. New York: Free Press, 1962.

Smith, David C. *H. G. Wells: Desperately Mortal*. New Haven: Yale University Press, 1986.

Smith, Steven C. *A Heart at Fire's Center: The Life and Music of Bernard Herrmann*. Berkeley: University of Calif. Press, 2002.

Velásquez, César Larrea. *70 Años de la Vida Nacional 1906–1975* (70 Years of National Life 1906–1975). Quito, Ecuador: Diario El Comercio, 1976.

Welles, Orson, and Peter Bogdanovich, *This Is Orson Welles*. London: HarperCollins, 1993.

Wells, H. G. *Experiment in Autobiography*, volume 1. London: Victor Gollancz, 1934.

West, Anthony. *H. G. Wells: Aspects of a Life*. New York: Penguin, 1985.

Zúñiga, Diego. "Guerra de los Mundos" (*The War of the Worlds*). *Pensar* 2, no. 4 (October/December 2005).

Radio Programs

All Things Considered. National Public Radio, 1988.

Theatre of the Imagination: The Mercury Company Remembers. 1988.

War of the Worlds. Radio Lab. WNYC, March 7, 2008.

Television Programs

The Making of WKBW's *War of the Worlds*. WNED-TV, Buffalo, N.Y., 1998.

Websites

Araújo, Ed Wilson Ferreira. A Guerra dos Mundos em São Luís do Maranhão (*The War of the Worlds in São Luís do Maranhão*). *Jornal da Rede Alfredo de Carvalho* 4, no. 48 (2004). http://www.redealcar.jornalismo.ufsc.br/boletins/jornal48.htm.

Bartholomew, Robert E. The Martian Panic Sixty Years Later. *Csicop*. http://www.csicop.org/si/9811/martian.html.

Boese, Alex. War of the Worlds. *Museum of Hoaxes*. http://www.museumofhoaxes.com/hoax/Hoaxipedia/War_of_the_Worlds.

Brown, Beverly. The Night the Martians Landed. *Appalachian Community Press*. http://www.greaterowego.com/communitypress/1998/11-98/WarOfTheWorlds.htm.

Carrascal, José Villamarín. La noche que los marcianos invadieron Cotocollao (The night the Martians invaded Cotocollao). *La Hora*. http://www.dlh.lahora.com.ec/paginas/temas/caleidoscopio28.htm.

Daly, Sean. "We Take You Now to Grover's Mill." *Washington Post*. http://www.washingtonpost.com/wp-dyn/content/article/2001/10/31/AR2005033116062.html.

The Estate of Orson Welles. http://home.bway.net/nipper/home.html.

Fill, David. *War of the Worlds. WKBW Radio*. http://www.wkbwradio.com/warintro.htm.

The H. G. Wells Society. http://hgwellsusa.50megs.com.

Hurtado, Julio. "Los marcianos llegaron ya... (The Martians have arrived)." *El Mercurio de Valparaíso*. http://www.mercuriovalpo.cl/prontus4_noticias/site/artic/20050829/pags/20050829143256.html.

Kingman, Nicolás. La invasión de los marcianos (The invasion of the Martians). *The Complete Works of Nicolás Kingman. La Hora*. http://www.dlh.lahora.com.ec/paginas/kingman/tomo66.htm.

Kosinski, Bob. "WKBW and the War of the Worlds." *Buffalo Broadcasters*. http://www.buffalobroadcasters.com/hist_kbwow.asp.

Lovgen, Stefan. "War of the Worlds": Behind the 1938 Radio Show Panic. *National Geographic*. http://news.nationalgeographic.com/news/2005/06/0617_050617_warworlds.html.

Maia, Matos. Como nasceu "A invasão dos marcianos" (How "The Martian invasion" was born). *Clássicos da Rádio*. http://www.classicosdaradio.com/InvasaoMarcianos.htm.

McCarthy, Caroline. Could the "War of the Worlds" scare happen today? *CNET News*. http://news.cnet.com/Could-the-War-of-the-Worlds-scare-happen-today/2100-1025_3-6216098.html.

The Mercury Theatre on the Air. http://www.mercurytheatre.info.

Moore, Don. The Day the Martians Landed. *Patepluma Radio*. http://donmoore.tripod.com/south/ecuador/martians.html.

Moucherek, Jaqueline, A versão maranhense da Guerra dos Mundos (The Maranhese version of *War of the Worlds*). *Jornal da Rede Alfredo de Carvalho* 4, no. 48 (2004). http://www.redealcar.jornalismo.ufsc.br/boletins/jornal48.htm.

O'Callaghan, Scott. *War of the Worlds*: Why the Hoax Worked. *Space.com*. http://www.space.com/sciencefiction/phenomena/war_worlds_hoax_991029.html.

Pérez, Rodolfo. Biography of Blanca Salazar Bautista. *Biographical Dictionary of Ecuador*. http://www.diccionariobiograficoecuador.com/tomos/tomo15/s1.htm

Stearns, Jerry. *War of the Worlds. Great Northern Radio*. http://www.greatnorthernaudio.com/sf_radio/wow.html.

Valim, Alexandre Busko. "Os Marcianos Estão Chegando! (The Martians Are Coming!)." *Revista de História da Biblioteca Nacional (Journal of History of the National Library)*. http://www.revistadehistoria.com.br/v2/home/?go=detalhe&id=336&pagina=1.

War of the Worlds Invasion. http://www.war-of-the-worlds.co.uk.

Wellesnet: The Orson Welles Web Resource. http://www.wellesnet.com.

INDEX

Numbers in *bold italic* indicate pages with photographs.